Interpreting Psychological Test Data

Interpreting Psychological Test Data

Associating personality
and behavior with responses
to the Bender–Gestalt,
Human Figure Drawing,
Wechsler Adult Intelligence Scale,
and the Rorschach Ink Blot Tests

Joseph Gilbert, Ph.D.

Volume I
Test Response Antecedent

VNR VAN NOSTRAND REINHOLD COMPANY
NEW YORK   CINCINNATI   ATLANTA   DALLAS   SAN FRANCISCO
LONDON   TORONTO   MELBOURNE

Van Nostrand Reinhold Company Regional Offices:
New York Cincinnati Atlanta Dallas San Francisco

Van Nostrand Reinhold Company International Offices:
London Toronto Melbourne

Library of Congress Catalog Card Number: 77-20593
ISBN: 0-442-25313-3

Manufactured in the United States of America

Published by Van Nostrand Reinhold Company
450 West 33rd Street, New York, N.Y. 10001

Published simultaneously in Canada by Van Nostrand Reinhold Ltd.

15 14 13 12 11 10 9 8 7 6 5 4 3 2 1

Library of Congress Cataloging in Publication Data

Gilbert, Joseph, 1920–
  Interpreting psychological test data.

  "Associating personality and behavior with responses
to the Bender-Gestalt, human figure drawing, Wechsler
adult intelligence scale, and the Rorschach ink blot
tests."
  Includes index.
  1. Personality assessment. 2. Bender gestalt
test. 3. Draw-a-person test. 4. Wechsler adult
intelligence scale. 5. Rorschach test. I. Title.
BF698.4.G46   155.2'8   77-20593
ISBN 0-442-25313-3

This book is affectionately dedicated to
Katherine Jennings Gilbert.

Introduction

The present volume abstracts and synthesizes from certain books regarded as standard references in the field those aspects of behavior which are assumed to be related to clinical psychological test productions.

The purpose of such a survey is (1) to provide a rapid useful reference source for both students and experienced practitioners who make inferences from psychological test data; (2) to systematize and integrate in one source interpretative material from a variety of recognized authorities in the area of clinical psychological testing; and (3) insofar as feasible to make uniform concepts utilized by different authors in a comparable way but so expressed as often to obscure the intrinsic similarity of the referents used.

It was originally contemplated that all the relevant basic reference books would be employed; this remains an objective for future volumes or an expanded edition of the present volume. The magnitude of the material compiled at this writing and the time required for abstraction, organization, and cross-indexing of the pertinent material in each source examined currently limits the references used in this edition to the following unquestionably preeminent works: *Psychodiagnostics*, by Herman Rorschach; *Personality Projection in the Drawing of the Human Figure*, by Karen Machover; *Rorschach Interpretation: Advanced Technique*, by Leslie Phillips and Joseph G. Smith; *Diagnostic Psychological Testing*, by David Rapaport, Morton M. Gilland, and Roy Schafer; *The Clinical Application of Projective Drawings*, by Emanuel F. Hammer and contributors; *The Hutt Adaptation of the Bender-Gestalt Test*, by Max L. Hutt; *A Visual Motor Gestalt Test and its Clinical Use*, by Lauretta Bender; *Evaluation of the Bender-Gestalt Test*, by Alexander Tolor and Herbert C. Schulberg; *Rorschach's Test*, Volumes II and III, by Samuel J. Beck; *The Rorschach Technique* and *Developments in the Rorschach Technique*, Volumes I and II, by Bruno Klopfer, Mary D. Ainsworth, Walter G. Klopfer, and Robert R. Holt; *The Clinical Application of Psychological Tests* and *Psychoanalytic Interpretation in Rorschach Testing*, by Roy Schafer; and chapters by various authors in *An Introduction to Projective Techniques*, by Harold H. and G. L. Anderson. Full citations for each of these are contained in the Bibliography at the end of the book, which also contains the code used for identifying the source in the text.

The author is well aware that this aggregation hardly exhausts the many authoritative texts which are also excellent references in the field and which are planned for inclusion later. For the moment, the foundation provided by the cited reference volumes must suffice.

To integrate the descriptive concepts from such diverse sources, it was essential to standardize three areas of approach. The first of these was the nomenclature used for diagnostic syndromes; the second was that for Rorschach scoring categories and symbols; the third was the terms employed to designate traits and behavioral attributes whenever the language of the reference source lacked brevity or clarity out of its original context.

In all instances the author's solution was as personal as it was pragmatic. For diagnostic syndromes the American Psychiatric Association's *Diagnostic and Statistical Manual of the Mental Disorders*, Second Edition (DSM-II), was used as the criterion, with syndrome nomenclature from DSM-I (first edition of the manual) equated to the second edition in accord with the position contained in the author's *Clinical Psychological Tests in Psychiatric and Medical Practice* (see Bibliography). For Rorschach scoring categories the basic system chosen was Beck's, since it seemed the best defined and least ambiguous. In the context of the Beck system were incorporated features of other systems that provide clinical interpretation and scoring conveniences which seemed to the author to supplement or improve upon some aspects of the Beck procedure. Scoring symbols employed in non-Beck systems are transposed to Beck symbols where this procedure is feasible as a result of the symbols' possessing logically comparable referents. Variations not encountered in some reasonable alternative guise in the Beck system were excluded, not to excommunicate them but simply because they could not be incorporated in the cross-reference scheme utilized. A table in the appendix presents the transpositions of non-Beck symbols to the Beck system and inclusion of symbols extending or modifying the system as indicated above.*

The third problem is that of selection of trait name and behavioral attribute designations which are both clinically meaningful and inclusive enough to be used synonymously for the diverse descriptive terminology encountered in the reference sources. Not only is the advantage of such uniformity self-evident in a systematic cross-comparison of interpretive inferences for clinical test responses, it would be realistically impossible to compile a practicable compilation of such inferences without it. Of course it is also apparent that the process of integration is contingent upon the author's judgment of congruence between the term selected and what the reference source actually meant. The potential semantic complexities are immense. How pertinently they are resolved in this compendium essentially can be assessed only in two ways: (1) by whether the present volume fulfills a useful role in the profession; and (2) by attentive examination of the original source.

Of these two criteria, the second is crucial. The danger that the present writer has misinterpreted material from an authoritative source is less disturbing in the long run (because of the availability of the original work and its familiarity to the profession) than the possibility that this compendium might be applied inappropriately by students, the inexperienced, and dilettantes to bypass the basic

*For Beck's own description of his scoring procedure, see Beck, Samuel J. *Rorschach's Test. Vol. I: Basic Processes.* New York, Grune, 1962.

reference sources, and in so doing to concoct a mélange of incompatible and inconsistent conclusions with minimal relevance to the dynamic subtleties presented by the subject's test performance. It is the way in which both consistencies and incongruities are accounted for that determines the validity of the conclusions drawn from psychological test data. The theoretical context, methodological rationale, and experimental evidence presented by the authoritative sources in the field are a necessary background to clinical test procedure. A professional should always begin and never end with basic reference sources; but without familiarity with both their content and their context, he can hardly question antecedents in his discipline. Hence the insistence upon the necessity for this compilation to function as a convenient reference and not to substitute for basic reference sources, the essence of which it can at best only incidentally suggest.

Each section of the present volume pertains to a particular test in the *basic clinical test* battery: the Bender-Gestalt, Human Figure Drawing, WAIS, and Rorschach, in the order named. Within each section the components or determinants of a particular test considered are indicated alphabetically in subheadings. Interpretations of the response from the various reference sources appear in adjacent columns, followed by identification of the source in question. The abbreviated names used, together with their source, are contained in the table in the appendix. This is Volume I of the book. Volume II will bring together in summary form the diagnostic syndromes or behavioral attributes suggested by test responses. It will list such syndromes or attributes first, followed by the test responses which suggest them, the reverse order of Volume I. Thus, for instance, catatonic schizophrenia or passive aggressive personality would appear in Volume II as a main category heading, followed by a compilation of test data considered by the reference sources to suggest the behavioral syndromes on traits in question. Volume II therefore will be a reorganization of the material in Volume I, arranged alphabetically by test involved as in the present volume.

The terms "increment" and "decrement" are to be understood as the degree to which the determinant or response tends to exceed the norm, which is cited in the "norms" category of each section or may be found in the reference sources. The term is of course relative. For sex content, increment, for instance, might be more than one such response, while for animal content it might pertain to 50 percent or more of the total response. The other designations used and departure from customary procedure are either self-explanatory or discussed in the table of symbols and scoring equivalents in the appendix.

JOSEPH GILBERT

Contents

Interpreting Psychological Test Data

Part I
Bender-Gestalt Test

Arrangement

Crowding:

Egocentricity; inappropriate assertion; lack of empathy; schizophrenia. (Anderson-Halpern)

Crowding remaining designs on page after most of room on page is utilized:

Anxiety, compulsive doubting, inadequacy feelings. (Hutt, 1969)

Large space between figures:

Oppositional tendency (Hutt, 1969); detachment from others; impulsivity; instability. (Anderson-Halpern)

Left to right placement of figures:

Unresolved need for sustaining interpersonal associations. (Hutt, 1969)

Markedly irregular use of space:

Retardation. (Hutt, 1969)

One figure on each page, in center:

Egocentricity, narcissism, oppositional tendency. (Hutt, 1969)

Several pages required:

Schizophrenia, prepsychosis. (Hutt 1969)

Vertical placement of figures, each below the preceding figure:

Anxiety and insecurity producing compulsive tendency (Anderson-* Halpern); conflict with authority figures. (Hutt, 1969)

Completion Impairment

Closure difficulty:

Emotional disturbance; difficulty in maintaining adequate interpersonal relationships; social anxiety (Hutt, 1969); interpersonal aggres-

*All names following "Anderson" refer to chapters by specific authors in that book. (See References).

Closure difficulty of diamond, figure 8, male subjects:

Figures on which closure difficulty may occur:

Gaps in closure:

Marked closure difficulty:

Omission major part of at least one design (especially figure 7):

Unstable closure:

sion on Rorschach, children as subjects (Tolor-Schulberg-Clawson**); neuroticism. (Tolor-Schulberg-Hutt)

Conflict with women; heterosexual anxiety. (Hutt, 1969)

A, 2, 4, 7, 8. (Hutt, 1969)

Difficulty in maintaining interpersonal relationships, possibly withdrawal. (Hutt, 1969)

Retardation; schizophrenia. (Hutt, 1969)

Brain-damaged retarded children. (Tolor-Schulberg-Baroff)

General emotional imbalance, as with catatonics. (Tolor-Schulberg-Guerwin)

Contiguity of Elements

Breakdown of gestalt:

Collision:

Collision of curved figures:

Collision tendency:

Component elements of figure drawn as separate (with intervening space) and with no effort at joining:

Correct rendition of parts with change of their relationship and direction:

Crossing difficulty:

Crossing difficulty; especially designs 6 and 7:

Brain damage. (Tolor-Schulberg-Halpern)

Brain damage, loss of control, marked anxiety (Hutt, 1969); organicity. (Hutt and Briskin-Masher and Smith)

Aggressive drives. (Hutt, 1969)

Retardation. (Hutt, 1969)

Organics, retardates, schizophrenics, young children. (Hutt, 1969)

Possible malingering. (Bender)

Neurosis. (Hutt, 1969)

Neuroticism. (Tolor-Schulberg-Hutt and Briskin)

**Names following book author names are those of persons cited in the book from literature in the field.

Crossing difficulty at juncture of figures 4, 5, 6:

Blocking, indecision, phobic tendency. (Hutt, 1969)

Design 6 drawn as nonintersecting separate lines:

Alcoholics (Hutt, 1969-Story); low frustration tolerance and withdrawal tendency. (Tolor-Schulberg-Story)

Design 7 hexagons drawn as separate and not overlapping:

Alcoholics (Hutt, 1969-Story); brain-damaged retarded children. (Tolor-Schulberg-Baroff)

Difficulty with intersecting figures:

Passivity. (Hutt, 1969)

Difficulty in joining diamond to side of hexagon, figure 8, male subjects:

Conflict with women, heterosexual anxiety. (Hutt, 1969)

Displacement of whole patterns:

Schizophrenic. (Tolor-Schulberg-Bender)

Drawing components of figure 7 as separated or with tips in contact:

Alcoholism, homosexual tendency, withdrawal tendency. (Tolor-Schulberg-Story)

Fragmentation:

Possible schizophrenia (Bender); organicity, schizophrenia, severe psychopathology (Hutt, 1969); disorganization, dissociation, psychotic factor. (Tolor-Schulberg-Guertin)

Fragmentation on figures 7 and 8:

Retardation. (Hutt, 1969)

Fragmentation or separation of open square and curve, figure 4:

Organicity, regression. (Hutt, 1969)

Gaps:

Withdrawal attempts. (Tolor-Schulberg-Hutt and Briskin)

Intrusion of design 6 into design 5:

Suicidal rumination. (Hutt, 1969-Sternberg)

Intrusion of one part into another:

Passive-dependent needs. (Tolor-Schulberg)

Nonintersecting curves, figure 6:

Social anxiety. (Hutt, 1969)

Overlapping difficulty:

Diffuse brain damage, severe psychopathology. (Hutt, 1969)

Separation of parts of designs:

Primitive gestalt principle. (Tolor-Schulberg-Schilder)

Separation of parts (fragmentation), preservation of gestalt:

With other signs possible dementia paralytica (chronic syphilitic meningoencephalitis). [Bender]

Variable spacing between columns, figure 2:

Emotional instability, unpredictability. (Anderson-Halpern)

Coordination

Poor coordination:

Anxiety, feeling of inadequacy (Hutt, 1969); organicity. (Hutt and Briskin-Masher and Smith)

Tremor:

Alcoholism. (Tolor-Schulberg-Kaldegg)

Well-articulated circles, figure 2:

Adequate functioning, although other indications may suggest a lower maturational level. (Hutt, 1969)

Distortion

Accentuated or sharpened angles:

Insecurity, psychopathology. (Anderson-Halpern)

Angulation difficulty:

Organicity in children. (Hutt, 1969-Weimer)

Asymmetry:

Alcoholism. (Tolor-Schulberg-Kaldegg)

Blunted or rounded angles:

Impulsivity, emotional lability. (Anderson-Halpern)

Careful execution, exaggeration of curves:

Rigidity alternating with impulsivity. (Anderson-Halpern)

Change in angulation:

Brain damage; impulse-control impairment; retardation. (Hutt, 1969)

Change in size of angulation, curvature, or design parts:

Neuroticism. (Tolor-Schulberg-Hutt)

Circles varying from loops to ovals, incorrect number of columns, figure 2:

Impulsivity. (Hutt, 1969)

Clockwise movement of angulation of circle columns progressively, figure 2:

Egocentricity, narcissism. (Hutt, 1969)

Curvature difficulty:

Organicity in children. (Hutt, 1969-Weimer)

Curvature difficulty on figures 4, 5, 6:

Emotional disturbance. (Hutt, 1969)

Curve of figure 6 larger than square: Feminine identification. (Hutt, 1969)

Curvilinear distortion: Impulsivity (Hutt, 1969; Tolor-Schulberg-Guertin); affect display and emotional disorganization as in hebephrenics. (Tolor-Schulberg-Guertin)

Dashes for dots: Impulsivity (Anderson-Halpern); primitive gestalt forms. (Hutt, 1969)

Dashes or lines for dots, distortion of curves: Emotional instability; organicity. (Anderson-Halpern)

Decreased angle (rotation of circle columns toward vertical) figure 2: Lower maturational level; or organicity; or reduction of affect expression (blandness). [Hutt, 1969]

Decreased angulation: Increased emotionality. (Hutt, 1969)

Decreased curvature: Constriction accompanying depression (Hutt and Briskin; Tolor-Schulberg); decreased emotionality, depression. (Hutt, 1969)

Decreased height of total figure, shortening of extension, figure 5: Problem with authority. (Hutt, 1969)

Decreased lateral size of figures: Withdrawal tendency. (Hutt, 1969)

Decreased lateral size of figure 1: Social anxiety, withdrawal. (Hutt, 1969)

Difficulty with angles: Emotional lability. (Hutt, 1969)

Difficulty with curved figures: Conflict over aggressive drives. (Hutt, 1969)

Difficulty with straight-line figures: Passive tendency. (Hutt, 1969)

Distortion of curves, dashes or lines for dots: Emotional instability; organicity. (Anderson-Halpern)

Dots for circles: Primitive gestalt form. (Hutt, 1969)

Elongation laterally of figure 2, correct number of circles: Interpersonal conflict, social anxiety. (Hutt, 1969)

Enlargement of square only, figure A: Masculinity striving. (Hutt, 1969)

Exaggeration alternating with flattening of curves: Emotional instability, unpredictability. (Anderson-Halpern)

Exaggeration of curves: Impulsiveness. (Anderson-Halpern)

Extension of circular portion of figure 5:

Insecurity, dependence. (Hutt, 1969)

Extension of vertical sides, open square of figure 4:

Problem with authority figures. (Hutt, 1969)

Extra loop at terminus of curve, figure 4:

Emotional instability, impulsivity. (Hutt, 1969)

Figure one dots lower on ends than in middle:

Egocentricity, narcissism. (Hutt, 1969)

Flattened curvature:

Retardation. (Hutt, 1969)

Flattening of curve, figure 4:

Flattening of affect. (Hutt, 1969)

Flattening of curves:

Flattening of affect tendency. (Anderson-Halpern)

Flattening of curves, figure 6:

Flattened affect tendency. (Hutt, 1969)

Gross distortion:

Organicity in children. (Hutt, 1969-Weimer)

Inconsistent direction of lines:

Neuroticism. (Hutt and Briskin; Tolor-Schulberg)

Incorrect number of units in designs 1, 2, 3, 5, 6:

Reading problems in children. (Tolor-Schulberg-Clawson)

Increase of angle of circles, figure 2:

Increased affectivity. (Hutt, 1969)

Increase of curvature:

Emotional lability; passivity. (Hutt, 1969)

Increase in height (vertical plane) of figures:

Anxiety relative to figures of authority. (Hutt, 1969)

Increase in size of circles of figure 2 progressively:

Impulsivity, acting-out tendency. (Hutt, 1969)

Increase in vertical sides of open square, figure 4:

Hostility toward authority figures, expressed indirectly. (Hutt, 1969)

Increased angulation:

Decreased emotionality, lack of spontaneity, overcontrol. (Hutt, 1969)

Increased size of diamond, figure 8:

Masculine striving. (Hutt, 1969)

Irregular curvature with increased curvature:

Hostile acting out. (Hutt, 1969)

Larger square than circle, with reduced size of square, figure A:

Masculine striving with felt masculine inadequacy. (Hutt, 1969)

Lateral elongation (stretching out) of figures:

Difficulty in interpersonal relationships; need to relate with social anxiety. (Hutt, 1969)

Marked angulation difficulty:

Intracranial damage. (Hutt, 1969)

Marked curvature difficulty:

Schizophrenia. (Hutt, 1969)

Marked isolated size change:

Neurosis. (Hutt, 1969)

Mild angulation difficulty:

Neurosis. (Hutt, 1969)

Mild curvature difficulty:

Neurosis. (Hutt, 1969)

Movement in deviant direction:

Neurosis. (Hutt, 1969)

Overextension of projection from circle, figure 5:

Paranoid features. (Hutt, 1969)

Overlapping of circle, design A:

Impulsivity. (Hutt, 1969)

Overlapping difficulty:

Intracranial damage. (Hutt, 1969)

Primitive gestalt forms:

Dashes for dots, dots for circles, loops for circles; schizophrenia (with regression). [Hutt, 1969]

Primitive gestalt forms:

Intensely anxious neurotics; schizophrenics; especially hebephrenics; severe psychopathology. (Hutt, 1969)

Reduction of number of curves on curve amplitude, figure 6:

Lack of spontaneity, possibly with withdrawal or flattened affect tendency; possible denial and isolation; repression. (Hutt, 1969)

Reduction of vertical dimension:

Passivity. (Hutt, 1969)

Small figures:

Inhibition. (Anderson-Halpern)

Small figures or elements within a figure, alternating with large:

Inhibition followed by impulsivity; emotional instability. (Anderson-Halpern)

Spiked curves, figure 6:

Problem with control of hostility. (Hutt, 1969)

Dynamic Significance

Circles:

May evoke feelings of castration and femininity in male, vaginal symbols. (Tolor-Schulberg-Hammer)

Significance of figure A:	Capacity for integrating conflictual elements. (Tolor-Schulberg-Suzcek and Kloffer)
Significance of figure 1:	Attitudes toward regularity and importance of detail. (Tolor-Schulberg-Suzcek and Kloffer)
Significance of figure 2:	Willingness to comply with externally imposed orderliness. (Tolor-Schulberg-Suzcek and Kloffer)
Significance of figure 3:	Handling of instinctual drives. (Tolor-Schulberg-Suzcek and Kloffer)
Significance of figure 4:	Reaction to ambivalence and incongruities within self and its emotional experiences. (Tolor-Schulberg-Suzcek and Kloffer)
Significance of figure 5:	Basic sexual identification. (Tolor-Schulberg-Suzcek and Kloffer)
Significance of figure 6:	Way individual copes with primitive instinctual drives or their derivatives. (Tolor-Schulberg-Suzcek and Kloffer)
Significance of figure 7:	Concept of one's adequacy. (Tolor-Schulberg-Suzcek and Kloffer)
Significance of figure 8:	Attitude toward one's phallic sexuality. (Tolor-Schulberg-Suzcek and Kloffer)

Elaboration

Adding facial features to curves, figure 6:	Paranoid tendency. (Hutt, 1969)
Addition of more complex elements:	Malingering. (Tolor-Schulberg-Blum and Nims)
Doodling and elaboration:	Psychotics with manic tendencies; severe disturbance of association functions (Tolor-Schulberg-Hutt-Briskin); impulse control disorder; intense overt anxiety; organics, retardates, schizophrenics. (Hutt, 1969)

Elaboration:	Intracranial damage. (Hutt, 1969)
Elaboration of figure 6 to resemble water:	Alcoholics; or alcoholic tendency. (Hutt, 1969; Tolor-Schulberg-Story)
Fanciful elaboration and ornamentation of the design; non-cryptic embellishment:	Manic state. (Bender)
Severe elaboration:	Schizophrenia. (Hutt, 1969)

Line Quality

Fine tremor:	Tension. (Hutt, 1969)
Gestalt preserved, outlines indefinite:	Chronic alcoholic hallucinatory states. (Tolor-Schulberg-Bender)
Tremors:	Intense anxiety; neurologic condition. (Hutt, 1969)
Tremulous line:	Possible alcoholic psychosis; or traumatic psychosis following head injury. (Bender)
Very heavy, very light or markedly inconsistent line quality:	Neurosis. (Hutt, 1969)

Margin

Excessive margin:	Anxiety; inadequacy feeling with efforts at self-mastery (Tolor-Schulberg-Hutt and Briskin); neuroticism. (Tolor-Schulberg-Hutt)
Margin-based drawings:	Anxiety, inadequacy, insecurity; atypical of schizophrenics unless intense anxiety is present or the condition is incipient; brain damage, paranoia. (Hutt, 1969)
Margin-based drawings, figures confined to upper half of page:	Insecurity, lack of confidence. (Anderson-Halpern)
Narrow margin:	Schizophrenia (paranoids). [Hutt, 1969]

Multiple Criteria

Collision; elaboration; fragmentation, incoordination; marked angulation difficulty; overlapping difficulty; perseveration; redrawing of total figure; severe rotation, especially when subject does not recognize rotation or is unable to correct it; simplification:

Intracranial damage. (Hutt, 1969)

Collision tendency; flattened curvature; fragmentation on figures 7 and 8; irregular sequence; marked closure difficulty; markedly irregular use of space; mild simplification:

Retardation. (Hutt, 1969)

Confused sequence; fragmentation; marked closure difficulty; moderate rotation, usually with capacity to correct; narrow margin (paranoids); perseveration; primitive gestalt forms (retrogression); redrawing of total figure; rotation, usually with ability to correct; several pages required (prepsychosis); severe elaboration; simplification (chronicity); very abnormal placement of first figure:

Schizophrenia. (Hutt, 1969)

Crossing difficulty; irregular sequence; marked isolated size change; mild angulation difficulty; mild curvature difficulty; mild rotation difficulty; movement in deviant direction; overly methodical sequence; very heavy, very light, or markedly inconsistent line quality:

Neurosis. (Hutt, 1969)

Difficulty with intersecting figures; difficulty with straight-line figures, increased curvature; light line drawings; reduction of vertical dimension:

Passivity. (Hutt, 1969)

Norms

Ability to copy square and triangle:

Four years. (Bender-Gesell)

Ability to imitate vertical stroke:	Two years. (Bender-Gesell)
Ability to mark with a pencil:	One year. (Bender-Kuhlman)
Ability to reproduce complex design from memory:	Ten years. (Bender-Stanford-Binet)
Ability to scribble imitatively:	Nine months to a year. (Bender-Gesell)
Ability to scribble spontaneously:	One to one-and-a-half years. (Bender-Gesell)
Age at which all designs are accurately reproduced:	Age eleven. (Bender)
Age at which rotation ceases:	Age seven. (Tolor-Schulberg)
Angles, diamonds and oblique lines, correctly rendered:	At least average intelligence. (Bender)
Circle copying:	Two-year-old child (Bender-Kuhlman); three-year-old child (Bender-Gesell); four-year-old child. (Bender-Buckler)
Cross copying:	Four-year-old child. (Bender)
Diamond copying:	Seven-year-old child. (Bender)
Ranges in which age and education have an effect on Bender-Gestalt performance:	Ages 15–50, at least ten years of education. (Tolor-Schulberg-Pascal and Suttell)
Scribble:	Children three years and under. (Bender)
Square copying:	Four-year-old child. (Bender)
Star copying:	Five-year-old child. (Bender)

Perceptual Impairment

Inability to copy angles:	Organicity. (Anderson-Halpern)
Inability to localize objects in space and separate them from their background:	Possible occipital lesion. (Bender)
Inability to recognize previously learned configurations, such as square, circle, and so on:	Alexia, aphasia. (Bender)

Probable areas most involved in visual-motor gestalt functions:

Adjoining occipital in temporal-parietal region; Wernicke's area or adjacency, probably left except in left-handed; the closer to occipital the lesion, the greater the gestalt disturbance. (Bender)

Perseveration

Absence of perseveration in presence of distortions atypical of usual diagnostic syndromes:

Possible malingering. (Bender)

Perseveration:

Organic brain damage (Hutt and Briskin-Masher and Smith); organic brain damage; schizophrenia (Hutt, 1969); possible schizophrenia. (Bender)

Perseveration on figure 1 and 2:

Organic brain damage. (Hutt, 1969)

Perseveration, more on figure 1 than 2:

Brain-damaged retardates. (Tolor-Schulberg-Baroff)

Perseveration with preservation of gestalt:

With other signs possible dementia paralytica (chronic syphilitic meningo-encephalitis). [Bender]

Redrawing of total figure:

Schizophrenia. (Hutt, 1969)

Severe perseveration:

Organicity, rigidity, schizophrenia. (Hutt, 1969)

Placement

Abnormal first figure placement:

Neuroticism. (Tolor-Schulberg-Hutt and Briskin)

First figure in center of page:

Marked egocentricity. (Hutt, 1969)

Placement of design A in extreme upper left-hand corner of page, especially with size reduction:

Anxiety, withdrawal. (Hutt, 1969)

Placement of design A in lower left or lower right page corner:

Borderline psychotic; malingering psychopath; schizophrenia. (Hutt, 1969)

Placement of designs in upper left-hand corner:

Anxiety, timidity. (Hutt, 1969)

Very abnormal placement of first figure:	Schizophrenia. (Hutt, 1969)

Pressure

Light line drawings:	Passivity. (Hutt, 1969)
Heavy line, impulsive execution:	Hostility externalized. (Anderson-Halpern)
Heavy pressure:	Externalized anxiety. (Hutt, 1969)
Very light pressure:	Inhibited or internalized anxiety. (Hutt, 1969)

Rotation

Awareness of rotation:	Transitional disturbance. (Hutt, 1969)
Change of circle columns, design 2, to the vertical plane or reverse direction:	Alcoholism; attempt to control affective stimuli. (Tolor-Schulberg-Story)
Clockwise rotation of first three figures:	Substantial depressive tendency. (Hutt, 1969)
Counterclockwise rotation:	Oppositional tendency. (Hutt, 1969)
Dip in figure 1; displacement of curve downward, figure 4; extension downward of curve on one side, figure 5:	Depressive tendency. (Anderson-Halpern)
Figure 1 dots drawn in downward angle to left:	Depression. (Hutt, 1969)
Figure 2 lower at right end than at left:	Depressive trend. (Hutt, 1969)
Figure 3 lower at right end than left:	Depressive trend. (Hutt, 1969)
Inability to correct rotation:	Organic; regressed schizophrenic. (Hutt, 1969)
Incidence of rotations:	Greater for epileptics than for other organics. (Tolor-Schulberg-Hovey with Graham-Kendall test)
Low incidence of rotations:	Characteristic of character disorders. (Tolor-Schulberg)
Marked perceptual rotation:	Psychosis, intracranial pathology, retardation. (Hutt, 1969)

Mild clockwise rotation:	Depression. (Hutt, 1969)
Mild rotation:	Neurosis. (Hutt, 1969)
Mild rotation (especially with depressives):	Neuroticism. (Tolor-Schulberg-Hutt and Briskin)
Moderate rotation, usually with capacity to correct:	Schizophrenia. (Hutt, 1969)
Probability of rotations:	Increases as intelligence decreases. (Tolor-Schulberg-Griffith and Taylor).
Reversal of design 45° or to mirror image of self:	Confusional state. (Bender)
Rotation:	Alcoholism (Tolor-Schulberg-Kaldegg); organics, retardates, schizophrenics (Tolor-Schulberg-Griffith and Taylor, Hutt and Briskin); possible alcoholic psychosis or traumatic psychosis following head injury (Bender); retardation. (Hutt, 1969)
Rotation of figure:	Severe psychopathology. (Hutt, 1969)
Rotation of horizontal gestalt to the vertical plane:	Reading difficulty in children. (Hutt, 1969; Tolor-Schulberg-Fabian)
Rotation 45°:	Schizophrenia. (Bender)
Rotation 90° to 180°:	Egocentricity, rigidity. (Hutt, 1969)
Rotation more than 180°:	Oppositional tendency. (Hutt, 1969)
Rotation with preservation of gestalt:	With other signs, possible dementia paralytica (chronic syphilitic meningoencephalitis). [Bender]
Rotation of upright hexagon of design 7 more than 5° but less than 20° to the left:	Alcoholics (Hutt, 1969-Story); attempt to control affective stimuli. (Tolor-Schulberg-Story)
Severe rotation, especially when subject does not recognize rotation or is unable to correct it:	Intracranial damage. (Hutt, 1969)
Slight clockwise rotation tendency:	Ambivalence toward same-sex parent, depressive tendency. (Hutt, 1969)
Unawareness of rotation:	Organic, schizophrenic. (Hutt, 1969)

Sequence

Atypical sequence:

Ambivalence, immaturity, rebelliousness. (Hutt, 1969)

Change of position, figure 8:

Conflict with women; heterosexual anxiety. (Hutt, 1969)

Confused sequence of BG drawings (right to left instead of left to right, bottom to top instead of top to bottom, or some combination of these):

Manic, schizophrenic, toxic psychosis. (Hutt, 1969)

Extreme orderliness of sequence:

Compulsivity. (Hutt, 1969)

Irregular sequence:

Inadequate impulse control; retardation. (Hutt, 1969)

Irregular or overly methodical sequence:

Neurosis. (Tolor-Schulberg-Hutt)

Right to left placement:

Negativism, rebelliousness. (Hutt, 1969)

Orderly sequence:

Good adjustment in children. (Hutt, 1969-Clawson)

Overly methodical or irregular sequence:

Neurosis. (Hutt, 1969)

Simplification

Mild simplification:

Retardation. (Hutt, 1969)

Simplification:

Intracranial damage; problems of impulse control; schizophrenics (with chronicity). [Hutt, 1969]

Simplification of drawing with correct slant:

Possible malingering. (Bender)

Part II
Human Figure Drawing

Activity

Active same sex figure:

Hysteric and manic tendency; pressure for motor activity; restlessness. (Hammer-Levy)

Figure depicted in motion:

Fantasy activity. (Anderson-Machover)

Male receiving something of value from female:

Dependence on maternal figure. (Hammer)

Age

Older figure than subject:

Identification with parent of same sex. (Machover)

Younger figure than subject:

Emotional fixation at age depicted or wish to return to youth (Machover); immaturity. (Hammer)

Alteration

Change of detail in drawing:

Change is defense against spontaneous reaction to situation as symbolized by detail first depicted. (Hammer)

Erasures:

Anxiety, restlessness: possible neurotic tendency (Machover); conflict area. (Hammer-Levy, Machover)

Excessive erasure:

Indecision, self-dissatisfaction. (Hammer)

Infrequent erasure:

Regression. (Machover)

Anomalies

Area depicted as broken, cut, damaged, or otherwise impaired:	Feeling of emasculation anxiety or masculine inadequacy. (Hammer)
Bizarre details:	Schizophrenia. (Hammer-Levy, Machover)
Body distortions:	Psychotic tendency. (Hammer-Levy)
Deviant drawing with little evidence of anxiety:	Character disorder, such as antisocial personality ("psychopathy") or psychosis. (Hammer-Levy)
Disheveled, unkempt figure:	Felt lack of status, low self-esteem. (Hammer)
Distortion of part:	Conflict relative to that part. (Hammer-Levy)
Elongated anatomical areas:	Phallic symbol. (Hammer)
Internal organs shown:	Schizophrenic (Machover); somatic delusions. (Anderson-Machover)
Less pathology suggested by drawing than by Rorschach:	Improved prognosis. (Hammer)
More pathology suggested by drawing than by Rorschach:	Less favorable prognosis. (Hammer)
Omission of part:	Conflict relative to that part. (Hammer-Levy, Machover)
Pathological drawing, less pathological Rorschach:	Latent severe pathology. (Hammer)
Pathological Rorschach, less pathological drawing:	Good prognosis. (Hammer)
Pathology about equally distributed in all drawings and in Rorschach:	Worst prognosis. (Hammer)
Transparency:	Poor judgment. (Anderson-Machover)
Unessential details emphasized:	Schizophrenia. (Machover)

Appurtenances

Aggressive content, as daggers, guns, spears:	Delinquent tendency possibly. (Hammer)

Belt emphasized:

Sexual conflict. (Machover)

Body emphasis (underclothed):

Egocentric; schizoid. (Machover)

Buckle:

Dependency. (Anderson-Machover)

Buttons:

Dependency (Hammer-Halpern); dependency, immaturity, inadequacy (Hammer-Levy); maternal dependence. (Anderson-Machover)

Buttons on clothing over breasts of figure:

Affectional deprivation, dependence; possible identification with mother. (Hammer-Levy)

Buttons on cuffs:

Obsessive element accompanying dependency. (Machover)

Buttons inconspicuous (as on cuffs):

Obsessive-compulsive. (Hammer-Levy)

Buttons in midline:

Maternal dependence (Machover); somatic preoccupation. (Hammer-Levy)

Buttons plus hat:

Regression. (Machover)

Cane:

Impotency (Anderson-Machover); involutional resistance to sexual decline, virility striving. (Machover)

Cigarette:

Sexual preoccupation, virility striving. (Machover)

Cigarette between lips:

Sophisticated oral-eroticism. (Machover)

Clothing carefully rendered:

Egocentric, immature; overconcern for material criteria for social status. (Hammer-Levy)

Clothing detail elaboration:

Homosexual trend. (Anderson-Machover)

Clothing elaboration, grooming:

Emphasis on possession and social prestige. (Machover)

Clothing foppish (overclothed):

Egocentricity, antisocial personality ("psychopathic") tendency; need for social approval and dominance. (Machover)

Clothes ill-fitting:	Unsatisfying social status. (Hammer)
Clothing transparent (body visible):	Voyeurism. (Machover)
Collar tight:	Problem with control of anger. (Hammer-Levy)
Disguise (clown, etc.):	Dissatisfaction with self. (Hammer)
Earrings:	Exhibitionism, sexual preoccupation. (Hammer-Levy)
Fireplace (with fire in it) before figure:	Need for emotional security and warmth. (Hammer)
Gun:	Aggressive tendency, hostility (Hammer); sexual preoccupation. (Machover)
Handkerchief of coat pocket emphasized:	Sexual inadequacy. (Machover)
Hat crease:	Fantasy relative to female genitalia. (Hammer-Buck)
Hat, no clothes:	Regression. (Machover)
Hat plus buttons:	Regression. (Machover)
Hat transparent:	Primitive sexual behavior. (Machover)
High heel on male, male subject:	Homoerotic tendency. (Hammer-Machover)
Knife:	Aggressive tendency, hostility. (Hammer)
Mask:	Cautious, secretive; possible feelings of depersonalization and estrangement. (Hammer)
Pants transparent (legs show through):	Homosexual anxiety. (Machover)
Pipe:	Sexual preoccupation, virility striving. (Machover)
Pipe between lips:	Sophisticated oral-eroticism. (Machover)
Pocket:	Affectional deprivation (Hammer-Machover); maternal dependence. (Anderson-Machover)
Pocket emphasis:	Dependent psychopath. (Machover)

Pockets, several (male figure, male subject).	Passive homosexual tendency. (Hammer-Levy)
Shoelaces, wrinkles, other unnecessary detailing:	Obsessive-compulsive. (Hammer-Levy)
Skirt ankle-length on female (male subject):	Maternal figure. (Machover)
Straw, toothpick between lips:	Primitive oral-eroticism. (Machover)
Tie:	Masculine striving (Hammer); sexual inadequacy. (Machover)
Tie, flying or swept-out:	Overt sexual aggression, sexual preoccupation. (Machover)
Transparencies:	Breaks in judgment, voyeurism (depending on area). [Machover]
Trousers fly:	Preoccupation with masturbation. (Machover)
Uniform of cowboy or soldier on male figure of male subject:	Need for greater status and recognition than subject feels he possesses. (Hammer)
V-neckline on female, male subject:	Breast fixation, voyeuristic tendency. (Machover)
Weapons:	Aggressiveness. (Hammer-Levy)
Wrinkles, shoelaces, other unnecessary detailing:	Obsessive-compulsive. (Hammer-Levy)
Yo-yo:	Immaturity, masturbatory fixation. (Hammer-Levy)

Context

Clouds:	Anxiety, depression. (Anderson-Machover)
Doodling of subject's name:	Egotism, narcissism. (Hammer)
Fence to lean on, ground line:	Need for support or help. (Hammer-Levy)
Ground line:	Insecurity. (Hammer-Machover)
Strong wind in scene of Human Figure Drawing:	Felt subjection to strong environmental pressure or stress, with fear of psychosis. (Hammer)

Sun added to HFD scene:

Need for affection, nurturing warmth. (Hammer)

Continuity

Broken lines:

Anxiety, insecurity. (Hammer-Buck)

Disconnected lines, displaced parts:

Psychotic trend. (Hammer)

Drawing Variations

Draw-a-person variation:

Draw-a-member-of-a-minority-group technique (reveals attitudes not only to minority group, but also subject's projected negative attitudes toward self). [Hammer]

Elaboration

Detail emphasized unessential:

Schizophrenic. (Machover)

Detail excessive:

Obsessive-compulsive tendency (Hammer); obsessive features. (Machover)

Detailing:

Compulsivity. (Hammer-Levy)

Detailing minute:

Constricted, pedantic. (Hammer-Waehner)

Reworking, with addition of excessive detail:

Compulsivity. (Hammer-Levy)

Extremities

Ankles and wrists small:

Effeminacy. (Machover)

Feet and hands dim or omitted:

Schizoid. (Machover)

Feet and legs drawn first:

Depression, discouragement. (Hammer-Levy)

Feet omitted:

Discouragement, withdrawal. (Machover)

Feet small, male subject:

Effeminacy, insecurity. (Anderson-Machover)

Finger omitted or overextended:

Masturbation guilt. (Anderson-Machover)

Fingernails, fingers, joints carefully depicted:

Compulsive body image problem as in early schizophrenic. (Hammer-Levy)

Fingers articulated carefully and cut off by line:

Repressed aggression; withdrawal. (Machover)

Finger, claw:

Overt aggression; paranoid. (Machover)

Fingers, grape:

Immaturity, infantile traits. (Machover)

Fingers with joints and nails carefully indicated:

Obsessive control of aggression. (Machover)

Fingers, large:

Assaultiveness. (Hammer-Katz)

Fingers, fewer than five:

Dependency, helplessness. (Hammer)

Fingers, long:

Overt aggression (Hammer); regression. (Machover)

Fingers, more than five:

Aggression, ambition. (Machover)

Fingers, no hands:

Assaultiveness (Hammer-Katz-Machover); infantile aggression (Machover)

Fingers, petal:

Immaturity; infantile traits. (Machover)

Fingers, scissor:

Subject is castrating or views maternal or paternal figures as castrating. (Hammer)

Fingers, shaded:

Guilt (as theft or masturbation). [Machover]

Fingers, spear:

Overt aggression, paranoia. (Machover)

Fingers, stick:

Assaultiveness (Hammer-Katz-Machover); infantile aggression. (Machover)

Fists clenched or closed:

Rebellion (close to body, repressed; out from body, overt) [Machover] ; repressed aggression. (Hammer-Levy)

Foot emphasized:

Assaultiveness. (Hammer-Katz-Machover)

Foot of male emphasized:

Involutional impotency. (Machover)

Foot phallic:

Sexual inadequacy and preoccupation. (Machover)

Hand of female figure in pelvic area, male subject:	Female regarded as sexually rejecting. (Hammer)
Hand at genital area:	Auto-eroticism. (Machover)
Hand, mitten:	Repressed aggression. (Machover)
Hands behind back or in pockets:	Evasion, guilt, lack of confidence; with hands in pocket may be psychopath. (Machover)
Hands dim:	Lack of confidence in productivity or social contact. (Machover)
Hands emphasized:	Externalized aggression. (Hammer-Levy)
Hands exaggerated:	Compensation for difficulty with interpersonal relations or masturbatory guilt. (Hammer-Levy)
Hands extended behind back in anal area:	Homoerotic conflicts. (Hammer)
Hands and feet dim or omitted:	Schizoid. (Machover)
Hands hidden:	Difficulty with interpersonal relations, masturbatory guilt. (Hammer-Levy)
Hands large:	Compensation for felt weakness, guilt. (Machover)
Hands omitted:	Inadequacy, withdrawal. (Hammer).
Hands omitted on female figure:	Maternal figure regarded as rejecting, unloving, unsupportive. (Hammer)
Hands powerful:	Aggressiveness. (Hammer)
Hands shaded:	Anxiety over difficulty with inter-personal relations or masturbatory guilt (Hammer); guilt over aggression or masturbatory guilt. (Machover)
Joint and knuckle emphasis:	Feeling of body disorganization: maternal dependence: psychosexual immaturity; schizoid, schizophrenic. (Machover)
Joints, fingers, fingernails carefully depicted:	Compulsive body image problem as in early schizophrenia. (Hammer-Levy)

Legs and feet drawn first:	Depression, discouragement. (Hammer-Levy)
Toes exposed:	Aggressiveness. (Machover)
Wrists and ankles small:	Effeminacy. (Machover)

Face

Brow (eyebrow) bushy:	Uninhibited. (Machover).
Brow (eyebrow) trim:	Disdain, refinement. (Machover)
Chin empasized:	Compensation for inadequacy, indecision, fear of responsibility (dim line elsewhere, fantasy) compensation). [Machover]
Chin emphasized on opposite sex:	Dependency on opposite sex; opposite sex regarded as stronger. (Machover)
Chin enlarged:	Aggressive drive. (Hammer-Levy)
Chin exaggerated:	Compensation for felt weakness, indecision. (Hammer-Levy)
Eye a circle (no pupil):	Egocentric hysteric (Anderson-Machover); egocentricity, immaturity, regression. (Machover)
Eye a dot with pressure, unenclosed:	Ideas of reference, paranoia. (Anderson-Machover)
Eye emphasized:	Externalized aggression (Hammer-Levy); paranoia. (Machover)
Eye prominent:	Assaultiveness. (Hammer-Katz-Machover)
Eye small:	Self-absorption, voyeuristic tendency. (Machover)
Eyes closed:	Schizoid. (Machover)
Eyes large, no pupil:	Voyeuristic tendency with guilt. (Hammer-Levy)
Eyes large, staring:	Paranoid trend. (Hammer-Levy)
Eyes and lashes large:	Homosexuality. (Hammer-Levy)
Eyes reinforced:	Assaultiveness. (Hammer-Levy)

Face dim:	Self-conscious, shy. (Hammer-Levy)
Facial expression:	May express attitude subject feels other people have toward him, rather than his attitude toward them (Hammer): prevailing mood and attitude. (Machover)
Facial expression placating:	Insecurity. (Hammer-Machover)
Facial expression self-preoccupied:	Schizoid. (Machover)
Facial scars on same sex figure:	May indicate expectation of aggression from environment or impaired self-esteem; may symbolize psychic trauma. (Hammer)
Features childlike:	Infantile social behavior. (Machover)
Features effeminate, male subject:	Homosexual trend. (Anderson-Machover)
Features masklike:	Cautious, secretive; possible feeling of depersonalization and estrangement. (Hammer)
Features overemphasized:	Inadequacy with compensatory fantasy. (Machover)
Features primitive, tiny:	Schizophrenic. (Machover)
Lashes and eyes large:	Homosexuality. (Hammer-Levy)
Lashes long:	Coquettishness, seductiveness, self-display. (Anderson-Machover)
Lashes on male:	Effeminacy, homoerotic tendency (Machover); homosexual tendency. (Hammer)
Lips full on male:	Effeminacy. (Machover)
Mouth clownlike:	Forced amiability, inappropriate affect. (Machover)
Mouth concave, oral-receptive:	Passive-dependency. (Machover)
Mouth emphasized:	Alcoholism, depression, regression. (Machover)
Mouth heavy line:	Oral-aggression, sadism. (Machover)
Mouth markedly full, open or oval:	Dependent, oral-erotic. (Hammer-Levy)

Mouth omitted on female subject: Possible scolding maternal figure. (Machover)

Mouth open: Orality. (Hammer)

Mouth line single: Oral-aggressive. (Hammer-Levy)

Nose broad, flared, hooked: Contemptuous attitude; tendency to think in terms of derisive social stereotypes. (Hammer-Levy)

Nose cut-off: Castration fears or wishes. (Anderson-Machover)

Nose large: Involutional melancholia, sexual impotency. (Adolescents: felt inadequate male role with striving for it.) [Hammer-Levy]

Nose long: Impotence (Machover); virility wish (Hammer-Levy)

Nose shaded: Castration; may be projected on opposite sex. (Machover)

Nose strong: Masculine assertion; or need for it. (Anderson-Machover)

Nostrils: Primitive aggression. (Machover)

Teeth shown: Oral-aggressive, sadistic (Hammer-Levy); oral-aggression, simple schizophrenic. (Machover)

Teeth well-defined: Aggressiveness. (Hammer)

Figure Type

Cartoon figure, clown: Adolescents with feelings of inadequacy or rejection; internalized hostility, self-contempt. (Hammer-Levy)

Drawing of male first, female subject: Female protest, feminine role rejection. (Machover)

Maternal figure rather than female sex object (male subject): Dependence on maternal figure. (Hammer)

Opposite sex drawn first: Sexual role conflict. (Machover)

Parental figures rather than self-image: Children; also adults preoccupied with past who are unable to emancipate themselves from their parents. (Hammer)

Peanut man, snowman, stick man:	Evasion of body problems. (Machover)
Peanut man, stick figure in subject capable of more advanced drawing:	Exhibitionistic tendency; secretive. (Anderson-Machover)
Puppet:	Compliance; feeling of domination by others. (Hammer)
Robot for male figure (male subject):	Depersonalization; feeling of being controlled by outside forces. (Hammer)
Stick figure:	May express evasion or negativism. (Hammer)
Type of person drawn:	Ideal self-perception of others; self-portrait. (Hammer)
Witches:	Hostility toward women, expressed overtly. (Hammer-Levy)

Hair

Balding male figure:	Felt lack of virility. (Hammer)
Beard, moustache, other facial hair (male subject):	Doubts about virility with compensatory virility striving; sexual inadequacy. (Hammer-Levy)
Hair area significance:	Virility striving. (Machover)
Hair emphasis:	Infantile or regressed sex drives. (Anderson-Machover); sensuality or sensual needs. (Hammer-Machover)
Hair emphasis (shaded):	Virility symbol (Machover); with heavy shading possible anxiety over sensual needs. (Hammer-Machover)
Hair on female, not on male:	Regression. (Machover)
Hair given much attention:	Narcissism; possible homosexual tendency. (Hammer)
Hair on jaw:	Schizoid. (Machover)
Hair mussed:	Sexual immorality. (Machover)
Hair parted in middle:	Feminine identification dealt with by

narcissism and obsessive-compulsive mechanisms. (Hammer-Levy)

Hair reinforced:

Assaultiveness. (Hammer-Katz)

Sparse, unpressured hair:

Inadequate virility. (Machover)

Hair white on male figure:

Felt lack of masculinity and virility. (Hammer)

Head

Ear emphasized or enlarged:

Auditory hallucinations: ideas of reference; paranoid or schizoid (Machover); auditory hallucinations in paranoid; ear injury or hearing disability; paranoia, sensitivity to attitudes of others (Anderson-Machover); passive homosexual conflict or tendency. (Hammer-Levy)

Ears large:

Sensitivity to criticism (children as subjects). [Hammer-Jolles]

Head dim:

Self-conscious, shy. (Hammer-Levy)

Head drawn last:

Conflict over interpersonal relations (Machover); possible thought disorder. (Hammer-Levy)

Head enlarged:

Concern about sufficiency of intellect (brain damaged, retarded), overideational (including paranoid), pride over intellect (Machover); emphasis on fantasy (children as subjects) [Hammer-Jolles]; intellectual aspirations (with possible grandiosity), introspective or fantasy preoccupied, somatic head symptoms. (Hammer-Levy)

Head large on figure of opposite sex:

Opposite sex regarded as smarter or as possessing greater social authority. (Machover)

Head malformed:

Organicity. (Anderson-Machover)

Head split:

Feminine identification dealt with by

narcissism and obsessive-compulsive mechanisms. (Hammer-Levy)

Limbs

Arm and leg distortion or reinforcement, left side, male subject, male figure:

Sexual role conflict. (Hammer-Levy)

Armless figure of male, male subject:

Strong genital drive associated with guilt; wish to be castrated. (Hammer-Levy)

Arms close to body:

Tension. (Machover)

Arms extended from body and overlong:

Externalized aggression. (Hammer-Levy)

Arms folded, short:

Rejecting maternal or paternal figure of opposite sex. (Machover)

Arms heavy, shaded, on opposite sex:

Opposite sex viewed as punishing. (Machover)

Arms and legs of male figure large:

Assaultiveness. (Hammer-Katz)

Arms and legs tapering:

Effeminacy. (Machover)

Arms long:

Ambition for accomplishment or acquisition (Machover); overt aggression. (Hammer)

Arms long and powerful:

Need for autonomy (children as subjects). [Hammer-Jolles]

Arms long, weak:

Dependency, nurturance needs. (Anderson-Machover)

Arms omitted:

Guilt, withdrawal (depressive, schizophrenic) [Machover]; withdrawal. (Hammer-Levy)

Arms omitted or short arms on opposite sex:

Rejection by maternal or paternal figure of the opposite sex. (Machover)

Arms overextended, reaching:

Dependency; desire for affection. (Machover)

Arms pressed to sides:

Difficulty in social contact; fear of aggressive impulses (Hammer); passivity

	as defense against aggressive impulses. (Hammer-Levy)
Arms reinforced:	Assaultiveness. (Hammer-Katz)
Arms short:	Lack of ambition. (Machover)
Arms strong, male subject:	Aggressive, energetic. (Anderson-Machover)
Arms thin, weak:	Lack of achievement. (Machover)
Elbows and joints stressed:	Compulsive; dependent, indecisive. (Hammer-Levy)
Joint emphasis:	Schizoid or schizophrenic (Machover); somatic preoccupation. (Anderson-Machover)
Legs and arms of male figure large:	Assaultiveness. (Hammer-Katz)
Legs and arms tapering:	Effeminacy. (Machover)
Legs long:	Need for autonomy (children as subjects). [Hammer-Jolles]
Legs masculine on female figure:	Sexual role conflict. (Machover)
Legs omitted:	Discouragement, withdrawal. (Machover)
Legs reinforced:	Assaultiveness. (Hammer-Katz)

Line Form

Angular body:	Aggression, criticality, masculinity. (Anderson-Machover)
Circular strokes:	Dependency, feminine tendency, lack of assertion (Hammer-Alschuler and Hattwick); dependent, emotional. (Hammer-Alschuler and Hattwick, children as subjects)
Curved lines on body of male:	Effeminacy. (Machover)
Emphasis on circles in depicting body:	Effeminate, narcissistic, submissive. (Anderson-Machover)
Few curves, many sharp edges:	Aggressive, poorly adjusted. (Hammer-Waehner)

Rounded lines: Femininity. (Hammer-Krout)

Straight lines: Aggressiveness. (Hammer-Krout)

Straight-line strokes: Assertiveness (children as subjects).
                                        [Hammer-Alshuler and Hattwick]

Line Quality

Combination of firm, heavy and light   Assaultiveness. (Hammer-Katz)
lines:

Constricted stroking: Tension, withdrawal. (Hammer-Levy)

Dim line: Timidity. (Machover)

Energetic, unhesitant stroke: Perseverance, security. (Hammer-Levy)

Fading line: Hysteric tendency. (Machover)

Fluctuating line: Tension. (Machover)

Heavy thick lines: Aggression: depersonalization fears.
                                        (Machover)

Horizontal stroke: Emphasis on fantasy; femininity, weak-
                                        ness. (Hammer-Levy)

Indeterminate vacillating stroke: Insecurity, lack of perseverance. (Ham-
                                        mer-Levy)

Jagged lines: Hostility. (Hammer-Krout)

Length of stroke movement: Decreases in excitable subjects, in-
                                        creases in inhibited ones. (Hammer-
                                        Mira)

Line break: Conflict area. (Machover)

Long strokes: Controlled behavior (children as sub-
                                        jects). [Hammer-Alschuler and Hatt-
                                        wick]

Reinforced line: Anxiety, insecurity (Hammer-Buck);
                                        conflict area (Hammer-Levy; Mach-
                                        over); repression, particularly with ref-
                                        erence to area reinforced. (Hammer)

Rhythmic stroking: Responsive, uninhibited. (Hammer-
                                        Levy)

Short sketchy strokes: Anxiety, uncertainty. (Hammer-Levy)

Short strokes:

Impulsive behavior (children as subject). [Hammer-Alschuler and Hattwick]

Sketchy lines:

Anxiety, timidity. (Hammer)

Thin, elongated line:

Tension. (Hammer)

Unbroken reinforced line outlining figure:

Isolation. (Hammer-Levy)

Uninterrupted straight lines:

Decisive. (Hammer-Levy)

Vertical stroke:

Assertive, determined, hyperactive. (Hammer-Levy)

Very faint line:

Depressed, inadequate (Hammer); withdrawn schizophrenic. (Machover)

Margin

Drawing near margin:

Dependency, lack of self-confidence. (Hammer)

Multiple Criteria

Bizarre features; confusion full face and profile; ear emphasis; emphasis on joints; failure to recognize grotesqueness of drawing; giraffe neck; gross disproportion; internal organs shown; omission of arms; sexual organ indicated; primitive features with tiny features; unessential detail emphasized; very faint line:

Schizophrenic. (Machover)

Breaks in line; erasures; omission; reinforcement, shading:

Conflict area. (Machover)

Breast emphasis; buckles; buttons; concave mouth; midline emphasis; pockets:

Dependency. (Machover)

Breast emphasis, buttock emphasis; effeminate features; elaboration of clothing detail; high heels on male figure, male subject:

Homosexual trend. (Anderson-Machover)

Breast emphasis; buttons; fingerless

Insecurity. (Machover)

hands; grape or petal fingers; midline emphasis:

Combination of firm, heavy and light lines; large arms and fingers; reinforced arms, eyes, fingers, and hair; stance with legs wide apart:

Assaultiveness. (Hammer-Katz)

Curved lines on body of male; full lips, high heel shoes, lashes, small ankles, feet and wrists, tapering arms and legs, all on male figure:

Effeminacy. (Machover)

Ear and eye emphasis; large grandiose figure; large head; speared or talon fingers:

Paranoid. (Machover)

Fingers without hands; foot emphasis; heavy line; prominent eye; stick fingers; wide stance:

Machover indices differentiating assaultive from nonassaultive subjects, as confirmed by Katz. (Hammer)

Ground line; placating facial expression; shaded shoes:

Insecurity. (Machover)

Hands in pocket; heavy shading; large figure:

Antisocial personality ("psychopath"). [Machover]

Powerful hands; squared shoulders; weapons; well-defined teeth:

Aggressiveness. (Hammer)

Neck

Adam's apple:

Masculinity striving; sexual role confusion (on opposite sex, that sex regarded as not virile). [Machover]

Neck emphasis:

Need for defensive intellectual control (children as subjects). [Hammer-Halpern]

Neck excessively large:

Awareness of physical impulses, with effort to control them. (Hammer-Buck)

Neck like giraffe:

Schizophrenic. (Machover)

Neck long (elongated):

Hysterical swallowing inhibition; problem in control of anger or of primitive drives; schizoid tendency. (Hammer-Levy)

Neck long, thin:	Inhibition, repression. (Machover)
Neck narrow:	Depression. (Hammer-Levy)
Neck omission:	Immaturity, lack of impulse control, regression. (Machover)
Neck short, thick:	Self-indulgence, uninhibited impulse expression. (Anderson-Machover)

Norms

Ability to draw recognizable figure of a man:	Five years of age. (Bender-Gesell)
Arms connected to trunk rather than head:	Six years of age. (Hammer-Halpern)
Change from segmented to unit body:	Eight years of age. (Hammer-Halpern)
Hands and fingers:	Five to six years of age. (Hammer-Halpern)
Head and limbs, little or no trunk:	Three to four years of age. (Hammer-Halpern)
Naval:	Four to five years of age. (Hammer-Halpern)
Row of buttons:	Six to seven years of age. (Hammer-Halpern)
Sexual differentiation of figures:	Five years of age. (Hammer-Halpern)
Shoulders:	Eight years of age. (Hammer-Halpern)
Two-dimensional arms and legs:	Eight years of age. (Hammer-Halpern)

Nudity

Idealized nude figures:	Voyeurism. (Hammer-Levy)
Nude figures with sexual parts:	Rebellion against sexual mores. (Hammer-Levy)
Same-sex figure nude and carefully rendered:	Body narcissism, egocentricity, immaturity. (Hammer-Levy)

Placement

Area variations:	High on page, optimism; low on page,

	depression; middle, aggression; left, self-oriented or introversive; right, environment-oriented or extroverted. (Machover)
Below-midpoint drawings:	Concretistic, depressed mood, feelings of inadequacy. (Hammer-Buck)
Centered drawing:	Emotional, self-centered (children as subjects); security. (Hammer-Alschuler-Hattwick)
Elevation of drawing above midpoint:	Aloofness; fantasy rather than reality satisfactions. (Hammer-Buck)
Feet on base of page:	Need for stability because of disturbance produced by a conflict. (Hammer)
High-on-page figure (looks adrift):	Insecurity, unrealistic euphoria. (Machover)
Large, centered figure:	Manic tendencies; paranoid grandiosity. (Machover)
Large figure shifted to left:	Aggressive psychopath with feelings of inadequacy. (Machover)
Left-side-of-page figure:	Introversive, self-oriented, tense. (Machover)
Middle placement:	Overt aggression. (Machover)
Right-side-of-page figure:	Environment-oriented. (Machover)
Upper-left-corner drawings:	Regression. (Buck)

Posture

Back of male figure to observer, male subject:	Desire to be a woman, feminine identification. (Hammer-Levy)
Confusion of full-face and profile (profile forehead and nose, full-face eyes and mouth):	Mental retardation ("mental defective"); primitive cultural origin; schizophrenics. (Machover)
Face turned toward page, so that back of head shows:	Withdrawal tendency. (Hammer)
Full-face figure:	Exhibitionistic tendency; social accessi-

bility. (Machover) Social communications, social dependency. (Anderson-Machover)

Off-balance figure: Preschizophrenic possiblility. (Hammer)

Profile figure: Evasiveness. (Machover)

Profile head, full-face body: Social anxiety with need for contact. (Machover)

Profile head and legs, full-face trunk: Poor judgment. (Machover)

Reclining or seated same-sex figure: Emotional exhaustion, lack of drive, low energy. (Hammer-Levy)

Rigid posture: Constriction, defensiveness, lack of assertion. (Hammer)

Rigid posture, profile figure: Defensive restriction of activity. (Hammer-Buck)

Seated figure: Inhibition, lack of drive. (Hammer)

Seated same-sex figure: Reduced drive and energy. (Hammer)

Self-conscious stance: Timid. (Machover)

Stance tight: Schizoid. (Machover)

Stance unbalanced: Tensions. (Machover)

Stance wide: Aggressive tendencies; assaultiveness. (Hammer-Katz)

Stiff posture: Rigid emotional controls. (Hammer-Levy)

Pressure

Excessive pressure: Antisocial personalities ("psychopaths"); organics (including retardates); paranoids. (Hammer-Payne)

Faint line: Apprehensive neurotics, catatonics, and chronic schizophrenics. (Hammer-Pfiester)

Firm lines: Ambition, drive. (Hammer-Levy)

Fluctuating pressure: Cyclothymic, impulsive, unstable. (Hammer-Levy)

Heavy line:

Assaultiveness. (Hammer-Katz-Machover)

Heavy pressure:

Energy, assertiveness (Hammer); extreme tension, organicity (Hammer-Buck); antisocial personalities ("psychopaths"); epileptics, organics. (Hammer-Pfiester)

Light lines:

Low energy. (Hammer-Levy)

Light pressure:

Low energy level, repression, restraint. (Hammer-Alschuler and Hattwick)

Pressure:

Aggression, sadism. (Machover)

Pressure variations:

Adaptibility, flexibility. (Hammer-Pfiester)

Pressured lines:

Aggressive, assertive. (Anderson-Machover)

Uneven line pressure:

Anxiety, insecurity. (Machover)

Varied pressure:

Emotionally unstable, moody. (Anderson-Machover)

Very faint line:

Schizophrenia. (Machover)

Sequence

Drawing opposite sex first:

Homosexuality, sexual identification conflict, strong attachment to or dependency upon parent or person of opposite sex. (Hammer-Levy)

Extreme discontinuity in drawing (as head, then feet; shoulders, then legs; etc.):

Psychopathology of incipient kind. (Hammer)

Normal succession in drawing:

Absence of thought disorder, adequate reality contact. (Anderson-Machover)

Sex

Average emphasis on female characteristics, female subject—neither over- nor underemphasized:

Genuine satisfaction in sexual role. (Hammer)

Emphasis on female sex characteristics, female subject:

Aggressive use of sexual characteristics, coquettishness. (Hammer-Machover)

Female characteristics underemphasized, female subject:

Constricted erotic response, limited heterosexual experience, somatic sexual dysfunction. (Hammer-Fisher and Fisher)

Female characteristics overstressed, female subjects:

More extensive sexual experiences up to promiscuity; unsatisfying erotic experience. (Hammer-Fisher and Fisher)

Shading

Heavy shading:

Aggressive tendency; antisocial personality ("psychopaths"). [Machover]

Profuse, smudgy shading:

Psychotic potential. (Hammer)

Shading:

Anxiety (Anderson-Machover, Hammer-Levy); aggression, anxiety (Machover); conflict area. (Hammer-Levy, Machover)

Shading in sexual areas:

Anxiety relative to sexual function. (Hammer-Levy)

Slight or minimal shading:

Relative freedom from anxiety. (Hammer-Levy)

Smudgy shading:

Anal-erotic interests. (Anderson-Machover)

Simplification

Abstract or stick figure:

Evasion; insecurity; self-distrustful. (Hammer-Levy)

Inadequate detailing:

Depression; lack of energy; withdrawal tendency. (Hammer)

Size

Decreased size of figure:

More common in men over thirty and women over forty. (Hammer-Lehner and Gunderson)

Drawing that fills the page:

Compensatory fantasy aggrandizement. (Hammer)

Figure too large for page:

Aspiration exceeds opportunities, environment viewed as excessively constraining. (Hammer-Machover)

Large, grandiose figure:

Paranoid. (Machover)

Large same-sex figure:

Aggressive, expansive. (Hammer-Levy)

Large-size drawing:

Antisocial personality ("psychopath") [Machover] ; narcissism (Hammer-Levy)

Obese patients who draw slim figures:

Improved prognosis for successful treatment of obesity. (Hammer)

Opposite-sex figure larger:

Possible passive trend (Hammer-Levy); opposite sex viewed as more powerful. (Machover)

Size of drawing large:

Expansiveness, grandiosity, self-esteem. (Hammer)

Small figures:

Anxiety, emotional dependence, feeling of discomfort and restriction (Hammer-Waehner, Hattwick, Elkisch); constricted ego (Machover)

Small same-sex figure:

Feelings of inadequacy. (Hammer-Levy)

Tiny drawings:

Feelings of inadequacy, withdrawal tendencies. (Hammer)

Space

Figures far apart in draw-a-family picture:

Lack of closeness in family situation. (Hammer)

Symmetry

Disturbed symmetry:

Inadequacy; incoordination. (Machover)

Excessive symmetry:

Depression; intellectualization; obsessive-compulsivity. (Hammer)

Gross disproportion:

Schizophrenia. (Machover)

Lack of symmetry: — Insecurity. (Hammer)

Marked symmetry: — Paranoid schizophrenia. (Machover)

Oversymmetrical drawings: — Compulsivity. (Machover)

Task Orientation

Ability appropriately to evaluate psychotic-looking drawing when asked to "criticize it": — Criterion for retained reality contact. (Hammer-Levy)

Acceptance of task with minimum protest, good initial performance followed by obvious fatigue and discontinuation of task: — Depressed state. (Hammer)

Apologetic of drawing: — Lack of confidence. (Machover)

Decreased pace and productivity as drawing continues: — Fatigability, possibly associated with depression. (Hammer)

Emphasis on left side of figure: — Feminine identification. (Hammer-Levy)

Labeling — Circumstantiality. (Machover)

Left-to-right strokes: — Extroversion, need for support. (Hammer-Levy)

Persistence with drawing despite difficulties: — Good prognosis; presence of drive. (Hammer-Buck)

Refusal or reluctance to draw figure of opposite sex: — Sexual role conflict. (Hammer-Levy)

Resistance to drawing figure: — Evasion of problems, reluctance to reveal self. (Anderson-Machover)

Right-to-left strokes: — Introversion, isolation. (Hammer-Levy)

Sitting on edge of chair: — Desire to escape from situation; fear, loneliness, mistrust. (Hammer)

Strokes away from subject: — Aggression; extroversion. (Hammer-Levy)

Stroking in (toward the body): — Introtensive. (Hammer-Levy)

Stylistic drawing, as caricatured, facetious, simplified: — Exhibitionistic; secretive tendency. (Anderson-Machover)

Unawareness of grotesqueness in drawing: — Schizophrenic tendency in drawing. (Machover)

Trunk

Body line heavy:

Apprehension with neurosis; depersonalization fears. (Machover)

Body line reinforced:

Explosive personality ("emotional instability"). [Anderson-Machover]

Body lower area of female visible through transparent skirt (male subject):

Involutional sex problems, sexual fantasies, sexual preoccupation. (Machover)

Body omitted (no trunk); appendages attached to head:

Denial or repression of physical drives (children as subject) [Hammer-Jolles]; immaturity; or regression, retardation, primitive character structure. (Machover)

Breast area emphasized:

Dependency; emotional and sexual immaturity (Machover); homosexual trend. (Anderson-Machover)

Breast emphasis, female subject:

Feminine identification with dominant mother. (Anderson-Machover)

Breast emphasis, male subject:

Maternal dependence and domination (Anderson-Machover); oral-dependency. (Hammer-Levy)

Breasts small:

Maternal figure unnurturing. (Machover)

Buttock emphasis:

Homosexual trend. (Anderson-Machover)

Buttocks and hips on male figure unusually emphasized or large and rounded:

Homosexual trend. (Hammer-Levy)

Genitalia, especially male:

Analysands; primitive culture; schizophrenics. (Anderson-Machover)

Hip emphasis:

Homosexual impulses. (Machover)

Hip emphasis on male figure, male subject:

Homosexual trend. (Anderson-Machover)

Hipline break:

Sexual conflict. (Hammer-Levy)

Hips and buttocks of male figure unusually emphasized or large and rounded:

Homosexual trend. (Hammer-Levy)

Measurement lines or stick frame for body:

Exhibitionism; perfectionism. (Machover)

Midline emphasis (stressed midline):	Conversion or somatic preoccupation; maternal dependence; possibly schizoid. (Machover)
Navel:	Dependency (Anderson-Machover); dependency (children as subject). [Hammer-Halpern]
Organs shown (internal anatomy):	Manic, schizophrenic (Hammer-Levy); schizophrenia, somatic delusions. (Machover)
Sex organs shown:	Analysands, professional artists, schizophrenics. (Machover)
Sexual anatomy area distorted or omitted:	Sexual conflict. (Hammer-Levy)
Shoulders broad:	Physical power drive. (Machover)
Shoulders drooping:	Dejection; feeling of guilt; lack of vitality. (Hammer)
Shoulders exaggerated or other masculine details:	Feeling of masculine insufficiency. (Hammer-Levy)
Shoulders massive on male (male subject):	Compensation for felt inadequacy. (Machover)
Shoulders squared:	Aggressiveness. (Hammer)
Shoulders wide on female (male subject):	Sexual conflict. (Machover)
Stick frame for body or measurement lines:	Exhibitionism, perfectionism. (Machover)
Torso of female upper half emphasized (male subject):	Dependence on maternal figure. (Machover)
Trunk angular or square:	Masculine tendencies. (Machover)
Trunk incomplete:	Regression. (Machover)
Trunk not closed at bottom:	Sexual preoccupation. (Machover)
Trunk rounded:	Feminine traits. (Machover)
Trunk rounded, narrow waist on male figure, male subject:	Homosexual trend. (Hammer-Levy)
Waist a heavy line:	Sex consciousness. (Machover)
Waist narrow, trunk rounded, on male figure, male subject:	Homosexual trend. (Hammer-Levy)

Waistline bound tightly:

Unstable emotional control. (Machover)

Waistline emphasized:

Sexual conflicts. (Machover)

Composite Criteria

Arms dangling by sides, entreating facial expression, tiny same-sex figure:

Conception of self as dependent, helpless, insignificant. (Hammer)

Arms long and hands prominent, female figure, male subject:

Wish for protective maternal figure. (Hammer-Levy)

Arms long and thin, mouth omitted:

Asthmatic. (Machover)

Arms out with fists clenched:

Aggressive tendencies. (Machover)

Curvilinear line interrupted:

Indecisive. (Hammer-Levy)

Features dim, with emphasis on head contour:

Timidity, withdrawal. (Machover)

Figure clothed with toes exposed:

Aggressive tendencies. (Machover)

Figure effeminate, tie emphasized:

Homesexual trend. (Hammer-Levy)

Figure minuscule, light line pressure:

Constriction, feeling of insignificance and lack of worth. (Hammer)

Figures micrographic, with detail shading, erasures, pressure variations:

Deep repression, neurotic depression. (Machover)

Figures tiny, primitive features:

Regressed schizophrenic; shrunken ego. (Machover)

Figures tiny, well-depicted features:

Alcoholic, involutional, senile patients. (Machover)

Full bodies with shaded or thin legs:

Feeling of decline associated with advancing age. (Shaded legs may be homosexual anxiety.) [Machover]

Hat on nude figure:

Regression. (Machover)

Head clearly indicated, dim line body or no body:

Compensatory fantasy, feeling of anxiety or of inferiority relative to body functions. (Hammer-Levy)

Inability to complete drawing, marked paucity of details:

Significant depression. (Hammer)

Rounded curves, small tie, male subject:

Sexual inadequacy. (Machover)

Shoes shaded:

Insecurity. (Hammer-Levy)

Part III
Wechsler Adult Intelligence Scale (WAIS)

Aptitudes

Decrement visual-motor coordination: Maladjustment. (Rapaport)

Arithmetic

Arithmetic: Measure of concentration. (Rapaport)

Decrement easy Arithmetic items: Psychotic depression; schizophrenia. (Rapaport)

Low Arithmetic: Antisocial personality ("psychopath," "narcissistic character disorder"); psychotic depression; simple schizophrenia. (Schafer-Clinical Application)

Block Design

Decrement Block Design: Depression. (Rapaport)

Comprehension

Comprehension subtest: Practical judgment. (Anderson-Mayman-Schafer-Rapaport; Rapaport)

Decrement Comprehension below Information: Impaired judgment. (Rapaport)

High Comprehension score: Strict moral code. (Schafer-Clinical Application)

"I don't know" responses to Comprehension: Self-deprecating attitude. (Schafer-Clinical Application)

Low Comprehension subtest score: May reflect inflexibility as well as impaired judgment. (Rapaport)

Misses on easy Comprehension items: Psychotic depression; schizophrenia. (Rapaport)

Retained Comprehension Score:

Paranoid schizophrenia. (Schafer-Clinical Application)

Well-retained Comprehension, low Performance, and low Similarities:

Paranoid schizophrenia. (Schafer-Clinical Application)

Digit Span

Digit Span:

Measure of attention. (Rapaport)

Digit Span decrement below Vocabulary:

Anxiety. (Rapaport)

Digit Span eight points or more below Vocabulary:

Possible incipient psychotic break. (Schafer-Clinical Application)

Digit Span equal to or above Arithmetic or Vocabulary:

Possible schizoid or schizophrenic tendency. (Rapaport)

Digit Span six or more points below Information:

Anxiety. (Schafer-Clinical Application)

Digits backward markedly superior to digits forward:

Schizophrenia. (Schafer-Clinical Application)

Elevated Digit Span:

Schizophrenia. (Schafer-Clinical Application)

High Digit Span:

Blandness in hysterics, antisocial personalities ("psychopaths"), chronic schizophrenics. With chronic schizophrenia may get high Object Assembly and Digit Symbol too, because of blandness. (Schafer-Clinical Application); phobia. (Schafer-Clinical Application)

Higher Digit Span than Arithmetic:

Antisocial personality ("narcissistic character disorder"), schizophrenia; impaired concentration, low anxiety tolerance. (Schafer-Clinical Application)

Inability to say Digit Span backward:

Chronic undifferentiated schizophrenia. (Rapaport)

Increment Digit Span backward above Digit Span forward:

Possible schizophrenia, especially paranoid schizophrenia. (Rapaport)

Low Digit Span:

Hysteria. (Schafer-Clinical Application)

Marked decrement of Digit Span:

Anxious undifferentiated schizophrenics; psychotic depression. (Rapaport)

No decrement of Digit Span:

Does not necessarily imply no impairment of recent memory. (Rapaport)

Digit Symbol

Decrement Digit Symbol:

Anxiety or depression; obsessive doubting; regressed schizophrenia. (Rapaport)

Increment Digit Symbol:

Possible schizophrenic blandness. (Rapaport)

Large decrement of Digit Symbol:

Possible psychotic depression. (Rapaport)

Peculiar distortion of Digit Symbol characters:

Possible schizophrenic element. (Rapaport)

Information

Decrement Information below Comprehension:

Hysteric. (Rapaport)

Decrement Information relative to Vocabulary:

Depression; hysteria; schizophrenia. (Rapaport)

Increment failures on easy items of Information, with increment passes on difficult ones:

Depression; hysteric; schizophrenic. (Rapaport)

Increment Information:

Intellectualization tendency; latent schizophrenic, obsessive-compulsive. (Rapaport)

Information below Comprehension and Vocabulary:

Repressive tendency. (Schafer-Clinical Application)

Missing easy Information items with average intelligence:

Possible chronic undifferentiated schizophrenia ("chronic schizophrenia"). [Schafer-Clinical Application]

Object Assembly

Low Object Assembly:

Tension. (Schafer-Clinical Application)

Performance Scale

Higher Performance than Verbal score: Antisocial personality ("narcissistic character disorder," "psychopath"); hysteria; simple schizophrenia. (Schafer-Clinical Application)

Low Performance Score: Possible depression. (Schafer-Clinical Application)

Picture Arrangement

Picture Arrangement: Anticipation and planning ability. (Rapaport)

Picture Arrangement decrement: Anxiety or depression; intellectualizing neurotics and paranoids; schizophrenia. (Rapaport)

Picture Arrangement high: Possible antisocial features. (Schafer-Clinical Application)

Picture Completion

Confusion in identification of objects on Picture Completion with good intelligence: Schizophrenia. (Schafer-Clinical Application)

Decrement Picture Completion, otherwise retained performance: Schizophrenia. (Rapaport)

Failing easy Picture Completion: Psychotic depression; undifferentiated schizophrenia. (Rapaport)

High Picture Completion: Antisocial personality ("psychopath"). [Schafer-Clinical Application]

Increment Picture Completion: Possible paranoid trend. (Rapaport)

Low Picture Completion: Simple schizophrenic. (Schafer-Clinical Application)

Very low Picture Completion: Psychotic depression; schizophrenia. (Rapaport)

Similarities

Similarities: A test of abstraction or concept formation. (Rapaport)

Similarities above other Verbal subtest scores:

Paranoid trend. (Schafer-Clinical Application)

Similarities decrement:

Cultural deprivation. (Rapaport)

Similarities decrement below Vocabulary:

Depression; organicity; schizophrenia. (Rapaport)

Similarities easy items failure:

Depression (neurotic and psychotic), schizophrenia (paranoid, simple, and undifferentiated). [Rapaport]

Similarities high:

Paranoid tendencies; acute paranoid schizophrenia. (Schafer-Clinical Application)

Similarities increment (19+):

Intellectualization. (Rapaport)

Similarities increment above Verbal and Vocabulary mean:

Paranoid tendency. (Rapaport)

Similarities low:

Chronic schizophrenia, especially chronic paranoid schizophrenia. (Schafer-Clinical Application)

Task Orientation

Absurd and impulsive responses:

Schizophrenia. (Schafer-Clinical Application)

Blandness, inappropriate affect:

Chronic undifferentiated schizophrenia ("chronic schizophrenia"). [Schafer-Clinical Application]

Breeziness, joking:

Avoidance tendencies, character disorder, denial of serious personal problems. (Schafer-Clinical Application)

Circumlocutious and irrelevant verbalizations:

Chronic undifferentiated schizophrenia ("chronic schizophrenia"). [Schafer-Clinical Application]

Circumlocutious, verbose verbalizations:

Contraindicates depression; suggests disorganization tendencies. (Schafer-Clinical Application)

Concepts based on absence rather than on presence of attributes:

Schizoid. (Schafer-Clinical Application)

Concern with what examiner writes down:

Paranoid tendency. (Schafer-Clinical Application)

Deferential, ingratiating, pseudo-conscientious:

Antisocial personality ("psychopath"). [Schafer-Clinical Application]

Devious associations:

Chronic undifferentiated schizophrenia ("chronic schizophrenia"). [Schafer-Clinical Application]

Difficulties in verbal expression, with anxious speech in broken phrases and trouble in remembering correct terms (may be decompensating obsessive-compulsive):

Anxiety neurosis. (Schafer-Clinical Application)

Distorted auditory and visual perceptions and misperceptions:

Possible paranoid tendency. (Schafer-Clinical Application)

Easy items often missed:

Alcohol addiction. (Schafer-Clinical Application)

Evasive, facetious, pretentious:

Antisocial personality ("narcissistic character disorder"). [Schafer-Clinical Application]

Evasiveness:

Paranoid tendencies. (Schafer-Clinical Application)

Even achievement:

Inhibited normal subject (with other ir dices). [Schafer-Clinical Applicat.on]

Failure on items patient should know by reason of training or interests:

Schizophrenia. (Schafer-Clinical Application)

Giving up easily, lack of persistence:

Possible depressive trend. (Schafer-Clinical Application)

Good overall Wechsler efficiency:

Inhibited normal subject (with other indices). [Schafer-Clinical Application]

Impulsive and absurd responses:

Schizophrenia. (Schafer-Clinical Application)

Inappropriate affect or blandness:

Chronic undifferentiated schizophrenia ("chronic schizophrenia"). [Schafer-Clinical Application]

Inappropriate solutions:

Schizophrenia. (Schafer-Clinical Application)

Incorrect solutions to arithmetic, with assertion by subject that he guessed when near correctness of response indicates that he did not:

Low anxiety tolerance and resistence to reflection, as with antisocial personality ("narcissistic character disorders"). [Schafer-Clinical Application]

Irrelevancies:

Schizophrenia. (Schafer-Clinical Application)

Irrelevant and circumlocutious verbalizations:

Chronic undifferentiated schizophrenia ("chronic schizophrenia"). [Schafer-Clinical Application]

Joking, breeziness:

Avoidance tendency, character disorder, denial of personal problems. (Schafer Clinical Application)

Lack of persistance, giving up easily:

Possible depressive trend. (Schafer-Clinical Application)

Moralizing content:

Hysteria. (Schafer-Clinical Application)

Nonimpulsive and nonpedantic to-the-point verbalizations:

Possible inhibited normal subject (with other indices). [Schafer-Clinical Application]

Objection to examiner's verbatim recording of patient's spontaneous remarks:

Possible paranoid trend. (Schafer-Clinical Application)

Overelaborate, overinclusive or redundant responses:

Doubt, indecision, intellectualization. (Rapaport)

Overelaboration:

Obsessive-compulsive tendency. (Anderson-Mayman-Schafer-Rapaport)

Peculiar literalness:

Schizophrenia. (Schafer-Clinical Application)

Peculiar verbalizations:

Schizophrenia, including paranoid schizophrenia. (Schafer-Clinical Application)

Pedantic response to WAIS, as "carnivora," "mammals," "quadrupeds" to animals item of similarities:

Ostentation, overmeticulousness, sophistication. (Rapaport)

Verbose, circumlocutious verbalizations:

Contraindicates depression; suggests disorganization tendency. (Schafer-Clinical Application)

Wild guessing: Blandness; impulsivity. (Anderson-
                                        Mayman-Schafer-Rapaport)

Variability

Extreme subtest scatter: Confusion. (Schafer-Clinical Applica-
                                        tion)

Extreme variability on and between   Schizophrenia. (Schafer-Clinical Appli-
subtests: cation)

Fail-easy, pass-hard variability: Schizophrenia. (Schafer-Clinical Appli-
                                        cation)

Marked scatter: Psychopathology. (Rapaport)

Relatively slight scatter (with much   Paranoid schizophrenia. (Schafer-Clin-
more scatter, confusion):   ical Application)

Verbal Scale

Verbal high, Peformance low: Possible depressive trend. (Rapaport)

Verbal I.Q. usually below superior   Hysteria. (Schafer-Clinical Applica-
range and may be borderline: tion)

Verbal markedly higher than Perfor-   Psychotic depressive trend. (Rapaport)
mance scores:

Verbal moderately higher than Perfor-   Depressive neurosis. (Rapaport)
mance:

Verbal subtests impairment: Schizophrenic tendency. (Rapaport)

Vocabulary

Associating to Vocabulary words: Schizophrenia. (Schafer-Clinical Appli-
                                        cation)

Clang associations to Vocabulary   Schizophrenia. (Schafer-Clinical Appli-
items: cation)

Misses on easy Vocabulary: Psychotic depression; schizophrenia.
                                        (Rapaport)

Vocabulary above other subtest   Psychotic tendency. (Rapaport)
scores:

Vocabulary definitions arbitrary, irrel-   Antisocial personality ("psycho-
evant: pathy") or psychosis. (Rapaport)

Vocabulary increment, adequate Verbal:

Intellectualization; latent schizophrenic, obsessive-compulsive, paranoid syndromes. (Rapaport)

Vocabulary score above Performance:

Chronic undifferentiated schizophrenia or psychotic depression. (Rapaport)

Vocabulary score generally above Performance:

Depression. (Rapaport)

Vocabulary score high:

Contraindicates chronic schizophrenia except paranoia; contraindicates depression. (Rapaport)

Vocabulary score low:

Contraindicates obsessive-compulsive states and paranoia. (Rapaport)

Composite Criteria

Ability to work effectively and appropriately; high Arithmetic, Picture Completion, Similarities:

Paranoia ("paranoid condition"). [Schafer-Clinical Application]

Clang associations on Vocabulary, impulsive guessing, supercilious attitude:

Antisocial personality ("narcissistic character disorder"). [Schafer-Clinical Application]

Clinical evidence of depression, increment of Similarities above Vocabulary:

Neurotic depression. (Rapaport)

Comprehension higher than Information, high Performance subtest scores:

Hysterical features. (Schafer-Clinical Application)

Decrement Arithmetic and Comprehension, retained Digit Span:

Acute schizophrenic episode or chronic undifferentiated schizophrenia ("unclassified schizophrenia"). [Schafer-Clinical Application]

Decrement Arithmetic and Digit Span below Vocabulary, decrement of Digit Span greater than Arithmetic:

Neurosis, including depression. (Rapaport)

Decrement Block Design below impaired Performance:

Psychotic depression. (Rapaport)

Decrement Comprehension below Vocabulary and Information:

Obsessives; psychotic depressives, psychotics. (Rapaport)

Decrement of Information and Comprehension:	Psychopathology. (Rapaport)
Decrement of Information and Vocabulary:	Repressive tendency. (Anderson-Mayman-Schafer-Rapaport)
Decrement Performance and Vocabulary, increment Picture Completion:	Hysterics, obsessive compulsives. (Rapaport)
Decrement Picture Arrangement below Vocabulary but not markedly below other Performance tests:	Depression. (Rapaport)
Decrement Picture Completion and Arithmetic, retained Picture Arrangement:	Character disorders, including antisocial personalities ("psychopaths") and addictions. [Rapaport]
Decrement Similarities below Vocabulary and Verbal mean, clinical evidence of depression:	Psychotic depression. (Rapaport)
Elevated scores on Information, Comprehension, and Vocabulary:	Intellectual striving. (Klopfer-Developments I)
Good Wechsler and absence of schizophrenic verbalizations with evidence of apprehension and fantasy withdrawal:	Latent ("incipient") rather than acute schizophrenia; fantasies rather than delusions. (Schafer-Clinical Application)
High Arithmetic and Picture Completion:	Possible paranoid alertness. (Schafer-Clinical Application)
High Arithmetic, Picture Completion, and Similarities:	Projective trend. (Schafer-Clinical Application)
High Arithmetic and/or Picture Completion in schizophrenic setting:	Paranoid overalertness. (Schafer-Clinical Application)
High Block Design with general drop of Performance level:	Paranoid schizophrenia. (Schafer-Clinical Application)
High Block Design with rest of Performance low:	Schizophrenia. (Schafer-Clinical Application)
High Digit Span and Performance:	Character disorders; hysterics. (Schafer-Clinical Application)
High Digit Span. Information and Vocabulary may be low:	Simple schizophrenia. (Schafer-Clinical Application)
High Digit Span, low Arithmetic:	Schizoid personality ("schizoid character"). [Schafer-Clinical Application]

High Digit Span with neurosis: — Ideational tendencies. (Schafer-Clinical Application)

High Information and Vocabulary, relatively low Comprehension and Performance, possible slight reduction of Similarities: — Obsessive-compulsive neurosis. (Schafer-Clinical Application)

High Picture Arrangement, flippancy: — Antisocial personality ("psychopathic") tendency. [Schafer-Clinical Application]

High Picture Completion, Similarities: — Paranoid schizophrenia. (Schafer-Clinical Application)

High Similarities, overmeticulous verbalization, preoccupation with minutia, often irrelevant details, high Arithmetic and Picture Completion. — Paranoid personality ("paranoid character"). [Schafer-Clinical Application]

Impulsive guessing, especially on Information and Vocabulary, good Block Design, high Digit Span, moralizing comments on Comprehension: — Antisocial personality ("psychopath"). [Schafer-Clinical Application]

Increment Block Design above Vocabulary and Performance means: — Schizoid, schizophrenia. (Rapaport)

Increment of both Arithmetic and Digit Span: — Possible obsessive-compulsive or schizoid tendency. (Rapaport)

Increment Information, mild decrement Vocabulary: — Latent schizophrenic; simple schizophrenic. (Rapaport)

Increment Information and Vocabulary, decrement rest of Verbal subtests: — Obsessive-compulsive; psychotic depression; undifferentiated schizophrenia. (Rapaport)

Increment Object Assembly, decrement other Performance tests: — Blandness; schizophrenia. (Rapaport)

Increment Vocabulary and Verbal, decrement Picture Completion: — Intellectualizing psychotics. (Rapaport)

Inertia and inability to concentrate on Arithmetic, with high Block Design and Object Assembly: — Acute paranoid schizophrenia. (Schafer-Clinical Application)

I.Q. in average range or lower; wild, bland guessing; perceptual vagueness: — Simple schizophrenia. (Schafer-Clinical Application)

Lack of qualification, elaboration, and verbal fluency; few peculiar verbalizations (even with psychotic depression); self-criticality; a few perceptual distortions in Picture Arrangement and Picture Completion for some psychotic depressives:

Depression. (Schafer-Clinical Application)

Limited perceptual distortions in Picture Arrangement and Picture Completion:

Paranoia (with other indices; "paranoid condition"). [Schafer-Clinical Application]

Low Arithmetic, Comprehension, Digit Span, and Similarities:

Depression. (Schafer-Clinical Application)

Low Arithmetic, with good Comprehension:

Contraindicates psychotic depression. (Schafer-Clinical Application)

Low Comprehension and Similarities, Performance above Verbal, good visual motor speed and coordination, high Picture Arrangement, especially with schemers:

Antisocial personality ("psychopath"). [Schafer-Clinical Application]

Low Digit Span and Object Assembly:

Depression, tension. (Schafer-Clinical Application)

Low Object Assembly, low Picture Completion:

Acute schizophrenic episode or chronic undifferentiated schizophrenia ("unclassified schizophrenia"). [Schafer-Clinical Application]

Low Performance plus low Similarities:

Paranoid schizophrenia. (Schafer-Clinical Application)

Low Picture Arrangement, Similarities:

Chronic undifferentiated schizophrenia ("chronic schizophrenia"). [Schafer-Clinical Application]

Low Vocabulary with good scores on Object Assembly and Digit Symbol:

Simple schizophrenia. (Schafer-Clinical Application)

Marked Verbal and Performance subtest scatter:

Schizophrenic tendency. (Rapaport)

Neurosis with decrement Information below Comprehension:

Repression in hysteroid states. (Rapaport)

Only Block Design and Object Assem-

Tension. (Schafer-Clinical Application)

bly of Performance moderately low, rest adequate, especially if response is rapid:

Orderly Wechsler responses. There may be extreme drop of one subtest, especially Digit Span, Arithmetic and Picture Completion, *occasional* odd verbalizations:

Schizophrenia, latent type ("incipient schizophrenia"). [Schafer-Clinical Application]

Performance equal to or above Verbal, high Picture Arrangement, low Arithmetic:

Antisocial personality ("narcissistic character disorder"). [Schafer-Clinical Application]

Performance equal to or above Verbal, or lower than it; high Comprehension, low Information:

Hysteria. (Schafer-Clinical Application)

Performance lower than Arithmetic and Information, the greater the reduction the greater the depression:

Depression. (Schafer-Clinical Application)

Performance lower than Verbal, mild Verbal scatter:

Neurotic tendency. (Rapaport)

Picture Arrangement and Picture Completion markedly below Block Design, Object Assembly:

Schizophrenia. (Schafer-Clinical Application)

Picture Arrangement and Picture Completion markedly below Block Design and Object Assembly, high Comprehension:

Paranoid schizophrenia. (Schafer-Clinical Application)

Possible sharp reduction Digit Span, Picture Arrangement, Picture Completion:

Schizophrenia. (Schafer-Clinical Application)

Psychosis with decrement Information below Comprehension:

Paranoid. (Schafer-Clinical Application)

Reduced Arithmetic, Picture Completion:

Schizophrenia. (Schafer-Clinical Application)

Reduction Vocabulary and Verbal:

Chronic undifferentiated schizophrenia ("chronic schizophrenia"); psychotic depression. (Rapaport)

Restricted formal education with high Information score; Comprehension

Intellectual striving. (Schafer-Clinical Application)

and Information above Similarities and Vocabulary:

Schizophrenia with high Object Assembly and Digit Span:

Blandness. (Schafer-Clinical Application)

Schizophrenia with large drop in Arithmetic and Similarities:

Chronicity. (Schafer-Clinical Application)

Schizophrenia, well-retained Comprehension:

Paranoid schizophrenia. (Rapaport)

Visual-motor coordination subtest scores higher than Picture Arrangement, Picture Completion, and Verbal; low Arithmetic and Comprehension:

Simple schizophrenia. (Schafer-Clinical Application)

Vocabulary above all other Verbal scales (intellectual deterioration); retained Block Design and Object Assembly; low Digit Span, Picture Arrangement, and Picture Completion:

Acute schizophrenic episode, chronic undifferentiated schizophrenia ("unclassified schizophrenia"). [Schafer-Clinical Application]

Vocabulary elevated, rest of Verbal and Performance reduced:

Alcohol addiction. (Schafer-Clinical Application)

Wild guessing with high intelligence:

Schizophrenia. (Schafer-Clinical Application)

Part IV
Rorschach

Anomalies

Abrupt change of an H to (H):

Latent schizophrenia ("incipient schizophrenia"). [Schafer-Clinical Application]

Absence of popular as initial response, inadequate form:

Unstable defense system tendency. (Schafer-Rorschach)

Absence of popular as initial response, inadequate form, but subsequent response F+ and/or no manifest anxiety clinically observable and no schizophrenic tendency:

Defense system adequate even if perhaps mildly unstable. (Schafer-Rorschach)

Absurd content presented in jovial manner, along with more sensible comments:

Brain tumor with elevated intracranial pressure; toxic states. (Klopfer-Developments II)

Absurdities, deviant verbalizations:

Schizophrenia. (Schafer-Clinical Application)

Accumulation of failures in Rorschach:

Blocked or paranoid schizophrenics; organics; severe depressives, (Schafer-Clinical Application)

Ambiguous sex differences:

Possible paranoid tendency. (Schafer-(Rorschach)

Anal and water content, projection, regression, susceptibility to fatigue:

May suggest severe brain damage. (Klopfer-Developments II)

Anger with self, feelings of worthlessness, inertia:

Depression. (Schafer-Clinical Application)

Anxiety or disgust evoked by insect percepts:

Phobic tendency; possible weakness of repressive defenses. (Schafer-Rorschach)

67

Anxiety or disgust reactions with arbitrary or diffuse form:

Inadequate defenses and reality testing; explosiveness ("emotional instability"). [Schafer-Rorschach]

Anxiety over death, killing, and mutilation responses:

Emasculation fears and wishes; feminine trend in men, masculine trend in women. (Schafer-Rorschach)

Asking for confirmation of a response ("Couldn't it?"):

Inappropriate, childish dependence. (Schafer-Clinical Application)

Avoidance of red areas:

An avoidance of emotionality; anxiety over hostility. (Schafer-Rorschach)

Avoidance of shading, shading denial:

Negative prognostic sign. (Klopfer-Developments I)

Belittling of conventional feminine activity or female figures:

Masculine identification in women. (Schafer-Rorschach)

Bizarre equivalents:

Schizophrenia. (Phillips and Smith)

Blandness, dependence on fantasy gratification, lack of object relations:

Schizoid personality ("schizoid character"). [Schafer-Clinical Application]

Blocking and delayed reaction on color or shaded cards:

Hysterical tendency. (Schafer-Clinical Application)

Body mutilation:

Castration fantasies or fears. (Schafer-Clinical Application)

Breakdown of reality testing, confusion, disorganized thinking:

Acute schizophrenic episode or chronic undifferentiated schizophrenia ("unclassified schizophrenia"). [Schafer-Clinical Application]

Both visual and motor disturbance:

Generalized cortical damage or subcortical involvement. (Klopfer-Developments II)

CF-, FC-:

Explosive ("emotional instability") tendency (Beck III); negative prognostic sign. (Klopfer-Developments I)

CF-W responses, color description, color symbolism:

Repressive tendency. (Klopfer-Developments I)

Calling colors black:

Possible depressive tendency. (Schafer-Rorschach)

Card description:

Obsessive anxiety. (Phillips and Smith)

Change of personality reported; evidence of brain damage:	May suggest frontal lesion. (Klopfer-Developments II)
Color avoidance and denial:	Withdrawal tendency. (Beck III)
Color denial:	Defense of isolation (Beck III); phobia tendency. (Klopfer-Developments I)
Color denial and avoidance:	Withdrawal tendency. (Beck III)
Color denial, shading denial:	Ego strength, although neurotic problems may be apparent. (Klopfer-Developments I)
Color description, CF-W responses, and color symbolism:	Repressive tendency. (Klopfer-Developments I)
Color description and color naming:	Intellectualization of affect. (Klopfer-Davidson)
Color naming:	Avoidance (Beck and Molish); organics; schizophrenics moving into remission (Klopfer-Developments I); possible organicity (Rapaport); rationalization, superficiality; children, psychotics, retardates. (Klopfer-Developments I)
Color naming, cool colors:	Depressive trend which is defended against. (Beck and Molish)
Color naming, denial of meaning in color, incidental references to color:	Potential for destructive acting-out. (Phillips and Smith)
Color naming and description:	Intellectualization of affect. (Klopfer-Davidson)
Color rejection:	Rejection of affective experience. (Beck III)
Color symbolism, CF-W responses, color description:	Repressive tendency. (Klopfer-Developments I)
Comments on hidden meanings and similarities in or between cards:	Paranoid tendency. (Schafer-Rorschach)
Concern about body image as reflected in comments on fragmentation of H content and deterioration responses:	Relatively valid sign for mild-to-moderate brain damage. (Klopfer-Developments II)
Confabulation and contamination:	Schizophrenia. (Schafer-Clinical Applications)

Confusion, blocking, disorganized thinking:

Acute schizophrenic episode or chronic undifferentiated schizophrenia ("unclassified schizophrenia"). [Schafer-Clinical Application]

Confusion, depersonalization, panic attacks (with delusions, psychotic break may be imminent):

Latent schizophrenia ("incipient schizophrenia"). [Schafer-Clinical Application]

Confusion of sexual characteristics:

Possible homosexual tendency. (Beck III)

Constriction, sterotypy:

Geriatric patients. (Klopfer-Developments I)

Contamination and confabulation:

Schizophrenia. (Schafer-Clinical Applications)

Contaminations, extreme vagueness, grandiosity, non sequiturs:

Schizophrenic bizarreness. (Phillips and Smith, citing Rapaport)

Crudeness, poor judgment, absence of other evidence of brain damage:

May suggest frontal lesion. (Klopfer-Developments II)

Damaged or impaired objects, male subject:

Possibly feeling or fear of loss of masculinity. (Schafer-Rorschach)

Decrease of anxiety with evidence of brain damage:

May suggest severe brain damage. (Klopfer-Developments II)

Decrement M, shading, texture; increment F:

Common in geriatric patients. (Klopfer-Developments II)

Decrement R, color cards:

Inhibition in emotionally provocative situations possibly. (Klopfer-Developments I)

Dehumanized content:

Schizophrenic, especially hebephrenic. (Rapaport)

Delayed reaction and blocking on color or shaded cards:

Hysterical tendency. (Schafer-Clinical Application)

Denial of meaning in color, color naming, incidental references to color:

Potential for destructive acting-out. (Phillips and Smith)

Dependent and demanding behavior, irresponsibility, lack of perseverance and attainment:

Alcohol addiction, with symptoms of gastrointestinal complaints and history of early drinking. (Schafer-Clinical Application)

Depreciation of H, especially male figures:

Possible female homosexual trend. (Beck and Molish)

Deterioration color:

Schizophrenic, especially hebephrenic. (Rapaport)

Determinant appearing only in minus forms:

Conflict areas with rigid and ineffective defensive system. (Klopfer-Developments I)

Disparaging of female sexual organ percepts, male subject:

Fear of inadequate masculinity; possible associated difficulty in experiencing tender affection in relationship with females. (Schafer-Rorschach)

Dysphoric content:

Suggests guilt. (Beck III)

Either or mixed sex figure:

Feminine identification, masculine inadequacy in men; masculine identification in women. (Schafer-Rorschach)

Emphasis on CF and C or lack of color:

Common in geriatric patients. (Klopfer-Developments II)

Emphasis on projections:

May suggest small focal lesion, usually accompanied by seizure. (Klopfer-Developments II)

Emphasis on sexual functions or organs of animal:

Possible homosexual tendency. (Beck III)

Emphasizing that one side or area of card is different in content from the other corresponding (almost identical) area or side:

Paranoid projection. (Schafer-Rorschach)

Evidence of anxiety despite security:

May suggest early brain damage. (Klopfer-Developments II)

Evidence of concreteness plus poor judgment:

May suggest frontal lesion. (Klopfer-Developments II)

Extreme vagueness, contaminations, grandiosity, non sequiturs:

Schizophrenic bizarreness. (Phillips and Smith, citing Rapaport)

Eyes perceived as "looking at" the subject:

Paranoid tendency. (Schafer-Rorschach)

F > 50%:

Constriction, repression. (Klopfer-Developments I)

F- responses to color:	Schizophrenics. (Klopfer-Developments II)
FC-:	Impairment of reality testing in emotionally stimulating situations. (Klopfer-Davidson)
FC-, CF-:	Explosive ("emotional instability") tendency (Beck III); negative prognostic sign (Klopfer-Developments I)
FM-:	Negative prognostic sign. (Klopfer-Developments I)
FT-, FY-:	Negative prognostic sign. (Klopfer-Developments I)
FY-, FT-:	Negative prognostic sign. (Klopfer-Developments I)
Feelings of worthlessness, anger with self, inertia:	Depression. (Schafer-Clinical Application)
Forgetting percepts:	Possible unstable defense system. (Schafer-Rorschach)
Form-minus color:	Acting-out tendency, impulsivity. (Klopfer-Developments I)
Genitalia increment:	Denial of sexual inadequacy or ineffectuality; immaturity; pregenital sexual fixations. (Klopfer-Developments I)
Good-form content perseveration with emphasis on projections:	May suggest focal lesions with accompanying seizures. (Klopfer-Developments I)
Good Wechsler, poor Rorschach performance:	May suggest multiple sclerosis or metastasized cerebral carcinoma. (Klopfer-Developments II)
Grandiosity, contaminations, extreme vagueness, non sequiturs:	Schizophrenic bizarreness. (Phillips and Smith)
Grossly deviant Rorschach responses interspersed with good quality responses:	Favorable prognostic sign. (Beck and Molish)
H called "persons":	Sexual identification conflict. (Klopfer-Developments I)

History of law violations or disregard for ethical conduct, with blandness; lack of long-range goals and of capacity for long-range goals:

Antisocial personality ("psychopathic character disorder"). [Schafer-Clinical Application]

Hostile designations for women:

Feminine identification, masculine inadequacy in men; masculine identification in women. (Schafer-Rorschach)

Impaired or damaged objects, male subject:

Possible feeling or fear of loss of masculinity. (Schafer-Rorschach)

Inability to give alternate interpretations for same blot area:

May suggest post-traumatic brain damage. (Klopfer-Developments II)

Incidental references to color, color naming, denial of meaning in color:

Potential for destructive acting-out. (Phillips and Smith)

Inconsistent evidence of hysteria:

May suggest multiple sclerosis. (Klopfer-Developments II)

Increment aggressive destructive fantasy:

Tenuous controls. (Schafer-Clinical Application)

Increment card turning:

Anxiety, tension. (Beck III)

Increment of precision alternatives:

Constriction, rigidity. (Beck III)

Increment of stereotyped phrases:

Constriction, rigidity. (Beck III)

Indifference to shading:

Contraindicates neurotic state; lack of need or indifference to need for affection, as in antisocial personality ("psychopathy"); poor prognostic sign. (Klopfer-Developments II)

Inertia, anger with self, feelings of worthlessness:

Depression. (Schafer-Clinical Application)

Initial avoidance or poor-form response to red areas, followed by form-plus response to red areas on the cards:

Resilience; adequate defense system despite anxiety trend. (Schafer-Rorschach)

Intratensive orientation with absence of color-shock and increment of FY shading:

May suggest flattened affect tendency. (Klopfer-Developments II)

Lack of color or emphasis on CF and C:

Common in geriatric patients. (Klopfer-Developments II)

Lack of rapport and emotional responsiveness, loss of interest, thinking peculiarities:

Simple schizophrenia. (Schafer-Clinical Application)

Latent schizophrenic symptoms with caution and constriction:

Paranoid schizophrenia. (Schafer-Clinical Application)

Long reaction time followed by reference on chromatic cards to meaninglessness of color:

Denial and repression. (Schafer-Rorschach)

M–:

Autism, regression (Beck III); negative prognostic sign (Klopfer-Developments I); paranoid ideas, especially with DW. (Schafer-Clinical Application)

Making large objects small (as "twig" for Card III, D5 area more often seen as tree "branch"):

Possible denial trend. (Schafer-Rorschach)

Making a percept a drawing, as a caricature, or making it lifeless, as preserved or a museum specimen:

Denial of threat the object presents. (Schafer-Rorschach)

Making things large that are usually seen as small ("a big mouse," etc.):

Possible grandiose trend. (Schafer-Rorschach)

Marked variability in quality and quantity of response:

Schizophrenia. (Schafer-Clinical Application)

Mixed or either sex figure:

Feminine identification, masculine inadequacy in men; masculine identification in women. (Schafer-Rorschach)

Mutilation:

Morbid sadistic preoccupation. (Schafer-Clinical Application)

Negative form responses; negative percepts ("It's not a"):

Denial of tendency the association implies (Schafer-Rorschach); schizophrenia. (Phillips and Smith)

No color associations:

Flat affect tendency. (Beck III)

Non sequiturs, contaminations, extreme vagueness, grandiosity:

Schizophrenic bizarreness. (Phillips and Smith)

O–:

Impairment of reality contact. (Klopfer-Davidson)

Opposite qualities ascribed to a percept, as "strong" and "weak":

Ambivalence; undoing mechanism. (Beck and Molish)

Passive-content Rorschach, aggressive TAT content:

May suggest grand mal seizures. (Klopfer-Developments II)

Peculiar and pedantic prefatory remarks:

Feeling of inadequacy; schizophrenia. (Phillips and Smith)

Perceiving cards "as evil" or "revolting"; loss of distance from percepts:

Emotional lability, naiveté; projection of anxiety over primitive id impulses; may be both paranoid and repressive. (Schafer-Rorschach)

Perceiving cards as inverted:

Possible brain damage, especially senile deterioration (Beck and Molish); schizoid tendency. (Schafer-Clinical Application)

Perceptual vagueness:

Inadequate reality testing; ineffective or weak defense systsm. (Schafer-Rorschach)

Perseverated F-color with detached affect:

Catatonic schizophrenics. (Klopfer-Developments II)

Piotrowski's automatic phrases, impotence, perplexity and repetition:

Best of the Piotrowski signs for mild-to-moderate brain damage. (Klopfer-Developments II)

Plural form for single percept (bats for bat, etc.):

Schizophrenia. (Schafer-Clinical Application)

Poor judgment, crudeness, absence of other evidence of brain damage:

May suggest frontal lesion. (Klopfer-Developments II)

Precision alternatives:

Indecision. (Phillips and Smith)

Precision alternatives with first rejected for second:

Absence of long-range goals, instability in sexual and social relationships, undoing mechanism. (Phillips and Smith)

Primitive bizarre content without anxiety:

Chronic undifferentiated schizophrenia ("chronic schizophrenia" or "latent chronic schizophrenia"). [Schafer-Rorschach]

Projection, anal and water content, regression, susceptibility to fatigue:

May suggest severe brain damage. (Klopfer-Developments II)

Regression, anal and water content, projection, susceptibility to fatigue:

May suggest severe brain damage. (Klopfer-Developments II)

Repulsion expressed to blot appearance:

Hysteric affect, neurasthenia. (Phillips and Smith)

Reversal of sex of figure or of sexual anatomy usually seen: Feminine identification, masculine inadequacy in men, masculine identification in women; possible paranoid tendency (Schafer-Rorschach); possible homosexual tendency. (Beck III)

Shading avoidance, shading denial: Negative prognostic sign. (Klopfer-Developments I)

Shading denial: Contraindicates psychosis, except guarded early paranoid schizophrenic (Klopfer-Developments II); possible denial of anxiety. (Schafer-Rorschach)

Shading-denial, color-denial: Ego-strength although neurotic problems may be apparent. (Klopfer-Developments I)

Shift from H to A content: Repressive tendency. (Schafer-Rorschach)

"Sinister" percepts: Paranoid or combined paranoid-phobic trend. (Schafer-Rorschach)

Stereotyped phrases: Brain-damage; stereotypy. (Beck III)

Stereotypy: May reflect depression. (Rapaport)

Stereotypy, constriction: Geriatric patients. (Klopfer-Developments II)

Susceptibility to fatigue, anal and water content, projection, regression: May suggest severe brain damage. (Klopfer-Developments II)

Transposition (perceiving usual F+ content of an area in an adjacent area where the form becomes F−): Catatonic and paranoid schizophrenics. (Klopfer-Developments II)

Unwillingness to admit perception until convinced others see it: Paranoid tendency. (Klopfer-Developments II)

Visual disturbance with evidence of crudity or motor disturbance or poor judgment: Parietal-occupital lesion possibly. (Klopfer-Developments II)

"Whirling" percepts: Possible homoerotic impulses. (Schafer-Clinical Application)

Blends (Determinants)

Blends: Painful affect; possible agitation potential. (Beck III)

CF.Y Blend: Agitation potential. (Beck and Molish)

C.Y Blend: Agitation; painful affect; suicidal potential. (Beck and Molish)

Color.M: Exciting or gratifying fantasy. (Beck III)

FM.FT: Anxiety associated with dependent tendencies. (Klopfer-Davidson)

FY.M: Dysphoric mood, probably expressed through fantasy. (Beck III)

Low-form color with low-form shading in Blend response: Painful affect; potential for agitation state. (Beck and Molish)

M with V in Blend: Possible suicidal tendency. (Beck and Molish)

M.Y: Agitation potential; dysphoric mood, painful affect. (Beck III)

Card-Specific Responses

CARD I
Absence of popular as first response, Card I: Possibly schizoid; social isolation; unconventional attitudes. (Phillips and Smith)

Animal as first response, Card I: Lack of insight. (Phillips and Smith)

Card I as face (cat, jack-o-lantern): Anxiety, insecurity, timidity. (Klopfer-Developments I)

Center D popular, Card I, seen from rear or as cloaked: Sexual role conflict. (Klopfer-Developments I)

Edging, shock, Card I: Acting out of hostility; ambivalence toward maternal figure; passive dependency, with suicidal gestures. (Phillips and Smith)

Excluding parts of popular, Card I: Criticality, insecurity. (Klopfer-Developments I)

F-, Card I: Probably psychopathology. (Phillips and Smith)

F+ on first response, Card I: Intact formal thought processes; if subject is psychotic, disturbance limited

	to delusional material. (Phillips and Smith)
Interior D as clouds, Card I:	Anxiety, apprehension; possible depressive trend. (Klopfer-Developments I)
Middle figure of Card I as man:	Feminine or masculine inadequacy; feminine identification in men, masculine identification in women. (Schafer-Rorschach)
Sex response to Card I, first response:	Schizophrenia. (Schafer-Clinical Application)
Sex response to first card:	Sexual preoccupation. (Schafer-Clinical Application)
Side D profiles, Card I:	Criticality; intellectualization. (Klopfer-Developments I)
Stereotyped popular response initiating Rorschach:	Guardedness. (Phillips and Smith)
Upper inner D, Card I, as hands:	Dependence, with associated feeling of helplessness. (Klopfer-Developments I)
W anatomy, Card I:	Hypochondriasis, somatization. (Klopfer-Developments I)

CARD II

Bizarre form-content, color areas, Card II:	Possible psychotic component or potential. (Klopfer-Developments I)
"Clowns," Card II:	Possible derogatory attitudes. (Klopfer-Developments I)
Edging, shock, Card II (men more often than women):	Destructive impulses expressed by excessive defensive constriction and constraint; episodic aggressive behavior; somatic symptoms secondary to suppressed hostility. (Phillips and Smith)
FT response to popular animal, Card II:	Sensitivity. (Klopfer-Developments I)
Response to inner space (DS5) of Card II, with black area (D6) as background:	Possible denial of anxiety and depression; oppositional trend may also be present. (Schafer-Rorschach)

CARD III

Card III popular H as minority group members:	Feeling of inadequacy or insecurity that may be denied or unconscious. (Klopfer-Developments I)
Color first on III:	Hysteria. (Rapaport)
D1 popular of III as animal:	Fear of males with disparagement of them. (Schafer-Rorschach)
Edging, shock, Card III:	Male: harsh, punitive paternal figure; economic and psychosexual maladjustment (exhibitionism, homosexuality); somatic complaints. Female: relationship with punitive or weak contemporary male, with depression and anxiety; traumatic heterosexual problems. (Phillips and Smith)
Female for Card III popular:	Feminine identification. (Phillips and Smith)
Inability to perceive D1 of Card III as human because of gap between upper and lower halves:	Repressive tendency. (Schafer-Rorschach)
Inability to perceive human popular, Card III:	Inability to empathize or identify with others. (Klopfer-Developments I)
Marionettes, puppets, Card III:	Schizoid. (Phillips and Smith)
One M on III, none elsewhere:	Suggests depressive trend. (Rapaport)
Perception of breast on D1 human, Card III:	Possible homosexual tendency. (Beck III)
Popular figure on Card III as woman or bisexual:	Feminine or masculine inadequacy; feminine identification in men, masculine identification in women. (Schafer-Rorschach)
Popular humans of III perceived as animals:	Difficulty with close relations with others; withdrawal. (Schafer-Rorschach)
Stylized figures, Card III, D1:	Detached, formal attitude toward others; lack of spontaneity. (Schafer-Rorschach)
Use of phrase *"trying* to lift something" on Card III, P:	Feelings of inadequacy. (Schafer-Clinical Application)

CARD IV

"Big feet" usual D on IV:	Apprehension and feelings of inadequacy relative to paternal figure, especially if response time is long for subject and there are self-disparaging comments relative to the quality of the response. (Schafer-Rorschach)
Card IV:	Especially likely to evoke T. (Beck and Molish)
Edging, shock, Card IV:	Punitive paternal figure; economic and sexual inadequacy, feelings of hopelessness and ineffectuality; women, sexual apprehension and inadequacy as well. (Phillips and Smith)
Emphasis on "big feet" of D2 area of Card IV:	Possible feelings of inadequacy. (Schafer-Rorschach)
Lack of W to Card IV, W's elsewhere:	In male subject, sexual role conflict, possible lack of masculine identification. (Klopfer-Developments I)

CARD V

D1, Card V, pig's foot:	Derogatory attitude toward femininity; view of woman as passive-oral in nature. (Schafer-Rorschach)
Inability to see Card V as bat or butterfly:	Impairment of reality testing. (Klopfer-Developments I)
Shock on Card V:	Possible depressive element. (Klopfer Developments I)
Side D, Card V, as crocodile head:	Passive-aggressive ("oral-aggressive") tendency. (Klopfer-Developments I)

CARD VI

Avoidance of projection, Card VI, male subject:	Difficulty with the male role. (Klopfer-Davidson)
Avoidance of projection, F− content, Card VI:	Sexual conflict. (Klopfer-Developments I)
Edging, shock, Card VI:	Aberrant sexual practices (tends to be shock on III as well with aberrant sexual practices); unsuccessful heterosexuality. (Phillips and Smith)

Egg, nest content, center upper D, Card VI:

Immaturity; infantile behavior or regressive potential. (Klopfer-Developments I)

Form-plus response to top projection, Card VI:

Potential for mature sexual relationships. (Klopfer-Developments I)

Increment responses to projection area of Card VI, not necessarily overtly sexual in content:

Sexual preoccupation. (Klopfer-Developments I)

CARD VII
Area D11 of Card VII as church:

Guilt over sexual impulses and needs; sexual inhibition and repression. (Schafer-Rorschach)

Area D11 of Card VII as house:

Dependency, nuturance needs. (Klopfer-Developments I)

Card VII popular human as animals or children:

Heterosexual inadequacy; immaturity; infantile social behavior. (Klopfer-Developments I)

Delay, evasion, Card VII:

Disturbance in mother-child relation. (Klopfer-Davidson)

Edging, shock, Card VII:

Conflicted or inadequate heterosexual relations; demanding, domineering, overprotective but not punitive maternal figure; immaturity. (Phillips and Smith)

Human popular elsewhere, no human popular on VII:

Impaired relationship with maternal figure. (Klopfer-Developments I)

Rejection female P, Card VII:

Possible rejection of women as sexual objects. (Beck and Molish)

CARD VIII
Anatomy, Card VIII:

Somatization tendency. (Klopfer-Development I)

Pure C on Card VIII:

Schizophrenic tendency. (Rapaport)

CARD IX
Color-shading Blends, Card IX (Klopfer-Spiegelmann):

Phobic anxiety. (Beck and Molish)

Color-shock on Card IX:

Neurotic affect. (Klopfer-Developments I)

FC on IX:

Good emotional control. (Rapaport)

Human popular D3 as clowns or witches, Cards IX:

Derogatory attitudes toward others. (Klopfer-Developments I)

CARD X
Single response on X:

Caution in presence of emotionally provocative situations. (Schafer-Clinical Application)

MULTIPLE CARDS
Absence of color responses in CARDS VIII–X:

Possible impairment of reality contact; withdrawal. (Beck and Molish)

Blood content on II and III:

Hysterical tendency. (Schafer-Clinical Application)

F– and shading responses, II, III, V:

Greater anxiety than when this occurs on IV, VI, VII. (Rapaport)

F+ and F–, RT and other determinants in relation to particular cards:

Conflict areas. (Klopfer-Davidson)

Good-quality responses on III and X after poor-quality responses on II and IX, respectively:

Adaptive potential. (Beck and Molish)

Immediate response to color on Cards II and III:

Impulsivity possibly. (Klopfer-Developments I)

Improved F+ quality on X after mediocre or poor quality responses on VIII and IX:

Adaptive resources, good prognostic sign. (Beck and Molish)

Increment pure C, IX and X:

Schizophrenic tendency. (Rapaport)

Lower middle Card I and upper middle Card II as vagina:

Feminine or masculine inadequacy; feminine identification in men, masculine identification in women. (Schafer-Rorschach)

Lower middle Cards II and VII, upper middle Card IV as penis:

Feminine or masculine inadequacy; feminine identification in men, masculine identification in women. (Schafer-Rorschach)

No response to color areas, Cards II and III:	Avoidance tendency. (Klopfer-Developments I)
Percent R VIII, IX, X > 10%:	Responsivity or potential for responsivity. (Klopfer-Developments I)
R Cards VIII, IX, X < 30%:	Detached, inhibited (Klopfer-Developments I); inhibited, unresponsive (Klopfer-Davidson)
R VIII, IX, X > 30-40%:	Appropriately responsive to emotionally provocative stimuli from the environment. (Klopfer-Developments I)
R VIII, IX, X > 40%:	Responsivity. (Klopfer-Davidson)

Composite Criteria

A > 50%; F% above 80; long reaction time; low C (possibly one pure C, usually blood, on II or III); low W; no more than one M; P > 30%; R below 20, often below 15; rejections, self-criticism or subtle criticism of tests or examiner:	Depression. (Schafer-Clinical Application)
Adx and Hdx:	Acute anxiety; organic brain damage (frontal lobe) or retardation; paranoid tendency. (Phillips and Smith)
Absence florid schizophrenic verbalizations, constrictive trend, decrement color, emphasis on M:	Paranoid schizophrenia. (Schafer-Clinical Application)
Absence M, emphasis on pure C, low F+:	Inappropriateness of affect and behavior rather than systematized delusions. (Schafer-Clinical Application)
Absence of pure C, presence FC, acceptable even if marginal F+ and P%:	Absence of incapacitating overt psychosis at the moment: some adaptive resources. (Schafer-Rorschach)
Abstractions, confabulation, decrement A, increment W, C, CF, Dd, S, shading, self-reference:	Hypomanic tendency. (Schafer-Rorschach)
Absurd form responses, F+ 60%, failures or perseverations, high A or At,	Simple schizophrenia. (Schafer-Clinical Application)

peculiar verbalizations (one or more M and Dd's suggest vague delusions):

Acute shizophrenic episode ("unclassified schizophrenia"), early dissappearance FC:

Unfavorable prognostic sign. (Schafer-Clinical Application)

Additional FM and M, increment F:

Inhibition. (Klopfer-Developments I)

Adequate block design and Bender performance, disturbed speech:

Possible parietal-temporal lesion. (Klopfer-Developments II)

Adequate F+ with occasional arbitrary form; arbitrary FC (early disappearance FC unfavorable prognostic sign); balanced color and M; CF; confabulation, contamination; peculiar verbalizations; R 20–30:

Acute schizophrenic episode ("unclassified schizophrenia"). [Schafer-Clinical Application]

Adequate F+, P, sequence:

Adequate reality contact. (Beck and Molish)

Affective ratio or percent color of about 80 or more:

Manic tendency, volatile. (Beck III)

Aggressive A; H with paranoid content themes; high Z score; decrement F+; increment S:

Displacement; or possible paranoid. (Beck III)

Ambiequal experience balance, S increment:

Ambivalence, doubt (Klopfer-Developments I); obsessive-compulsive state; doubt, perplexity, self-distrust (Beck III)

Ambiequal M:C; decrement R and Z; increment F+ and low-form shading; no more than one C and M; possibly vista responses; slow time 1R:

Depressive trend. (Beck III)

Anal percepts: decrement F+; "destructive" remarks about cards ("if you chop it off here," etc.); increment anxious, hostile imagery; color, shading:

Possible decompensating obsessive-compulsive defense system. (Schafer-Rorschach)

Anatomy content with increment color:

Hysteric tendency. (Beck III)

Anatomy content, low F+ combination:

Possible alcoholism and schizophrenia. (Beck and Molish)

Anxiety neurosis with circumstantiality, compulsivity and description:

Anxiety neurosis ("anxiety state") with decompensation. (Schafer-Clinical Application)

Apparent openness or sincerity with narcissistic use of color:

Antisocial personality ("psychopathy"). [Schafer-Rorschach]

Apprehension with evidence of fantasy withdrawal; many M's without high intelligence; recognition of Rorschach percept as untenable, followed by its reaffirmation:

Latent schizophrenia ("incipient schizophrenia") [Schafer-Clinical Application]

Approach narrow, rigid sequence:

Inflexibility. (Beck III)

Arbitrary color; eating, food and mouth content; F + level low:

Alcohol addiction. (Schafer-Clinical Application)

Asking for reassurance, decrement Dd, M, R, W; fabulization; increment color, texture and YF shading; long reaction time and rejection; personal references:

Repression; possible hysteria. (Schafer-Rorschach)

Average or decrement R; decrement M or W; increment color and shading; low F%:

Hysterical trend; repression. (Schafer-Rorschach)

Average or low R; avoidance intellectual effort; bland self-references; borderline F+ (60%); CF; decrement M; denial of obvious shading; evasion; food and ornamental content; leering sexual references; low W% or vague W; sensuous T:

Antisocial personality ("narcissistic character disorder" type). [Schafer-Clinical Application]

Avoidance of shading on shading cards, with increment of white space on the cards:

Negativistic or oppositional reaction to anxiety. (Rapaport)

Blood content followed by baby or domestic animal or religious content:

Hostile impulses defended against by reaction-formation against hostility. (Schafer-Rorschach)

Blood content followed by evasion:

Hostile impulses defended against by avoidance, resentful passive-compliance or withdrawal. (Schafer-Rorschach)

Blood content followed by over-deferential attitude toward the examiner:

Denial of hostility, undoing. (Schafer-Rorschach)

Blood stains; detectives or police; eyes; finger or footprints, finger pointing; sinister faces:

Paranoid tendency. (Schafer-Rorschach)

Botany or nature CF:

Lability, naiveté. (Schafer-Clinical Application)

C, CF associated with white space; literal content:

Oppositional tendency. (Beck III)

C, CF with depressive material:

Possible suicidal trend. (Beck and Molish)

C + CF > FC; few shading, M, R:

Narcissism. (Phillips and Smith)

C and CF with low affective ratio:

Explosiveness, inappropriate affect, lability; hysterics, organics, schizophrenics with excitement potential. (Beck III)

C, CF – increment; little or no FC; no M:

Possible primary narcissism; severely impaired emotional control. (Beck and Molish)

C, CF with shading:

Potential for agitation. (Beck III)

CF > FC; CF first on colored cards and appears first on II and III:

Hysterical tendency. (Schafer-Clinical Application)

CF exclusively; DW; D dominance; high animal %; low F + %; perseveration and sterotypy of content; R 10–20; shading absent:

Antisocial personality ("psychopathic character disorder"). [Schafer-Clinical Application]

CF limited to blood, botany, clouds, nature content:

Hysterical tendency. (Schafer-Clinical Application)

CF and space increment:

Impulsivity, narcissism, negativism. (Schafer-Rorschach)

C.Y. or V:

Restlessness, tension. (Beck III)

Circumstantial descriptions; high A, F, F+, P%; low or no color; low M; much Dd and S, overpreoccupation with similarities between cards:

Paranoid personality ("paranoid character"). [Schafer-Clinical Application]

Coherent language, grossly bizarre Rorschach associations:	More favorable prognosis than Rorschach content might suggest. (Beck and Molish)
Color abstractions, intense verbalized negative or positive reactions to color:	Manic tendency. (Beck III)
Color with high F%, M, shading:	Complex personality with capacity for matter-of-fact attitude. (Klopfer-Davidson)
Color-naming, poor-form red:	Sadism, temper. (Phillips and Smith)
Color, S, shading in schizophrenic record:	Catatonic tendency, with potential for excitement if color is present. (Beck and Molish)
Color with shading:	Very painful affect. (Beck III)
Color-shock in depression:	Indicates reactive depression. (Beck and Molish)
Color-shock in schizophrenic record:	Positive prognostic sign; possible latent or chronic undifferentiated schizophrenia ("pseudo-neurotic schizophrenia"). [Beck and Molish]
Confabulation; contamination; Dd increment; eyes; F+ adequate unless blocking or perseverations occur; high A, F%, P; ideas of reference; limited peculiar verbalizations; M−; M 2-3; no color; possible FC; symbols such as alphabet letters or geometric shapes; R below 25 or often below 15:	Paranoid schizophrenia. (Schafer-Clinical Application)
Confabulation tendency; decrement F+; increment W:	Expansiveness, possible grandiosity trend. (Schafer-Rorschach)
Confabulation, contamination; low F+; M−, pure C:	Schizophrenic tendency. (Schafer-Rorschach)
Confabulation, W below expectancy:	Social anxiety. (Phillips and Smith)
Confabulations, a couple of, with aggressive or sexual content; a few peculiar verbalizations which may be recognized as such; a few pure C's;	Latent schizophrenia ("incipient schizophrenia"). [Schafer-Clinical Application]

bizarre and dramatic abstractions of physical sensations; geometric shape or letter content; grossly disparate M:C ratios; many anal and sex responses; no more than two arbitrary FC (as green sheep); no more than two M−:

Confused content, low F+, space:

Severe emotional disturbance. (Beck and Molish)

Constricted EB; delayed reaction time; discrepancy between good intelligence and low R; excessive FC; high F+; low CF; single response to X:

Inhibition. (Schafer-Clinical Application)

Contaminated W's; increment M; little or no color; overconcern with similarities of cards; space responses in meager record; series of failures especially on last 3–4 cards; symbolic Dd:

Paranoia ("paranoid condition"). [Schafer-Clinical Application]

Cool color preference; form-dominance; M increment; shading:

Contraindicates acting-out; suggests inhibited motility. (Phillips and Smith)

Criticism of form adequacy of blot; decrement color with increment M; $F > 80\%$; $F+ > 80\%$; increment Dd, Dx, S; over 50% A; R above 35; symmetry comment:

Obsessive-compulsive neurosis. (Schafer-Clinical Application)

Dd high, F+ slightly below 65%:

Reality testing not necessarily impaired, as might be the case if Dd were not high. (Schafer-Clinical Application)

Dd increment; M increment or M without color:

Ideational tendency. (Schafer-Clinical Application)

DW; decrement M; $R < 15$:

Simple schizophrenia. (Schafer-Clinical Application)

DW; low F+, P, R, with blandness; peculiar verbalizations; perseveration:

Simple schizophrenia. (Schafer-Clinical Application)

Decay content, emotionality displayed without color on Rorschach:

Latent schizophrenia ("incipient schizophrenia"). [Schafer-Clinical Application]

Decrement A, F+, FC, H, M, P; increment C, CF−, S:

Probable acting-out psychosis with large labile, negativistic element and

	severely impaired emotional control. (Beck and Molish)
Decrement A + H, increment Ad + Hd:	Anxiety, compulsive trend, hostility with overcriticality. (Klopfer-Development I)
Decrement A, M, P, possibly with over-emphasis on certain content categories:	Absence of insight into motivations; egocentric withdrawal. (Beck III)
Decrement A and P; increment F+ D:	Practicality. (Beck III)
Decrement color (1–2 FC, CF) possibly; increase of Dd, increment At, FY, TF; moderately low F+, R > 20, rejection IX, X, and shaded cards; vague W:	Anxiety neurosis ("anxiety state"). [Schafer-Clinical Application]
Decrement color, good-form M:	Independence. (Klopfer-Developments I)
Decrement color, increment M:	Possible reality contact impairment. (Rapaport)
Decrement color, increment S:	Contraindicates acting-out. (Klopfer-Developments I)
Decrement color, M, shading; high F% (50–80):	Constriction, rigidity, (Klopfer-Davidson)
Decrement color, M and shading, increment F:	Constriction. (Klopfer-Developments I)
Decrement color, shading, texture:	Possible isolation defense. (Schafer-Rorschach)
Decrement D; increment vague W:	Geriatric patients. (Klopfer-Developments I)
Decrement D and P, poor form:	Impaired reality contact. (Klopfer-Developments I)
Decrement D; vague form:	Schizophrenia. (Klopfer-Developments I)
Decrement D and W, Dd increment:	Impaired reality testing. (Klopfer-Developments I)
Decrement F+ and animal; increment At and vague form responses:	Possible psychotic depression. (Rapaport)

Decrement F+, high Z score, increment S, paranoid content themes:

Possible paranoid tendency; with aggressive animal or human content may be possible paranoid tendency or represent displacement. (Beck III)

Decrement M, chronic undifferentiated schizophrenia. ("unclassified schizophrenia"):

Systematized delusional potential as M diminished with chronicity. (Schafer-Clinical Application)

Decrement M, color > M:

Extroversion, physical activity. (Phillips and Smith)

Decrement M and FM; increment F%:

Repressed tendency. (Klopfer-Davidson)

Decrement M and FM, mediocre or poor form:

Impulsivity without insight; irresponsibility, weak ego; children, psychopaths, psychotics. (Klopfer-Development I)

Decrement M and FM, form +:

Constriction, repression. (Klopfer-Developments I)

Decrement M; increment R:

Lack of creativity and imagination. (Beck III)

Decrement M, P; deterioration color responses; F+ below 60%; increment At, C, peculiar verbalization, sex, shading (with schizophrenic tendency increment of shading yields potential for bizarre panic attacks); neologisms, PO responses:

Chronic undifferentiated schizophrenia ("unclassified schizophrenia"). [Schafer-Clinical Application]

Decrement M+; FM, poor form:

Weak ego. (Klopfer-Davidson)

Decrement or no CF; increment FC:

Social graces without spontaneous emotional involvement. (Klopfer-Developments I)

Decrement P; delayed reaction time; increment A; reduction in productivity; rejections:

Anxiety indications. (Beck III)

Decrement R; increment time required for response:

Geriatric patients. (Klopfer-Developments II)

Decrement R, increment W:

Possible intellectualization defense. (Schafer-Rorschach)

Decrement R; W-to-D ratio 1:2:

Possible psychotic depression. (Rapaport)

Decrement R, W-to-D ratio 2:1: — Possible anxiety or schizoid state. (Rapaport)

Decrement S, increment of A and shading: — Lack of drive, mental inertia, possible discouragement. (Beck III)

Decrement W, increment M: — Escapist or wish-fulfilling fantasy. (Klopfer-Developments I)

Delayed reaction time; excessive C; low CF; low R in setting of good intelligence; M:C of 1:0; single response to Card X: — Inhibited normal subject. (Schafer-Clinical Application)

Deviant reasoning; low F+; no M; pure C: — Chronic undifferentiated schizophrenia ("chronic schizophrenia"). [Schafer-Clinical Application]

Dysphoric mood; painful affect; religiosity, serenity or tranquility associations: — Suicidal potential. (Beck and Molish)

Elaboration below expectancy; F% above expectancy, F+% above expectancy, R below expectancy: — Anxiety, guardedness, social isolation. (Phillips and Smith)

Elevated Z score and increment of F- with S: — Paranoid trend. (Beck III)

Emotionality displayed, without color on Rorschach: — Effort to maintain reality contact in latent schizophrenia ("incipient schizophrenia") with break probable. (Schafer-Clinical Application)

Emphasis on space or color as light, reacted to positively, while shading is reacted to negatively: — Cyclic moods swings; hypomanic trend. (Schafer-Rorschach)

Evasion, meager record, suspicion, symmetry comments: — Paranoid tendency. (Schafer-Rorschach)

Excessive qualification plus rapid initial response time: — Fear of impulses with inability to inhibit acting out; immaturity; impulsivity. (Phillips and Smith)

Expansiveness, grandiosity, high R, high W: — Intellectualizing paranoid. (Schafer-Clinical Application)

Extrotensive EB, with aggressive and S content: — Externalized hostility. (Beck III)

Extrotensive EB in hysteric with anatomy content:

Conversion tendency. (Beck III)

Extrotensive EB, increment F+:

Psychophysiologic tendency. (Beck III)

Extrotensive EB, increment S:

Immature aggressivity, impairment of emotional control. (Beck III)

F−, low-form color, rapid card turning, rapid speech, restlessness:

Emotional lability, impulsivity, irritability. (Beck III)

F% > 80, good form:

Compulsivity, depression, pathological constriction or lack of spontaneity. (Klopfer-Davidson)

Fm+, FM+ and M+:

Ego strength, although psychopathology may be present. (Klopfer-Developments I)

FT and FY increment

Possible feminine component; possible sexual identification conflict. (Beck and Molish)

FT−, FY−, T, TF:

Negative prognostic signs (Klopfer-Developments I)

FT plus color:

Need for dependent compliance. (Klopfer-Developments II)

Fabulization excessive, high W, inverted percepts (seeing figures upside down or without reversing card), no color or emphasis on color except limited arbitrary FC, perculiar verbalizations, several M; sex symbolism; with depression, low R; with sexual and somatic complaints, low F+, more At and sexual content:

Schizoid personality. (Schafer-Clinical Application)

Fabulizations, M− increment:

Obsessive (with space obsessive doubting). [Schafer-Clinical Application]

Form-minus color without subjective discomfort:

Lack of insight into emotional experiences or motivations; impairment of reality testing. (Klopfer-Developments I)

Form poor, rare Dd:

Lack of common sense; negativism. (Klopfer-Davidson)

Form + shading with M+:	Sublimatory striving; working out of anxiety in nonpathological fantasy activity and imagination. (Beck III)
High At, low F+ in some individuals, otherwise high F+%, perhaps some confabulation in persons with depressive pattern previously stated:	Psychotic depressive reaction ("psychotic depressives"). [Schafer-Clinical Application]
High F%, form good:	Control of emotions without involvement; impersonal, matter-of-fact approach. (Klopfer-Davidson)
High F+%, increment M, low color:	Caution, although impulsive acts may be sporadically expressed. (Schafer-Clinical Applications)
Hysteria with anatomy and paranoid projection:	Negative prognostic sign for therapy despite hysteric element. (Beck and Molish)
Hysterical features with anatomical content:	Conversion. (Schafer-Clinical Application)
Hysterical features with high F+:	Compulsive tendencies. (Schafer-Clinical Applications)
Hysterical features with increment M or M other than on III:	Phobic tendencies. (Schafer-Clinical Application)
Hysterical features with low F+:	Anxiety and lability. (Schafer-Clinical Application)
Hysterical features with usual sex content:	Sexual preoccupation. (Schafer-Clinical Application)
Good form M in optimal relation with FM; good H content:	Emotional stability, self-respect. (Klopfer-Developments I)
Good form, W above expectancy:	Ambition, perfectionism. (Phillips and Smith)
Guarded record, extratensive EB:	Negativism. (Klopfer-Developments I)
(H); Hd:	Criticality, egocentricity, hostility. (Klopfer-Developments I)
(H) M:	Immature, wish-fulfilling fantasy. (Klopfer-Developments I)
Hdx, slow response time:	Repressive tendency. (Beck and Molish)

High W% with schizophrenic disorganization:

Expansiveness; possible grandiosity. (Schafer-Clinical Application)

Hostility and sex themes, involving humans, without M:

Absence of conscious tension-reducing fantasy; lack of insight into complexes. (Beck and Molish)

Increment A, Ad, At, Hd:

Possible paranoid trend. (Schafer-Rorschach)

Increment A, At or perseveration of vague form:

Stereotypy. (Rapaport)

Increment A, D, orderly sequence:

Practicality. (Beck III)

Increment A and P:

Possible passive-compliance; repressive tendency. (Schafer-Rorschach)

Increment C with CF and FC:

Antisocial personality ("narcissistic character disorder" variety); decompensating compulsive; hysteric. (Schafer-Clinical Application)

Increment C with depression:

Psychotic depression. (Rapaport)

Increment D, F+:

Commonsense approach, practicality. (Klopfer-Developments I)

Increment Dd and F-:

Conflict between reaction-formation against hostility and narcissistic rebellious impulses, with defenses inadequate to contain the negativistic tendency. (Schafer-Rorschach)

Increment Dd and FC+:

Successful defense against hostility by compliance and meticulousness. (Schafer-Rorschach)

Increment Dd and R:

Obsessive tendency. (Beck III)

Increment F%; increment F+; decrement color and especially of CF; Fm, M-:

Paranoid trend with constriction and guardedness. (Schafer-Rorschach)

Increment F+ color with positively toned affective comments:

Elation potential. (Beck III)

Increment form-determined complex determinants (FC, FY, FT); decrement low-form complex determinants (C, CF, TF, YF, etc.):

Perfectionistic tendency; reaction-formation against hostility. (Schafer-Rorschach)

Increment form-determined and FC responses:

Possible overcontrol of impulses; possible reaction-formation against hostility. (Schafer-Rorschach)

Increment FV with increment R:

Effort to compensate for feelings of inadequacy. (Beck III)

Increment M, no color:

Delusional and obsessive symptoms. (Schafer-Clinical Application)

Increment M with depression:

Obsessive or schizoid trend. (Rapaport)

Increment M with low productivity:

Cautious paranoid; depressive; obsessive. (Schafer-Clinical Application)

Increment M with neurosis:

Obsessive tendency. (Rapaport)

Increment M without psychopathology:

Effective sublimation. (Rapaport)

Increment M (many M's) with psychosis (schizophrenic disorganization):

Delusional tendency. (Rapaport; Schafer-Clinical Application)

Increment M with space increment:

Hostility directed inward with dysphoric mood, oppressive anxiety and tension; possible suicidal tendency; punitive superego. (Beck and Molish)

Increment or optimum color sum, FT, FY, with increment F+:

At least minimal adaptability and emotional control. (Schafer-Rorschach)

Increment R, narrow content:

Possible compensation for feelings of inadequacy. (Beck III)

Increment rotation, variability in productivity and time from card to card:

Impatience, possible restless trend, tension. (Beck III)

Increment S, introtensive EB:

Inadequacy feelings, self-criticality, turning of hostility against self. (Klopfer-Developments I)

Increment W; mediocre but not vague form or increment F-:

Overcompensation, overgeneralization, unrealistic ambition. (Klopfer-Developments I)

Low F% in constricted record:

Anxiety, neurasthenia, severe depression. (Schafer-Clinical Application)

Low F% with optimal color, M, shading:

May be creative, sensitive, spontaneous or tend to overpersonalize reactions. (Klopfer-Davidson)

Low form red, expressed dislike or hesitancy in use:

Hysteria, impulsivity. (Phillips and Smith)

Low number color associations, high affective ratio:

Potential for affective response. (Beck III)

Low P with low sum color:

Blandness; generalized withdrawal. (Schafer-Clinical Application)

M in Dd:

Autism; withdrawal. (Phillips and Smith)

M in depression:

Suicidal rumination possibly. (Beck and Molish)

M in Hd:

Regressive tendency. (Beck and Molish)

M in Hd or Dd:

Regressive tendency. (Beck III)

M with psychosis:

Delusional trend. (Rapaport)

Menstrual or vaginal associations with revulsion:

Feminine inadequacy and masculine identification in women; rejection of feminine role. (Schafer-Rorschach)

No M or sharp form:

Impulsive, unreflective acts. (Schafer-Clinical Application)

0−, good form:

Probably eccentricity rather than psychosis. (Klopfer-Developments I)

0−, poor form:

Impairment of reality contact. (Klopfer-Developments I)

Overcriticalness of card, use of white space:

Negativism. (Klopfer-Davidson)

Pure C with low A% and F%:

Bizarre impulsive behavior; panic; potential excitement. (Schafer-Clinical Application)

Qualification, Y increment:

Passive trend. (Beck III)

Red shock followed by red-determined content (Boehm):

Hysterical neurosis ("anxiety hysteria"). [Beck and Molish]

Reduction R, mediocre W increment:

Acting-out disorders, psychophysiologic disorders ("psychosomatic"). [Philips and Smith]

Rigid sequence, increment of D:

Guardedness; stereotyped defenses and habits. (Beck III)

Rigid sequence, self-depreciation: Guilt. (Beck III)

Shading increment with C and S: Possible potential catatonic excitement. (Beck and Molish)

Shading increment with S increment: Possible catatonic trend. (Beck and Molish)

Shading increment, schizophrenic tendency: Potential for bizarre panic attacks. (Schafer-Clinical Application)

Shading with schizophrenic disorganization: Acute schizophrenic episode ("panic states"). [Schafer-Clinical Application]

Simple schizophrenic pattern with high R, no peculiar verbalizations: Antisocial personality ("psychopath") [Schafer-Clinical Application]

Space with increment color: Negativism, obstinacy. (Rapaport)

Space with increment Dd, P, M: Doubt, self-criticism, self-distrust (Rapaport)

Space increment with vista: Resistiveness as defense against inferiority feelings. (Beck III)

Symbolic content in sexual areas: Paranoid tendency. (Schafer-Clinical Application)

Two or more form-plus M in depressive state: Suggests reactive depression; good prognostic sign in depression. (Beck III)

Y with shading shock: Impairment of self-esteem. (Beck and Molish)

Confabulation

Confabulation (DW):   Schizophrenia; overgeneralization (Klopfer-Development I); schizophrenic trend (Rapaport)

Extreme confabulation: Catatonics, hebephrenics, organics. (Phillips and Smith)

Increment confabulation: Possible paranoid trend. (Schafer-Rorschach)

Contamination

Contamination: Schizophrenic trend. (Rapaport)

Content

ABSTRACTION

Abstract, irrelevant dichotomy responses, as "life-death":

Schizophrenic ambivalence. (Beck and Molish)

Abstract responses that require perceptual reorganization:

Paranoid tendency. (Schafer-Clinical Application)

Abstractions:

Contraindicates acting-out, immaturity, inadequacy; favorable prognosis for successful adjustment; ideational with moderate feeling tone and superior intelligence (Phillips and Smith); direct reflection of feeling tone, dysphoric or euphoric (Klopfer-Davidson); guardedness; inhibition, introspection. (Rapaport)

Chaos:

Emotional turmoil, volatility. (Schafer-Rorschach)

ANAL
Anal anatomy, buttocks:

Paranoid tendency possibly. (Klopfer-Developments I)

Anal associations (anus, rectum, colon, etc.):

Anality, feminine identification, masculine inadequacy in men, masculine identification in women. (Schafer-Rorschach)

Anal and buttock responses:

Paranoid tendency. (Klopfer-Davidson)

Animal or person defecating:

Anality; feminine identification and masculine inadequacy in men. (Schafer-Rorschach)

Buttocks:

Anality; masculine inadequacy and feminine identification in men, possible paranoid tendency. (Schafer-Rorschach)

Buttocks bumping or touching:

Anality; masculine inadequacy and feminine identification in men. (Schafer-Rorschach)

Emphasis on anal areas:	Passive-submissive; possible homosexual tendency. (Phillips and Smith)
Feces:	Anality; feminine identification and masculine inadequacy in men. (Schafer-Rorschach)
Snow-White buttocks:	Innocence and denial of guilt as a defense against superego conflict. (Schafer-Rorschach)
Toilet seat:	Anality; feminine identification and masculine inadequacy in men. (Schafer-Rorschach)

ANATOMY

Anatomy:	Destructive impulses which are not acted out directly because of fear of retaliation; hypochondriacal complaints. (Phillips and Smith)
Birth and reproductive images and organs, male subject:	Feminine identification tendency; or possible oedipal conflicts. (Schafer-Rorschach)
Bleeding, crushed, and mutilated anatomy:	Inadequacy, masochism, and negativism. (Schafer-Rorschach)
Bony anatomy:	Anxiety over repressed hostility; psychophysiologic tendencies; contraindicates acting-out (Phillips and Smith); blocking, rigidity. (Rapaport)
Cut:	Castration anxiety in men, castration feelings in women; feminine identification in men, masculine identification in women; negative feelings. (Schafer-Rorschach)
Crushed, bleeding, and mutilated anatomy:	Inadequacy, masochism, and negativism. (Schafer-Rorschach)
Decay anatomy:	Schizophrenia. (Schafer-Clinical Application)
Decayed or diseased anatomy:	Primarily schizophrenic. (Phillips and Smith)

Deteriorated or frayed anatomy:

Concern with aging and death. (Schafer-Rorschach)

Diseased anatomy:

Severe neurosis with felt neurotic distress. (Beck III)

Diseased or decayed anatomy:

Primarily schizophrenic. (Phillips and Smith)

Eroded pelvis:

Concern with aging and death; masochism; possible defeatist tendency. (Schafer-Rorschach)

Fangs:

Possible paranoid tendency. (Schafer-Rorschach)

Frayed or deteriorated anatomy:

Concern with aging and death. (Schafer-Rorschach)

Gangrenous tissue:

Concern with aging and death; masochism; possible defeatist tendency. (Schafer-Rorschach)

Gums and teeth:

Masturbation guilt; resentment over frustrated dependency; sibling rivalry; with absence of insight into these three conflict areas. (Phillips and Smith)

Increment anatomy:

Anxiety, blocking, somatization; possible schizophrenic element (Rapaport); conversion trend, hypochondriasis; possible phobic tendency. (Beck III)

Inflamed tissue:

Concern with aging and death; masochism; possible defeatist tendency. (Schafer-Rorschach)

Injuries and mutilation:

Anxiety; sadistic impulses. (Phillips and Smith)

Injury content:

Anxiety. (Beck and Molish)

Internal anatomy:

Anxiety (Beck and Molish); possible paranoid trend. (Beck III)

Mutilated, bleeding, crushed anatomy:

Inadequacy, masochism, negativism. (Schafer-Rorschach)

Mutilation and injuries:	Anxiety; sadistic impulses. (Phillips and Smith)
Neural anatomy:	Compensatory emphasis on intellectual attainment. (Phillips and Smith)
Non-P bony anatomy:	Reaction-formation against and denial of hostility; social constraint and anxiety; psychophysiologic states. (Phillips and Smith)
Original anatomy:	Pathologic concern with health. (Beck III)
Pregnancy:	Feminine identification, masculine inadequacy in men. (Schafer-Rorschach)
Pus:	Concern with aging and death; masochism; possible defeatist tendency. (Schafer-Rorschach)
Reproductive images and organs, birth, male subject:	Feminine identification tendency; or possible oedipal conflicts. (Schafer-Rorschach)
Scars and wounds:	Castration anxiety, feminine identification and masculine ineffectuality in men; castration feelings and masculine identification in women; inadequacy, negativism. (Schafer-Rorschach)
Skeletons, skulls:	Depressive or masochistic trend. (Klopfer-Developments I)
Skull, split-open:	Concern with aging and death; masochism; possible defeatist tendency. (Schafer-Rorschach)
Skulls:	Depressive or masochistic trend (Klopfer-Developments I); possible depressive tendency. (Schafer-Rorschach)
Spinal cord, spine:	Competitive women in involutional period; men, ineffectuality, fear of women. (Phillips and Smith)
Teeth:	Phobic tendency (Beck III); possible

	paranoid tendency. (Schafer-Rorschach)
Teeth and gums:	Masturbation guilt; resentment over frustrated dependency; sibling rivalry with absence of insight into these three conflict areas. (Phillips and Smith)
Umbilical cord:	Dependent, passive-receptive, rejection of adult role; concern with reproductive function. (Schafer-Rorschach)
Visceral anatomy:	Aggressive and sexual conflicts (Rapaport); passive-aggressive ("oral-aggressive") but otherwise contraindicates acting-out or assaultiveness; paranoid tendencies; resentment of maternal figures; antisocial personalities ("psychopaths") and schizophrenics. (Phillips and Smith, who comment that these observations are particularly indicated when visceral anatomy occurs on Cards I, VIII, IX, and X)
Wishbone, other than D3 on X:	Dependent, passive-receptive, rejection of adult role. (Schafer-Rorschach)
Wounds and scars:	Castration anxiety, feminine identification and masculine ineffectuality in men; castration feelings and masculine identification in women; inadequacy, negativism. (Schafer-Rorschach)
X ray:	Absence of negativism; morbid apprehension, strong inhibiting anxiety (Phillips and Smith); latent anxiety. (Beck III)

ANIMAL
A > 50%:

Low intelligence; narrow interests; stereotypy. (Klopfer-Davidson); conformity, immaturity; lack of introspection and lack of insight. (Phillips and Smith)

A increment:	Anxiety (declining M); depression; guardedness. (Phillips and Smith)
Aggressive A, as lions, tigers:	Aggressive impulses. (Klopfer-Davidson)
Aggressive animals:	Externalized hostility. (Beck III)
Alligator:	Negative attitudes. (Phillips and Smith)
Animal content:	Stereotypy. (Phillips and Smith).
Animal decrement:	Euphoria. (Phillips and Smith)
Animal held down:	Masochism; oppressive feeling; possible defeatist tendency. (Schafer-Rorschach)
Animal rear view:	Anality. (Schafer-Rorschach)
Animals devouring other animals or persons:	Dependent, demanding; sadism or possible masochism with rejection of adult role; with anal, oral, and sexual content, masculine and feminine inadequacy. (Schafer-Rorschach)
Animals fighting:	Aggressive impulses. (Beck and Molish)
Ape:	Ambivalence toward domineering father. (Phillips and Smith)
Attacking or devouring animals:	Denial of passive-aggressive ("oral-agressive") trend; possible emasculation conflicts. (Schafer-Rorschach)
Attacking horned animals:	Sadistic impulses. (Schafer-Rorschach)
Awkward or missing wings on birds (birds without wings):	Impotence, negative attitudes, weakness; feminine identification, masculine inadequacy in men. (Schafer-Rorschach)
Baby crocodiles:	Rejection of adult role. (Schafer-Rorschach)
Bacteria:	Regressive tendency; schizophrenia; severe hypochondriasis. (Phillips and Smith)
"Bat coming toward me":	Fearfulness, helplessness, weakness. (Schafer-Rorschach)

Bat (nonpopular area):

Oppressive, painful anticipation of un-pleasantness. (Phillips and Smith)

Bear:

Unresolved relationship with paternal figure viewed as domineering but sympathic. (Phillips and Smith)

Bee:

Industriousness (Klopfer-Davidson); regressive tendency; children paranoids, schizophrenics. (Phillips and Smith)

Bird:

Heterosexual inadequacy; immaturity; antisocial tendency ("psychopathy"). [Phillips and Smith]

Bison (or buffalo):

Ambivalence toward domineering father. (Phillips and Smith)

Biting animals:

Demanding, dependent, passive-aggressive ("oral-aggressive"), with rejection of adult role; possible masochism or sadism; with increment other anal, oral, sexual content, masculine and feminine inadequacy—with feminine identification in men, masculine identification in women (Schafer-Rorschach); phobic tendency. (Beck III)

Biting and stinging animals or insects:

Sadistic impulses. (Schafer-Rorschach)

"Black bat":

Phobic trend. (Beck III)

Black sheep:

Superego conflict with guilt. (Schafer-Rorschach)

Bleeding, crushed, mutilated animals:

Inadequacy; masochism, negativism. (Schafer-Rorschach)

Buffalo (or bison):

Ambivalence toward domineering father. (Phillips and Smith)

Bug (beetle):

Antisocial tendencies ("psychopathy") with acting-out, assaultiveness, lack of long-range goals; immaturity with anticipation of rejection, frustrated dependency needs, impulsivity; rejecting maternal figure with concomitant heterosexual inadequacy. (Phillips and Smith)

Bull:	Ambivalence toward domineering father. (Phillips and Smith)
Bunny:	Innocence and denial of guilt as a defense against superego conflict; rejection of adult role; regressive tendency. (Schafer-Rorschach)
Burdened animals:	Demanding, inadequate, negativistic; passive-aggressive ("oral-aggressive"); possibly masochistic. (Schafer-Rorschach)
Butterfly (non popular):	Mood of well-being; passive feminine tendency. (Phillips and Smith)
Calf:	Domination by father, with concomitant inhibition of aggression and lack of motivation for achievement; passive-feminine, possible homosexual tendency. (Phillips and Smith)
Camel:	Demanding, dependent, passive-aggressive ("oral-aggressive"); possible masochism, rejection of adult role. (Schafer-Rorschach)
Carcass:	Demanding, dependent, passive-aggressive ("oral-aggressive"); possible masochism; rejection of adult role. (Schafer-Rorschach)
Carnivorous animals and insects:	Demanding, passive-aggressive ("oral-agressive"); inadequacy, masochism, negativism. (Schafer-Rorschach)
Cat:	Immaturity, nostalgia for childhood dependency state (Phillips and Smith); passive-dependency. (Klopfer-Davidson)
Charging animals:	Active, lively. (Schafer-Rorschach)
Charging bull:	Destructiveness, hostility, sadism; feminine identification and masculine inadequacy in men; passive-submissive or defense against passive-submissive needs. (Schafer-Rorschach)
Chicken:	Deprivation of affection and feeling of

Chicks with open beaks:

Clawing animals:

Clipped French poodle:

Cockroach:

Colliding animals:

Cow:

Cows, sheep:

Coyote:

Crab:

rejection; immaturity. (Phillips and Smith)

Dependent, passive-receptive; rejection of adult role. (Schafer-Rorschach)

Demanding, dependent, passive-aggressive ("oral-aggressive"), with rejection of adult role; sadism, possible masochism; with increment of anal, oral and sexual content, feminine and masculine inadequacy—feminine identification in men, masculine identification in women. (Schafer-Rorschach)

Authoritarian attitudes with submission; inadequacy and negative attitudes. (Schafer-Rorschach)

Heterosexual inadequacy, immaturity, antisocial personality ("psychopathy"). [Phillips and Smith]

Sadistic impulses. (Schafer-Rorschach)

Dependent, passive-receptive, rejection of adult role (Schafer-Rorschach); indulgent maternal figure (Phillips and Smith); passive-dependency (Klopfer-Davidson); possible derision of women. (Beck III)

Passivity tendency. (Klopfer-Developments I)

Demanding, dependent, passive-aggressive ("oral-aggressive"); rejection of adult role; sadism or possible masochism. (Schafer-Rorschach)

Alcoholics, antisocial personalities ("psychopaths"), enuretics; acting-out of assaultive tendencies; rejecting maternal figure with concomitant anticipation of rejection, covert hostility and heterosexual inadequacy. (Phillips and Smith)

Crab (other than popular D1, D7 and D8 of Card X): — Dependent, demanding, passive-aggressive ("oral-aggressive"); rejection of adult role; sadism or possible masochism. (Schafer-Rorschach)

Crocodile: — Dependent, demanding, passive-aggressive ("oral-aggressive"); rejection of adult role; sadism, possible masochism (Schafer-Rorschach); negative attitudes. (Phillips and Smith)

Crouching animals: — Hostile impulses. (Schafer-Rorschach)

Crudely skinned animal: — Impotence, negative attitudes, weakness in men; feminine identification, masculine inadequacy in men. (Schafer-Rorschach)

Cub: — Domination by father with concomitant inhibition of aggression and lack of motivation for achievement; passive-feminine, possible homosexual tendency. (Phillips and Smith)

Damaged, diseased, deteriorated animals: — Inadequate, masochistic, negativistic. (Schafer-Rorschach)

Decrement A: — Impulsivity. (Rapaport)

Deer: — Indulgent maternal figure. (Phillips and Smith)

Deteriorated, damaged, diseased animals: — Inadequate, masochistic, negativistic. (Schafer-Rorschach)

Diminutive, passive, or plodding animals: — Caution, delayed response, timidity. (Schafer-Rorschach)

Diminutives (calf, colt, kitten, lamb, mouse, etc.): — Domination by father with concomitant constriction, inhibition of aggression and lack of motivation for achievement; passive-feminine, possible homosexual tendency. (Phillips and Smith)

Dinosaur: — May symbolize primitive hostile impulses. (Schafer-Rorschach)

Diseased, damaged, deteriorated animals: — Inadequate, masochistic, negativistic. (Schafer-Rorschach)

Dog:

Passive-dependency. (Klopfer-Davidson)

Dog scampering away:

Fearfulness, helplessness, weakness. (Schafer-Rorschach)

Eagle:

Ambivalence toward domineering father with concomitant suspicious attitudes, especially toward men; paranoid tendencies appearing involutionally; self-derogatory. (Common on Card I in paranoid syndromes.) [Phillips and Smith]

Elephant:

Immaturity; nostalgia for childhood dependency state. (Phillips and Smith)

Exceptionally low A:

Adults of superior intelligence without emotional pathology; also autism possibly; also some disturbed schizophrenics and some epileptics of a nonchronic and undeteriorated kind. (Beck III)

Falling bird shot in flight:

Concern with aging and death; masochism; possible defeatist tendency. (Schafer-Rorschach)

Fangs:

Dependent, demanding passive-aggressive ("oral-aggressive"); rejection of adult role; sadism, possible masochism. (Schafer-Rorschach)

Fat-cheeked pussy cat:

Rejection of adult role. (Schafer-Rorschach)

Feeding animals:

Passive-receptive trend. (Schafer-Rorschach)

Feeding, fighting, preying animals:

Demanding, dependent, passive-aggressive ("oral-aggressive"); possible masochism; rejection of adult role. (Schafer-Rorschach)

Fighting cocks:

Fearful, hostile conception of male role; feminine and masculine inadequacy; feminine identification in men, masculine identification in women. (Schafer-Rorschach)

Fighting, feeding, preying animals:	Demanding, dependent, passive-aggressive ("oral-aggressive"); possible masochism; rejection of adult role. (Schafer-Rorschach)
Fish:	Alcoholics; maternal overprotection; passive-dependency. (Phillips and Smith)
Fleeing animals:	Felt weakness with anxiety; inadequacy, negativism. (Schafer-Rorschach)
Fleeing dog:	Fearfulness, helplessness, weakness. (Schafer-Rorschach)
Fly:	Children, paranoids, schizophrenics; regressive tendency. (Phillips and Smith)
Fox:	Negative attitudes. (Phillips and Smith)
Foxes, rodents:	Antisocial or scheming tendency. (Klopfer-Developments I)
Frightening animals, as King-Kong, snakes, spiders:	Hysterical tendency. (Schafer-Clinical Application)
Frightening or sinister animals:	Felt weakness with anxiety; inadequacy, negativism. (Schafer-Rorschach)
Frog:	Alcoholics and enuretics; antisocial personalities ("psychopathy"); immaturity. (Phillips and Smith)
Germ:	Schizophrenics, severe hypochondriacs; regressive tendency. (Phillips and Smith)
Gorilla:	Ambivalence toward domineering father, with derogatory content; fearfulness, helplessness, weakness. (Schafer-Rorschach)
Helpless, powerless animals:	Inadequacy, negativism; superego conflict. (Schafer-Rorschach)
High A%:	Anxiety, depression, guardedness; stereotypy (Phillips and Smith); guarded-

ness, sense of guilt (Beck III); stereotypy. (Rapaport)

Horse:

Ambivalence toward domineering family. (Phillips and Smith)

Increment of animal content:

Anxiety indicator; phobic tendency possibly (Beck III); depression, inhibition, low intelligence; obsessive-compulsive; contraindicates chronic schizophrenia (Rapaport); geriatric patients (Klopfer-Developments I); may indicate lack of motivation for achievement; may indicate rigidity. (Beck and Molish)

Infant carnivorous animals:

Regression, rejection of adult role. (Schafer-Rorschach)

Jellyfish:

Alcoholics and enuretics; lack of assertion and initiative; passivity, perhaps as defense against hostility (Phillips and Smith); feminine identification, masculine inadequacy in men. (Schafer-Rorschach)

Lamb:

Dependent needs or need for innocence; denial of guilt and innocence as defense against superego conflict. (Schafer-Rorschach)

Large A:

Symbolizes parents. (Phillips and Smith)

Larva:

Passive-aggressive ("oral-aggressive") tendency; possible parasitic dependency tendency. (Schafer-Rorschach)

Lion:

Demanding, dependent, passive-aggressive ("oral-aggressive"); rejection of adult role; sadism; possible masochism. (Schafer-Rorschach)

Lions, panthers, tigers (Goldfarb):

Aggressive tendencies. (Klopfer-Developments I)

Lizard:

Negative attitudes (Phillips and Smith); rejection of adult role. (Schafer-Rorschach)

Lobster:	Alcoholics, antisocial personalities, enuretics; acting-out of assaultive tendencies; rejecting maternal figure with concomitant anticipation of rejection, covert hostility and heterosexual inadequacy. (Phillips and Smith)
Locusts:	Passive-aggressive ("oral-aggressive") tendency; possible parasitic dependency. (Schafer-Rorschach)
Mangled wings:	Concern with aging and death; defeatist tendency; masochism. (Schafer-Rorschach)
Mangy fur:	Concern with aging and death. (Schafer-Rorschach)
Maternal animals:	Passive-receptive trend. (Schafer-Rorschach)
Mice barely hanging on:	Feminine identification, masculine inadequacy in men; negative attitudes, impatience, weakness in men. (Schafer-Rorschach)
Monkey:	Ambivalence toward domineering father; antisocial personality ("psychopathy"), with sadism toward women; derisive attitudes and ineffectuality. (Phillips and Smith)
Mosquito:	Demanding, dependent, passive-aggressive ("oral-aggressive")—or denial of passive-aggressive trends; possible emasculation conflict. (Schafer-Rorschach)
Moth:	Passivity, perhaps as a defense against hostility. (Phillips and Smith)
Mother bird with worm:	Dependent, passive-receptive; rejection of adult role. (Schafer-Rorschach)
Mother hen:	Dependent, passive-receptive; rejection of adult role. (Schafer-Rorschach)
Mouse:	Cautious interpersonal relations; lethargy, timidity (Schafer-Rorschach);

feeling of inadequacy; passivity, timidity. (Phillips and Smith)

Mouse (with tail):

Lack of sexual aggressiveness. (Klopfer-Davidson)

Mule:

Demanding, dependent, passive-aggressive ("oral-aggressive"); obstinacy; possible masochism with rejection of adult role. (Schafer-Rorschach)

Neonate or small animals:

Need for help and protection, passive-dependency. (Beck III)

Nonaggressive animals (dog, sheep, turtle):

Possible suppression of hostility. (Klopfer-Developments I)

Nongeneric storybook animals (bee, cat, chicken, duck, horse, rabbit, etc.):

Immaturity. (Phillips and Smith)

Non-P bat:

Apprehension; morbid anticipation of unpleasantness. (Phillips and Smith)

Nursing lamb:

Dependent, passive-receptive; rejection of adult role. (Schafer-Rorschach)

Octopus:

Active striving for independence; alcoholics, enuretics; domineering, overprotective, possessive maternal figure; demanding, dependent, passive-aggressive ("oral-aggressive"); possible phobic trend (Beck III); rejection of adult role; sadism, possible masochism. (Schafer-Rorschach)

Optimal A content:

Adequate reality contact. (Beck and Molish)

Oral threat animal content, as crocodiles, wolves:

Possible propensity for panic states. (Beck and Molish)

Ostrich:

May symbolize use of denial as a defense. (Schafer-Rorschach)

Ox:

Demanding, dependent, passive-aggressive ("oral-aggressive"); masochism, possible defeatist tendency; oppressive feeling. (Schafer-Rorschach)

Parrot:

Authoritarian orientation with submission; inadequacy and negative attitudes; possible passive-submissive defenses against hostility. (Schafer-Rorschach)

Partially consumed animals:

Regression, rejection of adult role. (Schafer-Rorschach)

Passive A, as cats, cows, dogs, sheep:

Passive-dependency. (Klopfer-Davidson)

Peacock:

Narcissism, sensuality. (Schafer-Rorschach)

Percentage of animal resources:

Degree of stereotypy. (Rorschach)

Performing animals and pets:

Authoritarian attitude, with impersonal attitudes and masochistic-sadistic orientation; inadequacy, negativism. (Schafer-Rorschach)

Pig:

Dependent, passive-receptive; rejection of adult role. (Schafer-Rorschach)

Plant-devouring animals:

Demanding, passive-aggressive; possible parasitic dependency trend. (Schafer-Rorschach)

Polar bear:

Detached emotional tone; unfriendly, unresponsive. (Schafer-Rorschach)

Porcupine:

Defense against sado-masochistic tendency. (Schafer-Rorschach)

Powerful animals:

Passive-submissive needs which may be denied. (Schafer-Rorschach)

Pretty butterfly:

Reaction-formation against hostility. (Schafer-Rorschach)

Preying, feeding, fighting animals:

Demanding, dependent, passive-aggressive ("oral-aggressive"); possible masochism; rejection of adult role. (Schafer-Rorschach)

Protected animals like porcupine:

Defensive attitude, fearfulness. (Schafer-Rorschach)

Pup:

Domination by father with concomitant immaturity, inhibition of aggression and lack of motivation for achievement; passive-feminine, possible homosexual tendency. (Phillips and Smith)

Puppies nuzzling each other: Reaction-formation against hostility. (Schafer-Rorschach)

Puppy: Dependency needs. (Beck and Molish)

Pursuing animals: Demanding, dependent, passive-aggressive ("oral-aggressive"), with rejection of adult role; possible masochism or sadism; with increment other anal, oral, sexual content, masculine and feminine inadequacy—feminine identification in men. (Schafer-Rorschach)

Rabbit: Cautious interpersonal relations; lethargy, timidity (Schafer-Rorschach); feeling of inadequacy, lack of assertion, timidity; nostalgia for childhood dependency state; passivity, perhaps as defense againsty hostility. (Phillips and Smith)

Rat: Negative attitudes. (Phillips and Smith)

Rhinoceros: Destructiveness, hostility, sadism; feminine identification and masculine inadequacy in men. (Schafer-Rorschach)

Rodents, foxes: Antisocial or scheming tendency. (Klopfer-Developments I)

Scarab: Active striving for independence: domineering, overprotective, possessive maternal figure; superior intelligence. (Phillips and Smith)

Scorpion: Active striving for independence; domineering, overprotective, possessive maternal figure; superior intelligence. (Phillips and Smith)

Seahorse: Alcoholics and enuretics; immaturity; nostalgia for childhood dependency state. (Phillips and Smith)

Shark:	Demanding, dependent, passive-aggressive ("oral-aggressive"); possible masochism; rejection of adult role. (Schafer-Rorschach)
Sheep:	Feeling of inadequacy, timidity; indulgent maternal figure; passivity perhaps as defense against hostility, passive-dependency. (Klopfer-Davidson)
Sheep, cows:	Passivity tendency. (Klopfer-Developments I)
Shift from wild carnivorous animals to passive noncarnivorous animals:	Regression to passive-dependent role as defense against hostility; repression of hostility. (Schafer-Rorschach)
Sinister or frightening animals:	Felt weakness with anxiety; inadequacy, negativism. (Schafer-Rorschach)
Skin eaten away by bugs:	Rejection of adult role. (Schafer-Rorschach)
Sloth:	Inert, passive. (Schafer-Rorschach)
Small animals:	Symbolize children. (Phillips and Smith)
Snail:	Alcoholics, enuretics; domination by father with concomitant inhibition of aggression and lack of motivation for achievement; failure of man in heterosexual relationship, passive feminine tendency (Phillips and Smith); cautious interpersonal relations; lethargy, passivity, timidity. (Schafer-Rorschach)
Snake (and other named snake species:	Passive-aggressive ("oral-aggressive") tendency (Schafer-Rorschach); possible phobic tendency (Beck III); sexual symbolism. (Klopfer-Davidson)
Snakes, wolves, and other threatening animals:	Phobic tendency. (Beck and Molish)
Spider:	Active striving for independence; domineering, overprotective, possessive maternal figure; passive-dependency (Phillips and Smith) antagonism toward

	(and fear of) maternal figure (Klopfer-Davidson); conception of mother as destructive; demanding, dependent, passive-aggressive ("oral-aggressive"); projection of hostility. (Schafer-Rorschach)
Squashed tomcat:	Concern with aging and death; masochism; possible defeatist tendency. (Schafer-Rorschach)
Stork:	Concern with reproductive function. (Schafer-Rorschach)
Storybook animals (lamb, etc.), symbolic of innocence:	Superego conflict. (Schafer-Rorschach)
Tapeworm:	Demanding, dependent, passive-aggressive; rejection of adult role; sadism, possible masochism. (Schafer-Rorschach)
Tattered and torn butterflies:	Concern over body integrity; possible castration anxiety. (Schafer-Rorschach)
Tattered and worn skin:	Concern over body integrity; possible castration anxiety. (Schafer-Rorschach)
Teddy bear:	Domination by father with concomitant immaturity, inhibition of aggression and lack of motivation for achievement; passive-feminine tendency. (Phillips and Smith)
Tiger:	Ambivalence toward domineering father; fear of hostility of others (Phillips and Smith); demanding, dependent, passive-aggressive ("oral-aggressive"); rejection of adult role; sadism, possible masochism. (Schafer-Rorschach)
Tiny lions:	Rejection of adult role. (Schafer-Rorschach)
Tomato worm:	Demanding, dependent, passive-aggressive ("oral-aggressive"); rejection of adult role; possible masochism or sadism. (Schafer-Rorschach)

Torn and tattered butterflies:	Concern over body integrity; possible castration anxiety. (Schafer-Rorschach)
Toy dog:	Domination by father with concomitant immaturity, inhibition of aggression and lack of motivation for achievement; passive-feminine tendency. (Phillips and Smith)
Trained seal:	Authoritarian orientation with submission; inadequacy and negative attitudes. (Schafer-Rorschach)
Turkey:	Feeling of dejection and deprivation of affection; immaturity. (Phillips and Smith)
Turtle:	Alcoholics and enuretics (Phillips and Smith); cautious interpersonal relations, lethargy, timidity. (Schafer-Rorschach)
Vulture:	Demanding, dependent, passive-aggressive ("oral-aggressive"); lack of self-esteem; sadism or possible masochism. (Schafer-Rorschach)
Wild boar:	Demanding, dependent, passive-aggressive ("oral-aggressive"); rejection of adult role; sadism, possible masochism. (Schafer-Rorschach)
Wings too large or too heavy for body:	Feminine identification, masculine inadequacy in men; impotence, inadequacy and weakness. (Schafer-Rorschach)
Wolf:	Demanding, dependent, passive-aggressive ("oral-aggressive"); rejection of adult role; sadism, possible masochism (Schafer-Rorschach); negative attitudes (Phillips and Smith); possible phobic trend. (Beck III)
Worm:	Domination by father with concomitant immaturity, inhibition of aggression and lack of motivation for achieve-

ment; failure of man in heterosexual relationship; passive-feminine, possible homosexual tendency. (Phillips and Smith)

Worn or tattered skins:
Concern over body integrity, possible castration anxiety. (Schafer-Rorschach)

Worn-out skin:
Concern with aging and death. (Schafer-Rorschach)

ANIMAL DETAIL

Ad:
Avoidance. (Beck and Molish)

Artificial or missing antlers on a deer:
Disparagement of men, feminine inadequacy and masculine identification in women. (Schafer-Rorschach)

Dead, missing or mutilated animal limbs:
Feminine identification, masculine inadequacy in men, masculine identification in women; inadequacy, negativism. (Schafer-Rorschach)

Claws:
Dependent, demanding, passive-aggressive ("oral-aggressive"); rejection of adult role; sadism, possible masochism. (Schafer-Rorschach)

Eagle's beak:
Demanding, dependent, passive-aggressive ("oral-aggressive"); possible masochism or sadism; rejection of adult role. (Schafer-Rorschach)

Emaciated animal detail:
Regression; rejection of adult role. (Schafer-Rorschach)

Emaciated cow head:
Rejection of adult role. (Schafer-Rorschach)

Horns:
In female subject may represent masculine striving. (Schafer-Rorschach)

Missing or artificial antlers on a deer:
Disparagement of men, feminine inadequacy and masculine identification in women. (Schafer-Rorschach)

Missing, dead, or mutilated animal limbs:
Feminine identification, masculine inadequacy in men, masculine identification in women; inadequacy, negativism. (Schafer-Rorschach)

Mutilated, dead or missing animal limbs:	Feminine identification, masculine inadequacy in men, masculine identification in women; inadequacy, negativism. (Schafer-Rorschach)
Powerful wings:	Passive-submissive or defense against passive-submissive needs. (Schafer-Rorschach)
Stinger:	Destructiveness, hostility, sadism; feminine identification and masculine inadequacy in men. (Schafer-Rorschach)
Tusks:	Demanding, dependent, passive-aggressive ("oral-aggressive"), rejection of adult role; sadism or possible masochism. (Schafer-Rorschach)

ANTHROPOLOGY

"Ancient Tribal mask that once was frightening":	Counter-phobic resistance to passive-submissive needs. (Schafer-Rorschach)
Totem pole:	Average intelligence or above; normal males; potential for acceptable social adjustment (Phillips and Smith); sexual symbolism. (Klopfer-Davidson)

ANTIQUITY

Antiquity:	Absence of manifest anxiety; culture and social adjustment; potential for accomplishment. (Phillips and Smith)

ARCHITECTURE

Architecture content:	Ambition (Rapaport); feelings of inferiority, self-devaluation (Beck III); two groups: bridges—feeling of inadequacy relative to success of father, high level of aspiration, masculine identification; buildings and towers—insecurity with distrust of but desire for nurturing relationship. (Phillips and Smith)
Architecture content in women:	Masculine striving. (Rapaport)
"Base" percept:	Felt emotional instability guarded against by defense mechanisms; insecurity. (Schafer-Rorschach)

Bombed building:	Concern with aging and death; masochism; possible defeatist tendency. (Schafer-Rorschach)
Bridge:	Insecurity (see "Architecture content" above). [Phillips and Smith]
Building:	Maturity (see "Architecture content" above). [Phillips and Smith]
Castle:	Authoritarian orientation; concern with authority and elevated social status. (Schafer-Rorschach)
Crumpled wall:	Feeling of decay or of deterioration. (Schafer-Rorschach)
Fortress:	Defense against sado-masochistic tendency. (Schafer-Rorschach)
House:	Sexual symbolism. (Klopfer-Davidson)
Hut:	Authoritarian orientation with felt inferior social status; inadequacy and negative attitudes. (Schafer-Rorschach)
Lighthouse:	Felt weakness with need for guidance and support. (Schafer-Rorschach)
Palace:	Authoritarian orientation; concern with authority and elevated social status. (Schafer-Rorschach)
Prison bars:	Authoritarian orientation with submission; inadequacy and negative attitudes. (Schafer-Rorschach)
Protecting walls:	Paranoid tendency. (Schafer-Rorschach)
Protective structures:	Defensive attitude, fearfulness. (Schafer-Rorschach)
Ruined wall:	Concern with aging and death; masochism; possible defeatist tendency. (Schafer-Rorschach)
Supporting objects:	Felt weakness with need for support and guidance; inadequacy, negativism. (Schafer-Rorschach)

Tower:
Maturity (see "Architecture content" above). [Phillips and Smith]

Turrets:
Defense against sado-masochistic tendency. (Schafer-Rorschach)

Walls:
Constrained emotional tone; guarded interpersonal relations. (Schafer-Rorshach)

ART
Art:
Evasion, feminine traits, intellectualization. (Phillips and Smith)

ASTRONOMY
Astronomy (rare):
Regression and schizophrenia if F−; superior adjustment or intelligence if F+. (Phillips and Smith)

BLENDS (Content)
Amazon (Human. Mythology):
Destructiveness, hostility, sadism; feminine identification and masculine inadequacy with fear of women in men. (Schafer-Rorschach)

Angel (Inhuman Human. Religion):
Innocence and denial of guilt as defense against superego conflict; passive-receptive trend. (Schafer-Rorschach)

Atlas (Inhuman Human. Mythology):
Demanding, dependent, passive-aggressive ("oral-aggressive"); possible masochism; rejection of adult role. (Schafer-Rorschach)

Bestiality (Animal. Human. Sex):
Feminine identification in men, masculine identification in women; feminine or masculine inadequacy. (Schafer-Rorschach)

Bird on nest (Animal. Nature):
Dependent, passive-receptive; rejection of adult role. (Schafer-Rorschach)

Bleeding hymen (Anatomy. Sex):
Fearful hostile conception of male role; feminine identification in men, masculine identification in women; feminine or masculine inadequacy. (Schafer-Rorschach)

Bleeding rectum (Anal. Blood):

Anality; feminine identification and masculine inadeqaucy in men; sado-masochism. (Schafer-Rorschach)

Bleeding vagina (Anatomy. Sex):

Concern with aging and death; feminine identification in men, masculine inadequacy in men; masculine identification in women. (Schafer-Rorschach)

Breasts (Human Detail. Sex):

Passive-receptive trend. (Schafer-Rorschach)

Buddha (Human. Religion):

Passive-submissive; or intellectual defense against passive-submissive needs. (Schafer-Rorschach)

Cartoon woman (Human. Art):

Destructiveness, hostility, sadism. (Schafer-Rorschach)

Cathedral (Architecture. Religion):

Innocence and denial of guilt as a defense against supergo conflict. (Schafer-Rorschach)

Centaur (Inhuman Human. Mythology):

Destructiveness, hostility, sadism; feminine identification and masculine inadequacy in men. (Schafer-Rorschach)

Cherub (Inhuman Human. Religion):

Innocence and denial of guilt as defense against superego conflict. (Schafer-Rorschach)

Christ (Human. Religion):

Passive-submissive or intellectual defense against passive-submissive needs. (Schafer-Rorschach)

Christmas tree (Botany. Recreation):

Dependent, passive-receptive; rejection of adult role. (Schafer-Rorschach)

Cloaked women (Clothing. Human):

Demanding, passive-aggressive ("oral-aggressive"). [Schafer-Rorschach]

Creature with talons around anus (Anal. Animal):

Feminine identification and masculine inadequacy in men; sadomasochism. (Schafer-Rorschach)

Devil (Inhuman Human. Religion):

Authoritarian orientation with rebelliousness; destructiveness, hostility, sadism; superego conflict. (Schafer-Rorschach)

Dragon (Animal. Mythology):

Fearfulness, helplessness, weakness (Schafer-Rorschach); immaturity, nostalgia for childhood dependency state. (Phillips and Smith)

Dragons at the entrance to a building (Architecture. Mythology):

Defense against masculine penetration; feminine inadequacy and masculine identification in women. (Schafer-Rorschach)

Fireworks (Fire. Recreation):

Cheerful emotional tone; regression; rejection of adult role. (Schafer-Rorschach)

Flaming tail of jet plane or rocket (Fire. Travel):

Anality; feminine identification and masculine inadequacy in men; sadism. (Schafer-Rorschach)

Gargoyles over a doorway (Architecture. Inhuman Human):

Defense against masculine penetration; feminine inadequacy and masculine identification in women. (Schafer-Rorschach)

Gigantic penis (Anatomy. Sex):

Fearful, hostile conception of male role; feminine identification in men, masculine identification in women; possible paranoid tendency. (Schafer-Rorschach)

God (Inhuman Human. Religion):

Authoritarian orientation; concern with authority and power. (Schafer-Rorschach)

Good fairy (Inhuman Human. Mythology):

Innocence and denial of guilt as a defense against superego conflict. (Schafer-Rorschach)

Hell fire and brimstone (Fire. Religion):

Guilt, masochism, possible defeatist tendency. (Schafer-Rorschach)

House with hedge (Architecture. Botany):

May symbolize passive-receptive feminine trend—literally female genitalia. (Schafer-Rorschach)

Jehova (Inhuman Human. Religion):

Authoritarian orientation; concern with authority and power; superego conflict. (Schafer-Rorschach)

Jesus (Human. Religion):

Innocence and denial of guilt as defense against superego conflict. (Schafer-Rorschach)

Lesbians embracing (Human. Sex):
Feminine identification in men, masculine identification in women; feminine or masculine inadequacy. (Schafer-Rorschach)

Lighthouse (Architecture. Travel):
Inadequacy, negativism. (Schafer-Rorschach)

Loki (Inhuman Human. Mythology):
Authoritarian orientation with rebelliousness. (Schafer-Rorschach)

Madonna (Human. Religion):
Innocence and denial of guilt as defense against superego conflict. (Schafer-Rorschach)

Man with cosmetics (Human. Personal):
Feminine identification in men, masculine identification in women; feminine or masculine inadequacy. (Schafer-Rorschach)

Man weighted down by pack (Human. Implement):
Dependent, demanding, passive-aggressive ("oral-aggressive"); possible masochism; rejection of adult role. (Schafer-Rorschach)

Medusa (Inhuman Human. Mythology):
Destructiveness, hostility, sadism; feminine identification and masculine inadequacy with fear of women in men. (Schafer-Rorschach)

Men in gowns, as mandarins or monks (Human. Clothing):
Feminine identification in men, masculine identification in women; feminine or masculine inadequacy. (Schafer-Rorschach)

Mice tearing down a house (Animal. Architecture):
Rejection of adult role. (Schafer-Rorschach)

Miniature dragons (Animal. Mythology):
Denial of passive-aggressive ("oral-aggressive") trend; possible emasculation conflict. (Schafer-Rorschach)

Monk (Human. Religion):
Innocence and denial of guilt as a defense against superego conflict. (Schafer-Rorschach)

Nipples (Human Detail. Sex):

Passive-receptive trend. (Schafer-Rorschach)

Nun (Human. Religion):

Innocence and denial of guilt as defense against superego conflict. (Schafer-Rorschach)

Ovaries (Anatomy. Sex):

Concern with reproductive function. (Schafer-Rorschach)

Ovary content at child bearing age (Anatomy. Sex):

Anticipation, anxiety, and curiosity regarding reproduction. (Schafer-Rorschach)

Ovary content at end of childbearing age (after or near menopause) [Anatomy. Sex]:

Concern over loss of maternal role; feeling of decline. (Schafer-Rorschach)

People fighting and bleeding (Human. Blood).

Acting-out of hostility, impulse expression. (Schafer-Rorschach)

Person praying (Human. Religion):

Dependent; passive-receptive; rejection of adult role. (Schafer-Rorschach)

Person on a rack (Human. Implement):

Guilt; masochism; possible defeatist tendency. (Schafer-Rorschach)

Pregnant or swollen abdomen (Anatomy. Sex):

Concern with reproductive function. (Schafer-Rorschach)

Prophet (Human. Religion):

Superego conflict with concern over morality. (Schafer-Rorschach)

Rear end of animals (Animal Detail. Anal):

Feminine identification, masculine inadequacy in men. (Schafer-Rorschach)

Religious figures (Human. Religion):

Paranoid tendency; superego conflict. (Schafer-Rorschach)

Saint (Human. Religion):

Innocence and denial of guilt as a defense against superego conflict. (Schafer-Rorschach)

Satan (Inhuman Human. Religion):

Superego conflict with guilt. (Schafer-Rorschach)

Scantily-clad women (Human. Clothing):

Feminine identification, masculine inadequacy in men; masculine identification in women. (Schafer-Rorschach)

Scarecrow (Inhuman Human. Rural):

Castration fears, impotence, weakness;

demanding, dependent, passive-aggressive ("oral-aggressive") feminine identification, masculine inadequacy in men. (Schafer-Rorschach)

Skull of steer in desert (Anatomy. Landscape).

Demanding, dependent, passive-aggressive ("oral-aggressive"); negative attitudes; rejection of adult role. (Schafer-Rorschach)

Smeared slide (Science. Stain):

Feminine identification, masculine inadequacy in men; impotence, negative attitudes, weakness. (Schafer-Rorschach)

Snow-White (Human. Mythology):

Innocence and denial of guilt as a defense against superego conflict; regressive tendency; rejection of adult role. (Schafer-Rorschach)

Straw man (Inhuman-Human. Rural):

Castration fears, impotence, negative attitudes; feminine identification, masculine inadequacy in men. (Schafer-Rorschach)

Swollen or pregnant abdomen (Anatomy. Sex):

Concern with reproductive function. (Schafer-Rorschach)

Tattered figures (Clothing. Human):

Demanding, dependent, passive-aggressive ("oral-aggressive"); inadequacy, masochism, negativism. (Schafer-Rorschach)

Unfinished figures (Art. Human):

Castration anxiety in men, castration feeling in women; feminine identification in men, masculine identification in women. (Schafer-Rorschach)

Uterus (Anatomy. Sex):

Concern with reproductive function. (Schafer-Rorschach)

Vagina with hooks in it (Anatomy. Implement. Sex):

Feminine identification, masculine inadequacy in men; masculine identification in women. (Schafer-Rorschach)

Volcano (Fire. Landscape):

Emotional turmoil, volatility. (Schafer-Rorschach)

Woman masturbating man (Human. Sex):

Feminine or masculine inadequacy; feminine identification in men, masculine identification in women. (Schafer-Rorschach)

Womb (Anatomy. Sex):

Concern with reproduction function. (Schafer-Rorschach)

Women with enveloping cloak (Clothing. Human):

Demanding, dependent, passive-aggressive ("oral-aggressive"); possible masochism; rejection of adult role. (Schafer-Rorschach)

Yoke (Implement. Rural):

Authoritarian orientation with submission; demanding, dependent, passive-aggressive ("oral-aggressive") with rejection of adult role; possible masochism. (Schafer-Rorschach)

BLOOD
Blood:

Aggression, which may either take the passive form of somatization or be expressed by temper tantrums (Rapaport); anxiety (Beck and Molish); anxiety; hostile and sadistic impulses (Schafer-Rorschach); destructive impulses; sadistic but contraindicates direct acting-out; "blood" to achromatic areas is hysteric and may indicate conversion tendencies (Phillips and Smith); impulsivity (Klopfer-Developments I); poorly controlled emotional impulses. (Klopfer-Davidson)

Blood stains:

Paranoid tendency. (Schafer-Rorschach)

BOTANY
Botany:

Feminine tendencies; passive-dependency (Phillips and Smith); pleasantly toned affect, if not countered by negative determinants. (Beck and Molish)

Damaged, deteriorated, diseased, and frayed plants:

Concern with aging and death; possible masochism. (Schafer-Rorschach)

Dead branch:

Feminine identification in men, masculine identification in women; negative attitudes; possible ambivalence

Dead, missing or mutilated plant limbs:

concerning male figure or aging, death or impotence of male figure. (Schafer-Rorschach)

Feminine identification in men, masculine identification in women; inadequacy, negativism. (Schafer-Rorschach)

Flower bud:

Birth and youth associations; concern over advancing age or childbearing function. (Schafer-Rorschach)

Frayed, damaged, deteriorated, or diseased plants:

Concern with aging and death; possible masochism. (Schafer-Rorschach)

Missing, dead, or mutilated plant limbs:

Feminine identification in men, masculine identification in women; inadequacy, negativism. (Schafer-Rorschach)

Old plant:

Feeling of decline or loss of reproductive function with advancing age. (Schafer-Rorschach)

Orchid:

Narcissism, passive-receptive tendency. (Schafer-Rorschach)

Pistil:

Concern with reproductive function. (Schafer-Rorschach)

Pollen:

Concern with reproductive function. (Schafer-Rorschach)

Pretty flowers:

Feminine identification, masculine inadequacy in men. (Schafer-Rorschach)

Seed:

Concern with reproductive function. (Schafer-Rorschach)

Stamen:

Concern with reproductive function. (Schafer-Rorschach)

Thicket:

Defense against sado-masochistic tendency. (Schafer-Rorschach)

Tree stump:

Castration anxiety in men, castration feeling in women; feminine identification in men, masculine identification in women; negative attitudes. (Schafer-Rorschach)

Withered leaves:

Concern with aging and death; feeling of decay and deterioration; masochism. (Schafer-Rorschach)

CLOTHING
Armor:

Defense against sado-masochistic tendency; paranoid tendency. (Schafer-Rorschach)

Badly tied bow tie:

Inadequacy, impotence, negative attitudes; feminine identification in men. (Schafer-Rorschach)

Bed jacket:

Feminine identification, masculine inadequacy in men. (Schafer-Rorschach)

Brassiere:

Demanding, dependent, passive-aggressive ("oral-aggressive"); defense against sado-masochism with rejection of adult role; inadequacy, negativism. (Schafer-Rorschach)

Breastplate:

Demanding, dependent, passive-aggressive ("oral-aggressive"); defense against sado-masochism with rejection of adult role; inadequacy, negativism. (Schafer-Rorschach)

Bustle:

Anality; feminine identification, masculine inadequacy in men. (Schafer-Rorschach)

Children's garments:

Regression, rejection of adult role. (Schafer-Rorschach)

Cloaking garment:

Paranoid tendency. (Beck III)

Clothing:

Concern over sexual or social role; female subject, clothing other than undergarments or enveloping cover on nonhuman form indicates healthy narcissism, good adjustment, high intelligence (Phillips and Smith); narcissism, sensuality. (Schafer-Rorschach)

Corset:

Feminine identification, masculine inadequacy in men. (Schafer-Rorschach)

Derby:

Authoritarian orientation, concern

	with authority and elevated social status. (Schafer-Rorschach)
Dress form:	Narcissism, sensuality. (Schafer-Rorschach)
Dunce cap:	Feminine identification, masculine inadequacy in men; impotence, inadequacy; negative attitudes. (Schafer-Rorschach)
Feminine clothing content:	Pleasantly toned affect if not countered by negative determinants. (Beck and Molish)
Frayed garment:	Concern with aging and death: (Schafer-Rorschach)
Gown:	Feminine identification, masculine inadequacy in men. (Schafer-Rorschach)
Helmet:	Defense against sado-masochistic tendency. (Schafer-Rorschach)
Hip guards:	Defense against sado-masochistic tendency. (Schafer-Rorschach)
Leggings:	Cheerful emotional tone; regressive tendency; rejection of adult role. (Schafer-Rorschach)
Mask:	Cautious interpersonal relations; lethargy, timidity; paranoid tendency (Schafer-Rorschach); concealment of true self. (Klopfer-Davidson)
Mink coat:	Authoritarian orientation; concern with authority and elevated social status. (Schafer-Rorschach)
Protective clothing:	Defensive attitude; fearfulness. (Schafer-Rorschach)
Ragged boot:	Concern with aging and death. (Schafer-Rorschach)
Ragged or torn clothes:	Authoritarian orientation with felt inferior social status; inadequacy and negative attitudes. (Schafer-Rorschach)

Shoulder pads:	Defense against sado-masochistic tendency. (Schafer-Rorschach)
Silk:	Feminine identification, masculine inadequacy in men. (Schafer-Rorschach)
Stockings:	Feminine identification, masculine inadequacy in men. (Schafer-Rorschach)
Taffeta:	Feminine identification, masculine inadequacy in men. (Schafer-Rorschach)
Tattered clothes:	Concern with aging and death; masochism; possible defeatist tendency. (Schafer-Rorschach)
Top hat:	Authoritarian orientation; concern with authority and elevated social status. (Schafer-Rorschach)
Visor:	Defense against sado-masochistic tendency. (Schafer-Rorschach)

CLOUDS

Clouds:	Anxiety, depressive tendency (Schafer-Rorschach); dependence, insecurity, passivity; evasion, guardedness (Phillips and Smith); free-floating anxiety. (Rapaport)
Floating clouds:	Lack of long-range goals; passivity. (Schafer-Rorschach)
Storm clouds:	Emotional turmoil, volatility. (Schafer-Rorschach)

DEATH

Damage, death:	Depression. (Phillips and Smith)
Death:	Anxiety, depresssion (Phillips and Smith); externalized hostility; or depersonalization tendency. (Beck III)
Death and decay:	Depressed, dysphoric mood (Schafer-Rorschach); suicidal. (Phillips and Smith)
Decay (including fungus):	Morbidity, possibly schizophrenic

Mourning content:

Mummy:

Mutilation:

Poison:

(Schafer-Clinical Application); severe depression, suicidal impulses. (Phillips and Smith)

Sadness, unhappy emotional tone. (Schafer-Rorschach)

Concern with aging and death; masochism; possible defeatist tendency. (Schafer-Rorschach)

Depersonalization tendency; or externalized hostility. (Beck III)

Paranoid tendency. (Schafer-Rorschach)

EMBLEM
Coat of arms:

Confederate flag:

Communist emblem:

Crest:

Crown and other kingly paraphernalia:

Emblem:

Scepter:

Authoritarian orientation; concern with authority and elevated social status; paranoid tendency. (Schafer-Rorschach)

Authoritarian orientation with rebelliousness. (Schafer-Rorschach)

Authoritarian orientation with rebelliousness. (Schafer-Rorschach)

Authoritarian orientation; concern with authority and elevated social status. (Schafer-Rorschach)

Concern with authority and power; paranoid tendency; passive-submissive or defense against passive-submissive needs. (Schafer-Rorschach)

Anxiety, dependence, inferiority feelings (Phillips and Smith); inhibition for fear of injury; submission to authority (Klopfer-Developments I); paranoid tendency (Schafer-Rorschach); submissive attitude toward authority. (Klopfer-Davidson)

Concern with authority and power; paranoid tendency. (Schafer-Rorschach)

Seal of state:	Authoritarian orientation; concern with authority and power. (Schafer-Rorschach)
Throne:	Authoritarian orientation; concern with authority and power; paranoid tendency. (Schafer-Rorschach)

FIRE

Devastating fires:	Anxious adolescents, schizophrenics; nihilistic fantasy possibly. (Beck III)
Erupting lava:	Anality; feminine identification and masculine inadequacy in men; sadism. (Schafer-Rorschach)
Explosion:	Destructiveness, hostility, sadism, possibly with anxiety; emotional turmoil, volatility. (Schafer-Rorschach)
Explosion, fire:	Pyromaniac possibly. (Phillips and Smith)
Explosion, red area:	Acting-out of hostility, impulse expression. (Schafer-Rorschach)
Explosions, volcanic eruptions:	Acting-out, impulsivity, with felt inability to restrain oneself. (Klopfer-Developments I)
Fire:	Anxiety (Beck and Molish); emotional turmoil, volatility; inadequacy, negativism (Schafer-Rorschach); enuretics, pyromaniacs; indirect aggression, passivity (Phillips and Smith); impulsivity. (Klopfer-Developments I)
Fire content in children:	Insecurity, phobic tendency. (Beck III)
Smoke:	Children, retardates; with average or above average intelligence, apprehension, depression, social maladjustment (Phillips and Smith); free-floating anxiety. (Rapaport)
Volcanic eruptions, explosions:	Acting-out, impulsivity, with felt inability to restrain oneself. (Klopfer-Developments I)

Volcano:

Destructiveness, hostility, sadism: emotional turmoil (Schafer-Rorschach); possible explosiveness (Beck and Molish)

FOOD
Badly baked cookie:

Impotence, inadequacy, negative attitudes; feminine identification in men. (Schafer-Rorschach)

Bone or chicken neck with the meat removed:

Rejection of adult role. (Schafer-Rorschach)

Candy:

Regression; rejection of adult role. (Schafer-Rorschach)

Food:

Dependency needs (Klopfer-Davidson); dependency, with indifference to adult role and poor prognosis; manipulation of others for nurturance needs; retardates, schizophrenics (Phillips and Smith); oral-dependency (Beck III); oral-dependent, passive-receptive needs (Schafer-Rorschach); parasitic tendencies, strong oral needs. (Schafer-Clinical Application)

Food service associations (cook, waiter):

Passive-receptive trend. (Schafer-Rorschach)

Ice cream:

Regression, rejection of adult role. (Schafer-Rorschach)

Partially consumed objects:

Regression, rejection of adult role. (Schafer-Rorschach)

GEOGRAPHY
Bay, harbor:

Above average intelligence; good social and vocational adjustment but with residual passive-dependent wishes. (Phillips and Smith)

Canyon:

Feelings of rejection, suicidal attempts. (Phillips and Smith)

Dark cave:

Fearfulness, helplessness, weakness. (Schafer-Rorschach)

Geography content:

Intellectual inadequacy feelings possibly (Klopfer-Davidson); sterotypy if form is vague. (Rapaport)

Island:

Deprivation; feeling of isolation and rejection (Phillips and Smith); sense of isolation. (Beck III)

Lake:

Alcoholics; dependence, inadequacy. (Phillips and Smith)

Little island:

Constriction; feeling of isolation. (Schafer-Rorschach)

Map:

Alcoholics, antisocial personalities ("psychopaths"); chronic maladjustment with dysphoric mood, isolation from others, frustrated dependence with resentment; evasion, guardedness (Phillips and Smith); evasion, guardedness. (Klopfer-Davidson)

Map with vista element, as aerial map:

Feelings of personal inadequacy. (Phillips and Smith)

Peninsula:

Above average intelligence; assertive, successful adjustment, but with fear of rejection from others. (Phillips and Smith)

Valley:

Defense against sado-masochistic tendency. (Schafer-Rorschach)

HOUSEHOLD
Bed linen hung out to dry:

Passivity; possible sexual conflict and guilt. (Schafer-Rorschach)

Candelabra:

Feminine identification, masculine inadequacy in men. (Schafer-Rorschach)

Chandelier:

Feminine identification, masculine inadequacy in men. (Schafer-Rorschach)

Cradle:

Cheerful emotional tone; dependent needs or need for reassurance; regression, rejection of adult role. (Schafer-Rorschach)

Decanter: Dependent, passive-receptive, rejection of adult role. (Schafer-Rorschach)

Food utensils: Passive-receptive trend. (Schafer-Rorschach)

Frying pan: Dependent, passive-receptive; rejection of adult role. (Schafer-Rorschach)

Household: Domestic interests; possible dependency needs (Beck III); predominantly domestic interests; restraint; women. (Phillips and Smith)

Syrup jar: Dependent, passive-receptive, rejection of adult role. (Schafer-Rorschach)

Table setting: Dependent, passive-receptive, rejection of adult role. (Schafer-Rorschach)

Worn-out rug: Feeling of decay and deterioration. (Schafer-Rorschach)

Vases: Feminine identification, masculine inadequacy in men. (Schafer-Rorschach)

HUMAN
Absence female H: Impaired relationship with female figures. (Klopfer-Developments I)

Absence male H: Impaired relationship with paternal figures. (Klopfer-Developments I)

Admiral: Authoritarian orientation; concern with authority and power. (Schafer-Rorschach)

Aggressive humans: Externalized hostility. (Beck III)

Aggressively active H (football player, etc.):   Assertiveness, successful adjustment, but with sensitivity to authority. (Phillips and Smith)

Alice in Wonderland: Innocence and denial of guilt as a defense against superego conflict, regressive tendency, rejection of adult role. (Schafer-Rorschach)

American Indian: Authoritarian orientation with rebelliousness. (Schafer-Rorschach)

Andy Gump:

Disparagement of men; feminine inadequacy and masculine identification in women. (Schafer-Rorschach)

Apeman:

Fearful, hostile conception of masculine role; feminine and masculine inadequacy; feminine identification in men, masculine identification in women. (Schafer-Rorschach)

Arguing or deriding people:

Passive-aggressive ("oral-aggressive"), demanding. (Schafer-Rorschach)

Authoritative, savage, threatening figures:

Authoritarian attitude; impersonal and sadistic-masochistic relationships; sadistic impulses. (Schafer-Rorschach)

Avoidance of H:

Avoidance of others. (Klopfer-Davidson)

Baby, child, infant:

Feeling of immaturity with adult responsibility. (Phillips and Smith)

Baker:

Dependent, passive-receptive; rejection of adult role. (Schafer-Rorschach)

Beard, hair emphasis:

Possible homosexual impulses. (Beck and Molish)

Beggar:

Demanding, passive-aggressive ("oral-aggressive"); or passive-receptive trend. (Schafer-Rorschach)

"Bending over":

Conforming, passive-submissive; sexual identification conflict. (Phillips and Smith)

Bleeding, crushed, mutilated persons:

Inadequacy, negativism; masochistic. (Schafer-Rorschach)

Body without backbone:

Impotence, inadequacy, negative attitudes; feminine identification, masculine inadequacy in men. (Schafer-Rorschach)

Bowed, debased, powerless, slovenly, subjugated persons:

Authoritarian attitude; impersonal relationships and sadistic-masochistic orientation; inadequacy, negativism. (Schafer-Rorschach)

Bowing, conversing, listening H: Submissive feelings. (Klopfer-Davidson)

Bowing H: Masculine attributes. (Klopfer-Developments I)

Boys or "little boys," female subject: Disparagement of men; feminine inadequacy and masculine identification in women. (Schafer-Rorschach)

Burdened people: Inadequacy, negativism. (Schafer-Rorschach)

Butlers: Authoritarian orientation; concern with authority and elevated social status. (Schafer-Rorschach)

Cannibals: Demanding, dependent, passive-aggressive ("oral-aggressive"); possible masochism or sadism; rejection of adult role. (Schafer-Rorschach)

Caricatured or inanimate human: Externalized hostility. (Beck III)

Cartoon and virago women: Sadistic impulses. (Schafer-Rorschach)

Cavemen: Destructiveness, hostility, sadism; feminine and masculine inadequacy; feminine identification in men, masculine identification in women. (Schafer-Rorschach)

Celebrated and powerful persons: Paranoid tendency; passive-submissive needs which may be denied. (Schafer-Rorschach)

Child, baby, infant: Feeling of immaturity with adult responsibility. (Phillips and Smith)

Children: Regression and rejection of adult role. (Schafer-Rorschach)

Children bundled up: Cheerful emotional tone; regressive tendency; rejection of adult role. (Schafer-Rorschach)

Clown: Cheerful emotional tone; disparagement of men; friendly, responsive. (Schafer-Rorschach)

Comments regarding percept of head as detached from body of person:
Intellectualization; possible defense of isolation. (Schafer-Rorschach)

Concealed or obscured figures:
Paranoid tendency. (Schafer-Rorschach)

Cook:
Dependent, passive-receptive; rejection of adult role. (Schafer-Rorschach)

Crouching or fleeing figures:
Paranoid tendency. (Schafer-Rorschach)

Crushed, bleeding, or mutilated persons:
Inadequacy, negativism; masochistic. (Schafer-Rorschach)

Crushed or squashed figure:
Authoritarian orientation with inadequacy, negative attitudes, submission. (Schafer-Rorschach)

Damaged, deteriorated, diseased persons:
Inadequacy, negativism; masochistic. (Schafer-Rorschach)

Dancing:
Active, lively. (Schafer-Rorschach)

Dandies:
Disparagement of men; feminine inadequacy and masculine identification in women. (Schafer-Rorschach)

Dead, missing, or mutilated human limbs:
Concern over bodily injury, possible castration anxiety; inadequacy, negativism; feminine identification, masculine inadequacy in men, masculine identification in women. (Schafer-Rorschach)

Deriding or arguing people:
Demanding, passive-aggressive ("oral-aggressive"). [Schafer-Rorschach]

Deteriorated, damaged, diseased people:
Inadequacy, negativism; masochistic. (Schafer-Rorschach)

Diseased, damaged, deteriorated people:
Inadequacy, negativism; masochistic. (Schafer-Rorschach)

Double-sex H:
Possible homosexual trend. (Beck III)

Drowning and hanging content:
Possible suicidal tendency. (Beck and Molish)

Dunces:
Disparagement of men; feminine inad-

equacy and masculine identification in women. (Schafer-Rorschach)

Dwarf:

Disparagement of men; feminine inadequacy and masculine identification in women. (Schafer-Rorschach)

Einstein:

Passive-submissive; or intellectual defense against passive-submissive needs. (Schafer-Rorschach)

Emaciated figures:

Demanding, passive-aggressive ("oral-aggressive"); inadequacy, negativism; masochistic. (Schafer-Rorschach)

Embryo, fetus:

Concern with reproductive function; passive-receptive and passive-regressive orality; rejection of adult role. (Schafer-Rorschach)

Emphasis on short arms on male figures, female subject:

Disparaging hostility toward men; emasculation impulses. (Schafer-Rorschach)

Engulfing figures:

Possible paranoid tendency. (Schafer-Rorschach)

Eskimos:

Detachment, irresponsibility, lack of empathy; possible rejection of intimacy, including in the sexual relationship. (Schafer-Rorschach)

Facial expression of hostility on same-sex figure:

Paranoid tendency. (Beck III)

Fairy tale entities:

Immaturity; may be phobic if H is frightening. (Beck and Molish)

Fat persons:

Dependent, passive-receptive; rejection of adult role. (Schafer-Rorschach)

Female figures on other than Card VII:

Feminine identification, passive-conforming attitudes. (Phillips and Smith)

Female in masculine activity or role:

Sexual role conflict. (Klopfer-Developments I)

Fetus, embryo:

Concern with reproductive function; passive-receptive and passive-regressive orality; rejection of adult role. (Schafer-Rorschach)

Figure of authority (politician, etc.): Assertiveness, successful adjustment but with sensitivity to authority. (Phillips and Smith)

Figure facing away from subject: Frustrated dependency, heterosexual maladjustment. (Phillips and Smith)

Figure kissing: Dependent, passive-receptive; oral-eroticism; rejection of adult role. (Schafer-Rorschach)

Figures exercising: Possible narcissism or somatization tendency. (Schafer-Rorschach)

Figures seen from behind or with backs turned: Anality; feminine identification and masculine inadequacy in men; possible paranoid tendency. (Schafer-Rorschach)

Flat- or small-bosomed woman: Demanding, dependent, passive-aggressive ("oral-aggressive"); disparagement of maternal figures, with feminine inadequacy and masculine identification in women; negativism, possible masochism. (Schafer-Rorschach)

Franklin or Teddy Roosevelt: Passive-submissive or defense against passive-submissive needs. (Schafer-Rorschach)

Frightening or sinister figures: Felt weakness with anxiety; inadequacy, negativism. (Schafer-Rorschach)

Gangster: Authoritarian orientation with rebelliousness. (Schafer-Rorschach)

General: Authoritarian orientation; concern with authority and power. (Schafer-Rorschach)

George Washington: Passive-submissive or defense against passive-submissive needs. (Schafer-Rorschach)

Gossip: Feminine identification, masculine inadequacy in men. (Schafer-Rorschach)

H carrying basket:

Feminine attributes; in men, sexual role conflict. (Klopfer-Developments I)

H equal to or > expectancy:

Form dominance over color. (Phillips and Smith)

H < expectancy:

Color dominance over form; social isolation. (Phillips and Smith)

H seen at distance:

Sense of isolation from others. (Beck III)

Hair, beard emphasis:

Possible homosexual impulses. (Beck and Molish)

Hanging and drowning content:

Possible suicidal tendency. (Beck and Molish)

Headless figure:

Hostility toward that figure (Beck III); possible anxiety over loss of intellectual control. (Schafer-Rorschach)

Headless woman:

Concern with aging and death; masochism; possible defeatist tendency (Schafer-Rorschach); hostility toward maternal figure. (Beck III)

Helpless, powerless figures:

Inadequacy, negativism; superego conflict. (Schafer-Rorschach)

Heroic leaders and persons:

Passive-submissive needs which may be denied. (Schafer-Rorschach)

Humans in combat:

Sadistic impulses. (Schafer-Rorschach)

Human content:

Interest in others and sensitivity to them. (Phillips and Smith)

Ice skaters:

Feminine inadequacy and masculine identification in woman. (Schafer-Rorschach)

Inanimate or caricatured human:

Externalized hostility. (Beck III)

Incomplete or small male figure:

Female subject: competitiveness toward and disparagement of men; male subject: feeling of masculine inadequacy. (Schafer-Rorschach)

Increment children's storybook characters and figures:

Regression; rejection of adult role. (Schafer-Rorschach)

Increment diminutive and disparaged male figures, or male figures in absurd or demeaning acts or postures (female subject):

Hostile disparagement of males, masculine identification in women. (Schafer-Rorschach)

Increment women engaged in feminine or passive activities:

Feminine identification, masculine inadequacy in men; masculine identification in women. (Schafer-Rorschach)

Indian percept:

Possible defiance, rebelliousness. (Schafer-Rorschach)

Infant:

Passive-receptive orality. (Schafer-Rorschach)

Infant, baby, child:

Feeling of immaturity with adult responsibility. (Phillips and Smith)

Joseph Stalin:

Destructiveness, hostility, sadism; feminine identification and masculine inadequacy. (Schafer-Rorschach)

Judge:

Fear of punishment or masochistic wish for punishment; guilt. (Schafer-Rorschach)

King:

Authoritarian orientation; concern with power and authority; passive-submissive or defense against passive-submissiveness. (Schafer-Rorschach)

Kneeling position:

Authoritarian orientation with submission; inadequacy and negative attitudes. (Schafer-Rorschach)

Ku Klux Klan figures:

Concern with authority and power; destructiveness, hostility, sadism; feminine identification and masculine inadequacy in men. (Schafer-Rorschach)

Lincoln:

Passive-submissive or intellectual defense against passive-submissive needs. (Schafer-Rorschach)

Listening or staring:

Paranoid tendency. (Beck III)

"Little boys" or "boys," female subject:

Disparagement of men; feminine inadequacy and masculine identification in women. (Schafer-Rorschach)

Little Lord Fauntleroy:

Disparagement of men; feminine inadequacy and masculine identification in women. (Schafer-Rorschach)

Little man:

Condescending attitudes toward and disparagement of males; feminine inadequacy and masculine identification in women; masculine striving and rivalry with men. (Schafer-Rorschach)

Loss of grip associations:

Impotency; felt weakness; inadequacy, negativism. (Schafer-Rorschach)

Lumberjack:

Passive-submissive or defense against passive-submissive needs. (Schafer-Rorschach)

Lying or sitting down:

Inert, passive. (Schafer-Rorschach)

Man with no chin or receding chin:

Disparagement of men; feminine inadequacy and masculine identification in women. (Schafer-Rorschach)

Maternal persons:

Passive-receptive tendency. (Schafer-Rorschach)

Men embracing:

Feminine identification in men, masculine identification in women; feminine or masculine inadequacy. (Schafer-Rorschach)

Menacing female figure:

Destructiveness, hostility, sadism. (Schafer-Rorschach)

Midget:

Disparagement of men. (Schafer-Rorschach)

Missing, dead, or mutilated human limbs:

Concern over bodily injury, possible castration anxiety; feminine identification in men, masculine identification in women; inadequacy, negativism. (Schafer-Rorschach)

Missing or small mouth comments:

Possible denial of orality. (Schafer-Rorschach)

Mountain climbers:

Feminine inadequacy and masculine identification in women. (Schafer-Rorschach)

Muscular figures:

Passive-submissive or defense against passive-submissive needs. (Schafer-Rorschach)

Mutilated, bleeding, crushed persons:

Inadequacy, negativism; masochism. (Schafer-Rorschach)

Mutilated, dead, or missing human limbs:

Concern over bodily injury, female castration anxiety; feminine identification in men, masculine identification in women; inadequacy, negativism. (Schafer-Rorschach)

Napoleon:

Authoritarian orientation; concern with power and authority; passive-submissive or defense against passive-submissive needs. (Schafer-Rorschach)

No H:

Impulsivity; lack of empathy. (Klopfer-Developments I)

Non-children's literature H:

Contraindicates acting-out; superior intelligence. (Phillips and Smith)

Norseman:

Passive-submissive or defense against passive-submissive needs. (Schafer-Rorschach)

Nurse:

Dependent, passive-receptive; rejection of adult role. (Schafer-Rorschach)

"Old hen" (woman):

Feminine identification, masculine inadequacy in men. (Schafer-Rorschach)

Outstretched hands on H:

Desire for support and nurturance. (Phillips and Smith)

Overweight persons:

Passive-receptive trend. (Schafer-Rorschach)

Peasant:

Authoritarian orientation with felt inferior social status; inadequacy and negative attitudes. (Schafer-Rorschach)

Peering, staring:

Possible paranoid trend; possible voyeuristic tendency. (Beck III)

Peg-leg sailor:

Concern with aging and death; masochism; possible defeatist tendency. (Schafer-Rorschach)

People with attributes suggesting weakness:

May reflect subject's own projected feeling of inadequacy or weakness. (Schafer-Rorschach)

People in conflict:

Hostile impulses. (Klopfer-Davidson)

"Person":

Bisexuality; sexual identification conflict. (Phillips and Smith)

Person addressing multitude:

Authoritarian orientation; concern with power and authority. (Schafer-Rorschach)

Person being torn in half:

Concern with aging and death; masochism; possible defeatist tendency. (Schafer-Rorschach)

Person eating:

Dependent, passive-receptive; rejection of adult role. (Schafer-Rorschach)

Person giving orders:

Concern with authority and power; authoritarian orientation. (Schafer-Rorschach)

Person sticking tongue out:

Authoritarian orientation with rebelliousness; demanding, dependent, passive-aggressive ("oral-aggressive"). [Schafer-Rorschach]

Persons back to back:

Anality; feminine identification and masculine inadequacy in men. (Schafer-Rorschach)

Policeman:

Concern with authority and power; paranoid tendency; superego conflict. (Schafer-Rorschach)

Powerful or celebrated persons:

Paranoid tendency; passive-submissive needs which may be denied. (Schafer-Rorschach)

Powerless, bowed, debased, slovenly, subjected persons:

Authoritarian attitude; impersonal relationships and masochistic-sadistic

	orientation; inadequacy, negativism. (Schafer-Rorschach)
Powerless, helpless figures:	Inadequacy, negativism; superego conflict. (Schafer-Rorschach)
Primitive aggressive males (apeman, caveman):	Feminine identification, masculine inadequacy in men; masculine identification in women. (Schafer-Rorschach)
Primitive people:	May symbolize primitive impulses. (Schafer-Rorschach)
Prussian:	Authoritarian orientation; destructiveness, hostility, sadism; feminine identification, masculine inadequacy in men. (Schafer-Rorschach)
Puritan:	Superego conflict with concern over morality. (Schafer-Rorschach)
Queen:	Authoritarian orientation; concern with power and authority. (Schafer-Rorschach)
Resting:	Inert, passive. (Schafer-Rorschach)
Savage, authoritative, or threatening figures:	Authoritarian attitude; impersonal relationships and masochistic-sadistic relationships; sadistic impulses. (Schafer-Rorschach)
Savages:	Destructiveness, hostility, sadism; feminine identification and masculine inadequacy in men. (Schafer-Rorschach)
Sensuous emphasis on appearance of female figures:	Masculine identification in women. (Schafer-Rorschach)
Servant:	Authoritarian attitude with felt inferior social status and submission; impersonal relationships and masochistic-sadistic orientation; inadequacy and negative attitudes. (Schafer-Rorschach)
Shakespeare:	Passive-submissive or intellectual defense against passive-submissive needs. (Schafer-Rorschach)

Sinister or frightening figures:

Felt weakness with anxiety; inadequacy, negativism. (Schafer-Rorschach)

Sitting or lying down:

Inert, passive. (Schafer-Rorschach)

Slave:

Authoritarian orientation with felt inferior social status and submission; inadequacy, negativism; masochism, possible defeatist tendency with feeling of depression. (Schafer-Rorschach)

Sleeping:

Inert, passive. (Schafer-Rorschach)

Sleeping infant:

Dependent needs; or need for innocence. (Schafer-Rorschach)

Sleeping males, female subject:

Hostile view of male as implicitly inert and passive. (Schafer-Rorschach)

Slovenly, bowed, debased, powerless, subjugated persons:

Authoritarian attitude; impersonal relationships and masochistic-sadistic orientation; inadequacy, negativism. (Schafer-Rorschach)

Small- or flat-bosomed woman:

Demanding, dependent, passive-aggressive ("oral-aggressive"); disparagement of maternal figures with feminine inadequacy and masculine identification in women; inadequacy, negativism, possible masochism. (Schafer-Rorschach)

Small or incomplete male figures:

Female subject, competitiveness toward and disparagement of men; male subject: feeling of masculine inadequacy. (Schafer-Rorschach)

Small or missing mouth comments:

Possible denial of orality. (Schafer-Rorschach)

Snow-White and seven dwarfs:

Childhood fantasy concept of heterosexual associations; conception of female as innocent, sexually repressed, and indulged by gallant but depreciated males. (Schafer-Rorschach)

Socrates:

Passive-submissive or intellectual defense against passive-submissive needs. (Schafer-Rorschach)

Squashed or crushed figure:	Authoritarian orientation with submission; inadequacy and negative attitudes. (Schafer-Rorschach)
Squatting posture:	Anal tendency. (Schafer-Rorschach)
Staring or listening:	Paranoid tendency. (Beck III)
Staring, peering:	Possible paranoid trend; possible voyeuristic tendency. (Beck III)
Statesmen and wise men:	Passive-submissive needs which may be denied. (Schafer-Rorschach)
Subjugated, bowed, debased, powerless, slovenly persons:	Authoritarian attitude; impersonal relationships and masochistic-sadistic orientation; inadequacy, negativism. (Schafer-Rorschach)
Symmetrical females as male-female instead of same sex:	Homosexual impulses. (Rapaport)
Symmetrical figures identified as one sex on one side and the opposite sex on the other:	Feminine identification in men; masculine identification in women; feminine or masculine inadequacy. (Schafer-Rorschach)
Tears content:	Sadness, unhappy emotional tone. (Schafer-Rorschach)
Teddy or Franklin Roosevelt:	Passive-submissive or defense against passive-submissive needs. (Schafer-Rorschach)
Threatening, authoritative, or savage figures:	Authoritarian attitude; impersonal relationships and sadistic-masochistic relationships; sadistic impulses. (Schafer-Rorschach)
Toothless old man:	Feeling of decay and deterioration. (Schafer-Rorschach)
Tortured persons:	Inadequacy, negativism, possible masochism; paranoid tendency. (Schafer-Rorschach)
Truck driver:	Passive-submissive or defense against passive-submissive needs. (Schafer-Rorschach)
Umpire:	Feminine inadequacy and masculine

	identification in women. (Schafer-Rorschach)
Vacuous-looking woman:	Feminine inadequacy and masculine identification in women; rejection of adult role. (Schafer-Rorschach)
Virago and cartoon women:	Sadistic impulses. (Schafer-Rorschach)
Waiter:	Dependent, passive-receptive; rejection of adult role. (Schafer-Rorschach)
Warrior:	Passive-submissive or defense against passive-submissive needs. (Schafer-Rorschach)
Weeping:	Depressed or dysphoric mood. (Schafer-Rorschach)
Wise men and statesmen:	Passive-submissive needs which may be denied. (Schafer-Rorschach)
Witches:	Hostile attitude toward women; tendency to project hostility (Beck and Molish); hostility toward the maternal figure. (Beck III)
Wizards:	Cheerful emotional tone; regressive tendency; rejection of adult role. (Schafer-Rorschach)
Women in delivery position:	Concern with reproductive function. (Schafer-Rorschach)
Women engaged in trivial gossip:	Feminine inadequacy and masculine identification in women; rejection of female role. (Schafer-Rorschach)

HUMAN DETAIL

Big belly:	Dependent, passive-receptive; rejection of adult role. (Schafer-Rorschach)
Blind or missing eyes:	Castration anxiety in men, castration feelings in women; feminine identification in men, masculine identification in women; negative attitudes. (Schafer-Rorschach)
Bony chest:	Disparagement of maternal figures; feminine inadequacy and masculine

	identification in women. (Schafer-Rorschach)
Colliding limbs:	Sadistic impulses. (Schafer-Rorschach)
Dangling legs:	Feminine identification in men; impotence, inadequacy, negative attitudes. (Schafer-Rorschach)
Drooping arms:	Feminine identification in men; impotence, inadequacy; negative attitudes, weakness. (Schafer-Rorschach)
Ears:	Superego conflict. (Schafer-Rorschach)
Ears and eyes content:	Paranoid tendency, suspicion. (Beck and Molish)
Emaciated face:	Demanding, dependent, passive-aggressive ("oral-aggressive"); rejection of adult role with inadequacy and negative attitudes. (Schafer-Rorschach)
Eyes:	Alert caution, apprehension, suspicion; paranoid tendency (Beck III); ideas of reference or influence; paranoia, suspicion (Phillips and Smith); paranoid schizophrenic (Schafer-Clinical Application); paranoid tendency, superego conflict (Schafer-Rorschach); paranoid trend. (Beck and Molish)
Face:	Above average intelligence, ideational; obsessive-compulsive. (Phillips and Smith)
Face and head Hd:	Compulsive tendency; intellectualization. (Klopfer-Developments I)
Facial expression:	Reflect patient's attitude, mood, and self-conception. (Rapaport)
Full-face Hd in space:	Aberrant thought processes; paranoid schizophrenic (except IX, Dds 29, seen by eccentric normals). [Phillips and Smith]
Hd:	Anxiety, guardedness (Rapaport); apprehension, social anxiety (Phillips and

Hd facial expressions:

Hd limbs (arms, legs):

Hd other than faces and heads:

Hdx:

Hands raised in supplication:

Head and face Hd:

Headless female figure:

Increment faces, heads:

Lips:

Missing or blind eyes:

More than two faces:

Mouth:

Smith); avoidance (Beck and Molish); constriction, inhibition, produced by anxiety; displacement (Beck III); doubt, self-criticality. (Klopfer-Developments I)

Phobic if aggressive in content; with increment and in Dd areas represent obsessive-compulsive denial, reaction-formation, undoing. (Beck and Molish)

Fear of injury from others; contraindicates assaultiveness, destructiveness. (Phillips and Smith)

Compulsivity; inept social behavior. (Klopfer-Developments I)

Anxiety. (Beck and Molish)

Dependent, passive-receptive; inadequacy, negative attitudes; rejection of adult role. (Schafer-Rorschach)

Compulsive tendency; intellectualization. (Klopfer-Developments I)

Hostility toward the maternal figure. (Beck III)

Compulsivity, intellectualization; over-emphasis on intellect. (Klopfer-Davidson)

Dependent, oral-erotic, passive-receptive; rejection of adult role (Schafer-Rorschach); possible homoerotic impulses; sexual preoccupation. (Schafer-Clinical Application)

Castration anxiety in men, castration feelings in women; feminine identification in men, masculine identification in women; negative attitudes. (Schafer-Rorschach)

Apprehension, suspicion. (Phillips and Smith)

Frustrated dependency, passive-aggres-

	sive ("oral-aggressive") tendency; hostility, suspicion; obsessive, paranoid, and (with mouth alone) schizophrenia (Phillips and Smith); oral-dependent, passive-receptive needs (Schafer-Rorschach); phobic tendency. (Beck III)
Mouthless or toothless face:	Demanding, dependent, passive-aggressive ("oral-aggressive"); possible masochism; rejection of adult role. (Schafer-Rorschach)
Navel:	Dependent, passive-receptive; rejection of adult role. (Schafer-Rorschach)
Nipples:	Dependent, passive-receptive; rejection of adult role. (Schafer-Rorschach)
Pixie heads in red:	Reaction-formation against hostility. (Schafer-Rorschach)
Pointing finger:	Possible paranoid tendency; superego conflict with projection as defense. (Schafer-Rorschach)
Profile increment:	Social anxiety. (Klopfer-Davidson)
Sinister faces:	Paranoid tendency. (Schafer-Rorschach)

IMPLEMENT

Arrow:	Destructiveness, hostility, sadism; feminine and masculine inadequacy. (Schafer-Rorschach)
Arrowhead:	Possible paranoid tendency. (Schafer-Rorschach)
Beacon:	Weakness with need for guidance and support. (Schafer-Rorschach)
Bludgeoning and penetrating tools and weapons:	Feminine identification, masculine inadequacy in men; masculine identification in women. (Schafer-Rorschach)
Bomb:	Destructiveness, hostility, sadism. (Schafer-Rorschach)
Broken chains:	Authoritarian orientation with rebelliousness. (Schafer-Rorschach)

Camouflage: Defense against sado-masochistic tendency. (Schafer-Rorschach)

Cane: Weakness with need for guidance and support. (Schafer-Rorschach)

Cannon: Destructiveness, hostility, sadism; feminine identification, masculine inadequacy in men; possible paranoid tendency. (Schafer-Rorschach)

Chains: Authoritarian orientation with submission; inadequacy, negative attitudes. (Schafer-Rorschach)

Club: Destructiveness, hostility, sadism; feminine identification in men, masculine identification in women; feminine or masculine inadequacy. (Schafer-Rorschach)

Cracked yoke: Authoritarian orientation with rebelliousness. (Schafer-Rorschach)

Crushing objects: Sadistic impulses. (Schafer-Rorschach)

Crutch: Weakness with need for support and guidance. (Schafer-Rorschach)

Cutting or squeezing implements: Feminine identification, masculine inadequacy in men, masculine identification in women; inadequacy, negativism, sadistic impulses. (Schafer-Rorschach)

Destroyed objects: Paranoid tendency. (Schafer-Rorschach)

Double-barreled shotgun: Feminine and masculine inadequacy; feminine identification in men, masculine identification in women; hostile, fearful conception of masculine role. (Schafer-Rorschach)

Enclosing objects: Emphasis on emotional control. (Schafer-Rorschach)

Explosive devices: Sadistic impulses. (Schafer-Rorschach)

False teeth: Demanding, dependent, passive-aggressive ("oral-aggressive"); possible mas-

	ochism with rejection of adult role. (Schafer-Rorschach)
Gas mask:	Anality; feminine identification and masculine inadequacy in men; sadism. (Schafer-Rorschach)
Governor on steam engine:	Constrained emotional tone; guarded interpersonal relations. (Schafer-Rorschach)
Guns:	Possible suicidal tendency, especially in intelligent persons who display painful affect (Beck and Molish); sadistic impulses. (Schafer-Rorschach)
Hammer:	Sadistic impulses, especially if in space area. (Schafer-Rorschach)
Handles:	Weakness with need for support and guidance. (Schafer-Rorschach)
Hatchet:	Destructiveness, hostility, sadism; feminine identification and masculine inadequacy in men. (Schafer-Rorschach)
Horseshoe:	Dependent, passive-receptive; rejection of adult role. (Schafer-Rorschach)
Implement:	Masculine activity, possibly compensatory; aggressive implements (machine gun, etc.) with other sadistic content: overt sadistic acting-out, psychopathy; rare. (Phillips and Smith)
Knives:	Possible suicidal tendency, especially in intelligent persons who display painful affect. (Beck and Molish)
Military armament:	Sadistic impulses. (Schafer-Rorschach)
Missing part comment:	Apprehension, conventionality, inhibition (Phillips and Smith); feminine identification, masculine inadequacy in men, masculine identification in women. (Schafer-Rorschach)
Named mechanical objects, as wings of DC-3:	Feminine inadequacy and masculine identification in women. (Schafer-Rorschach)

Nutcracker:	Castration anxiety in men, castration feeling in women; feminine and masculine inadequacy with negative attitudes; feminine identification in men, masculine identification in women. (Schafer-Rorschach)
Old post:	Concern with aging and death. (Schafer-Rorschach)
Penetrating and bludgeoning tools and weapons:	Feminine identification, masculine inadequacy in men; masculine identification in women. (Schafer-Rorschach)
Pliers:	Castration anxiety or feelings in men and women; masculine inadequacy, negative attitudes, sadism. (Schafer-Rorschach)
Poison gas:	Destructiveness, hostility, sadism. (Schafer-Rorschach)
Protective devices:	Defensive attitude, fearfulness. (Schafer-Rorschach)
Reference to exhaust systems of machinery:	Anality. (Schafer-Rorschach)
Regulating objects:	Emphasis on emotional control. (Schafer-Rorschach)
Rifle:	Destructiveness, hostility, sadism; feminine identification and masculine inadequacy in men. (Schafer-Rorschach)
Ropes:	Possible suicidal tendency, especially in intelligent persons who display painful affect. (Beck and Molish)
Saw:	Destructiveness, hostility, sadism; feminine identification and masculine inadequacy in men. (Schafer-Rorschach)
Shears:	Destructiveness, hostility, sadism; feminine identification, masculine inadequacy in men. (Schafer-Rorschach)
Shield:	Defense against sado-masochistic or paranoid tendency; feminine inadequacy and masculine identification in

	women with defense against masculine penetration. (Schafer-Rorschach)
Spear:	Destructiveness, hostility, sadism; feminine identification, masculine inadequacy in men; possible paranoid tendency. (Schafer-Rorschach)
Spearhead:	Acting-out of hostility, impulse expression. (Schafer-Rorschach)
Squeezing or cutting implements:	Feminine identification, masculine inadequacy in men, masculine identification in women; sadistic impulses. (Schafer-Rorschach)
Steamroller:	Sadistic impulses. (Schafer-Rorschach)
Tanks:	Sadistic impulses. (Schafer-Rorschach)
Torpedo:	Destructiveness, hostility, sadism. (Schafer-Rorschach)
Trap:	Demanding, dependent, passive-aggressive ("oral-aggressive"); feminine identification, masculine inadequacy in men, masculine identification in women; paranoid tendency. (Schafer-Rorschach)
Truss:	Castration anxiety in men, castration feelings in women; feminine and masculine inadequacy with negative attitudes; feminine identification in men, masculine identification in women. (Schafer-Rorschach)
Tweezers:	Castration anxiety in men, castration feelings in women; feminine and masculine inadequacy with negative attitudes; feminine identification in men, masculine identification in women. (Schafer-Rorschach)
Vise:	Demanding, dependent, passive-aggressive ("oral-aggressive"); possible masochism; rejection of adult role. (Schafer-Rorschach)
Weapons:	Sadistic impulses. (Schafer-Rorschach)

Yoke:

Authoritarian orientation with sub-mission, inadequacy and negative attitudes; masochism with defeatist tendency and oppressive feeling. (Scha-fer-Rorschach)

INHUMAN HUMAN
Angel:

Possibly symbolizes innocent attitudes, or reaction-formation mechanism as defense against hostile impulses. (Scha-fer-Rorschach)

Arguing or deriding animals:

Demanding, passive-aggressive ("oral-aggressive"). [Schafer-Rorschach]

Automaton:

Authoritarian attitude; impersonal re-lationships and masochistic-sadistic orientation; inadequacy, negativism. (Schafer-Rorschach)

Cartoon, statue:

Homosexual tendency. (Phillips and Smith)

Children's literature (H):

Children, immaturity. (Phillips and Smith)

Comic-book monster:

Counter-phobic resistance to passive-submissive needs. (Schafer-Rorschach)

Dehumanization:

Depersonalization tendency; or exter-nalized hostility. (Beck III)

Demon:

Destructiveness, hostility, sadism; fem-inine identification, masculine inade-quacy in men. (Schafer-Rorschach)

Deriding or avenging animals:

Demanding, passive-aggressive ("oral-aggressive"). [Schafer-Rorschach]

Devil:

Anxiety, hostility. (Schafer-Rorschach)

(The) devil:

Paranoid tendency. (Beck III)

Dracula:

Demanding, dependent, passive-aggres-sive ("oral-aggressive"); fearfulness, helplessness, sadism, possible mas-ochism. (Schafer-Rorschach)

Elves:

Cheerful emotional tone; regressive

tendency; rejection of adult role. (Schafer-Rorschach)

Fat-bellied devils:

Rejection of adult role. (Schafer-Rorschach)

Ghost:

Fearfulness, helplessness, weakness (Schafer-Rorschach); paranoid. (Phillips and Smith)

Good fairy:

Dependent, passive-receptive; regressive tendency; rejection of adult role. (Schafer-Rorschach)

Gnome:

Disparagement of men; feminine inadequacy and masculine identification in women. (Schafer-Rorschach)

Gremlin:

Disparagement of men; feminine inadequacy and masculine identification in women. (Schafer-Rorschach)

(H):

Doubt, self-criticality (Klopfer-Developments I); inability to sustain close relationships. (Klopfer-Davidson)

(H) (+1):

Avoidance of social interaction; sensitivity to and interest in others but with social anxiety. (Phillips and Smith)

(Hd):

Lonely; possibly schizoid; social isolation. (Phillips and Smith)

Hercules:

Passive-submissive or defense against passive-submissive needs. (Schafer-Rorschach)

King Kong:

Feminine identification, masculine inadequacy in men; sadism. (Schafer-Rorschach)

Leprechaun:

Disparagement of men. (Schafer-Rorschach)

Little demons:

Rejection of adult role. (Schafer-Rorschach)

Male puppet:

Disparagement of men. (Schafer-Rorschach)

Marionette: Authoritarian orientation with submission; inadequacy and negative attitudes. (Schafer-Rorschach)

Mermaid, female subject: Repudiation of feminine sexual role; sexual identification conflict. (Schafer-Rorschach)

Monster: Fearfulness, helplessness, weakness (Schafer-Rorschach); phobic tendency. (Schafer-Clinical Application)

Mr. Hyde (from *Dr. Jekyll and Mr. Hyde*).   Destructiveness, hostility, sadism; feminine identification and masculine inadequacy in men. (Schafer-Rorschach)

Ogres: Cheerful emotional tone; regressive tendency; rejection of adult role. (Schafer-Rorschach)

Pans and satyrs: Possible homosexual tendency. (Beck III)

Pinocchio: Disparagement of men. (Schafer-Rorschach)

Protective angel: Dependent, passive-receptive; rejection of adult role. (Schafer-Rorschach)

Puppet: Possible passive-submissive defenses against hostility. (Schafer-Rorschach)

"Ridiculous ghost":   Counter-phobic resistance to passive-submissive needs. (Schafer-Rorschach)

Robot: Authoritarian orientation; inadequacy and negative attitudes. (Schafer-Rorschach)

Santa Claus: Dependent, passive-receptive; rejection of adult role. (Schafer-Rorschach)

Satyrs and pans: Possible homosexual tendency. (Beck III)

Savage and threatening inhuman figures: Sadistic impulses. (Schafer-Rorschach)

Statue, cartoon: Homosexual tendency. (Phillips and Smith)

Supernatural figures: Authoritarian orientation; impersonal relationships and masochistic-sadistic orientation. (Schafer-Rorschach)

Threatening and savage inhuman figures:

Sadistic impulses. (Schafer-Rorschach)

"Trained elephants performing an act," female subject:

Possible hostile disparaging attitude toward males. (Schafer-Rorschach)

Trained monkey:

Authoritarian attitude with submission; inadequacy and negative attitudes. (Schafer-Rorschach)

Vampire:

Demanding, dependent, passive-aggressive ("oral-aggressive"); sadism, possible masochism; rejection of adult role. (Schafer-Rorschach)

Witch:

Demanding, dependent, passive-aggressive ("oral-aggressive"); feminine identification and masculine inadequacy with fear of women in men; possible masochism with maternal figure conceived of as destructive (Schafer-Rorschach); hostility toward maternal figure (Beck III); inimical maternal figure. (Klopfer-Davidson)

LANDSCAPE

Arctic and winter associations:

Coldness, detachment. (Schafer-Rorschach)

Canyon, chasm, cliff:

Feeling of being abandoned; insecurity; suicidal potential. (Phillips and Smith)

Desert:

Concern with childlessness or loss of reproductive function in women; deprivation and isolation feelings; feeling of constriction. (Schafer-Rorschach)

Desolate landscapes (swamps, etc.), desolation:

Depressed or dysphoric mood (Schafer-Rorschach); depressive element, sense of isolation. (Beck III)

Frightening or sinister places:

Felt weakness with anxiety. (Schafer-Rorschach)

Harbor:

Passive-regressive tendency. (Schafer-Rorschach)

Hills: | Dependency needs with inferiority feelings; neurotic alcoholics. (Phillips and Smith)

Hostile environment comments: | Anxiety, insecurity. (Phillips and Smith)

Lake or river bank: | Possible suicidal tendency, especially in intelligent persons who display painful affect. (Beck and Molish)

Lake, river, stream: | Alcoholism; dependence, ineffectuality, sexual inadequacy in men. (Phillips and Smith)

Landscape: | Stereotypy, if form is vague. Rapaport)

Moat: | Defense against sado-masochistic tendency. (Schafer-Rorschach)

Mountain: | Inferiority feelings. (Phillips and Smith)

Pit: | Demanding, dependent, passive-aggressive ("oral-aggressive"); possible masochism; rejection of adult role. (Schafer-Rorschach)

River or lake bank: | Possible suicidal tendency, especially in intelliegent persons who display painful affect. (Beck and Molish)

River, lake, stream: | Alcoholism; dependence, ineffectuality, sexual inadequacy in men. (Phillips and Smith)

Rocks: | Organicity possibly. (Phillips and Smith)

Rubble: | Concern with aging and death; masochism; possible defeatist tendency. (Schafer-Rorschach)

Ruins: | Sadness; unhappy emotional tone. (Schafer-Rorschach)

Shangri-la percept: | In older patients possible concern over aging; passive-regressive dependency wishes. (Schafer-Rorschach)

Sheltering terrain:	Defensive attitude; fearfulness. (Schafer-Rorschach)
Sinister or frightening places:	Felt weakness with anxiety. (Schafer-Rorschach)
Stream, lake, river:	Alcoholism; dependence, ineffectuality, sexual inadequacy. (Phillips and Smith)
Tranquil LS content:	Possible suicidal tendency. (Beck and Molish)
War-torn and devastated terrain:	Concern with aging and death; masochism, possible defeatist tendency. (Schafer-Rorschach)
Wasteland:	Constriction with feeling of isolation and loneliness; demanding, dependent, passive-aggressive ("oral-aggressive"); inadequacy and negative attitudes. (Schafer-Rorschach)
Winter and arctic associations:	Coldness, detachment. (Schafer-Rorschach)

MINERAL

Iron ore:	Superior intelligence. (Phillips and Smith)
Mineral:	Rare content. (Phillips and Smith)
Stone:	Organicity. (Phillips and Smith)

MULTIPLE CONTENT

Adornment associations and objects; exotic associations with the Arabian Nights; nude or scantily dressed women (chorus girl, sunbather); peacock:	Narcissism; sensuality. (Schafer-Rorschach)
Affectionate gestures; funnies; candy and ice cream; carnival; children and children's garments; circus; clown; dancing; fireworks; increment of children's storybook characters and figures:	Cheerful mood. (Schafer-Rorschach)

Ambiguous sex differences; lipstick, sex reversal:

Possible paranoid tendency. (Schafer-Rorschach)

Anatomy and animal content:

May indicate rigidity. (Beck and Molish)

Anatomy, geography, science content:

Intellectual inadequacy feelings possibly. (Klopfer-Davidson)

Animal and anatomy content:

May indicate rigidity. (Beck and Molish)

Animal and people rear view:

Anality. (Schafer-Rorschach)

Animals or persons arguing, spitting, sticking tongues out, yelling:

Demanding, dependent, passive-aggressive ("oral-aggressive"); possible masochism; rejection of adult role. (Schafer-Rorschach)

Arguing or deriding animals or people:

Demanding, passive-aggressive ("oral-agressive"). [Schafer-Rorschach]

Armor, crouching or fleeting figures, masks, shells of animals, protecting walls:

Paranoid tendency. (Schafer-Rorschach)

Artificial or missing biting and punching surfaces (false teeth, toothless faces); devouring or attacking animals (miniature dragons, mosquitoes).

Denial of passive-aggressive ("oral-aggressive") trend; possible emasculation conflicts. (Schafer-Rorschach)

Athletic or mechanical associations with masculine connotations:

Feminine identification, masculine inadequacy in men, masculine identification in women. (Schafer-Rorschach)

Authoritative, supernatural, or threatening figures:

Authoritarian attitudes, impersonal relationships; sadistic-masochistic orientation. (Schafer-Rorschach)

Bacteria content; increment anatomy content:

Hypochondriasis. (Phillips and Smith)

Barren and deserted places:

Feeling of isolation, loneliness. (Schafer-Rorschach)

Barriers (dragons at entrance of building, gargoyles over doorway, shield):

Masculine identification in women. (Schafer-Rorschach)

Beacons, guiding beams, light house, supporting objects:

Felt weakness with need for support and guidance. (Schafer-Rorschach)

Biting A; mouths; teeth:

Phobic tendency. (Beck III)

Bleeding, crushed, mutilated anatomy, animals and persons:

Inadequacy, negativism; masochistic. (Schafer-Rorschach)

Blood, fire:

Impulsivity. (Klopfer-Developments I)

Blood, fire, internal anatomy, injury content:

Anxiety. (Beck and Molish)

Botany, feminine clothing, nature content:

Pleasantly toned affect, if not countered by negative determinants. (Beck and Molish)

Botched or poorly prepared adornments, materials, and specimens:

Felt weakness, impotence, inadequacy; negativism. (Schafer-Rorschach)

Burdened animals and people:

Demanding, passive-aggressive ("oral-aggressive"); inadequacy, masochism, negativism. (Schafer-Rorschach)

Buttocks, figures seen from rear:

Possible paranoid tendency. (Schafer-Rorschach)

Celebrated or powerful persons or religious figures; coat of arms, crowns, emblems, and other kingly paraphernalia; monuments:

Paranoid tendency. (Schafer-Rorschach)

Chaos; explosion and fire; threatening or violent weather; volcano:

Emotional turmoil. (Schafer-Rorschach)

Cloaking garments; eyes; facial expression of hostility on same-sex figure; listening or staring H or Hd; the devil:

Paranoid tendency. (Beck III)

Coat of arms, crowns, emblem, and kingly paraphernalia; celebrated or powerful persons or religious figures; monuments:

Paranoid tendency. (Schafer-Rorschach)

Colliding animals and limbs:

Sadistic tendencies. (Schafer-Rorschach)

Concealed, engulfing, and obscured figures; electrical waves or rays; concealing darkness, fangs, jaws, pits, poison, teeth, traps, and webs:

Paranoid tendency. (Schafer-Rorschach)

Crab; fish; flower; frog; jellyfish; lobster; octopus; seahorse; snail; turtle; water content; lake; river; stream:

Alcoholics. (Phillips and Smith)

Cradle, lamb, sleeping infant:

Dependent needs or need for innocence. (Schafer-Rorschach)

Crouching or fleeing figures, armor, masks, shells, shields, protecting walls:

Paranoid tendency. (Schafer-Rorschach)

Crowns, coat of arms, emblem, and other kingly paraphernalia, celebrated or powerful persons or religious figures; monuments:

Paranoid tendency. (Schafer-Rorschach)

Crumbled wall, toothless old man, withered leaf, worn-out rug:

Feeling of decay or deterioration. (Schafer-Rorschach)

Crushed, bleeding, mutilated anatomy, animals and persons:

Inadequacy, negativism; masochistic. (Schafer-Rorschach)

Crushed objects and military armament (tanks, steamroller):

Sadistic impulses. (Schafer-Rorschach)

Damaged, deteriorated, diseased animals, objects, and plants:

Inadequacy, negativism; masochistic. (Schafer-Rorschach)

Dead, missing, or mutilated animal, human, and plant limbs; missing parts:

Concern over body integrity; possible castration anxiety; feminine identification in men, masculine identification in women. (Schafer-Rorschach)

Death, dehumanization, mutilation:

Depersonalization tendency; or externalized hostility. (Beck III)

Decay and desolation; mourning and weeping:

Depressed or dysphoric mood. (Schafer-Rorschach)

Deriding or arguing animals or people:

Demanding, passive-aggressive ("oral-aggressive"). [Schafer-Rorschach]

Deserted and barren places:

Feeling of isolation, loneliness. (Schafer-Rorschach)

Desolation and decay; mourning and weeping:

Depressed or dysphoric mood. (Schafer-Rorschach)

Destroyed objects, instruments of torture or tortured persons, mutilated parts:

Paranoid tendency. (Schafer-Rorschach)

Deteriorated, damaged, diseased animals, persons, plants, and objects:

Inadequacy, negativism; masochistic. (Schafer-Rorschach)

Deteriorated and frayed anatomy, objects, and plants:

Concern with aging and death. (Schafer-Rorschach)

Devastating fires; objects collapsing:

Anxious adolescents, schizophrenics; possible nihilistic fantasy. (Beck III)

Diminutive, passive, or plodding animals; mask:

Caution, delayed response, timidity. (Schafer-Rorschach)

Dirt and mess associations:

Anality. (Schafer-Rorschach)

Diseased, damaged, deteriorated animals, objects, and plants:

Inadequacy, negativism; masochistic. (Schafer-Rorschach)

Drooping or limp limbs and organisms:

Felt weakness; impotence, inadequacy. (Schafer-Rorschach)

Ears and eyes:

Superego conflict. (Schafer-Rorschach)

Electrical rays and waves; concealed, engulfing, or obscured figures; concealing darkness; fangs, jaws, pits, poison, teeth, traps, webs:

Paranoid tendency. (Schafer-Rorschach)

Emaciated or tattered figures (beggar, scarecrow):

Demanding, passive-aggressive ("oral-aggressive"); inadequacy, negativism; masochistic. (Schafer-Rorschach)

Emblem, coat of arms, crowns, and other kingly paraphernalia; celebrated or powerful persons and religious figures; monuments:

Paranoid tendency. (Schafer-Rorschach)

Enclosing, geometrically exact, and regulating objects:

Emphasis on emotional control. (Schafer-Rorschach)

Explosion and fire; chaos; threatening or violent weather; volcano:

Emotional turmoil. (Schafer-Rorschach)

Explosions, mutilations, weapons:

Sadistic impulses. (Schafer-Rorschach)

Extremely large penis; phallic symbols, as arrowhead, cannon, spear:

Possible paranoid tendency. (Schafer-Rorschach)

Eyes and ears:

Superego conflict. (Schafer-Rorschach)

Fangs; concealing darkness and concealed, engulfing, or obscured figures;

Possible paranoid tendency. (Schafer-Rorschach)

electrical rays or waves; jaws, poison, pits, teeth, traps, webs:

Feminine adornment, garments and objects:

Feminine identification, masculine inadequacy in men; masculine identification in women. (Schafer-Rorschach)

Feminine clothing; botany, nature content:

Pleasantly toned affect, if not countered by negative determinants. (Beck and Molish)

Feminine garments, adornment, and objects:

Feminine identification, masculine inadequacy in men; masculine identification in women. (Schafer-Rorschach)

Figures seen from rear, buttocks:

Possible paranoid tendency. (Schafer-Rorschach)

Fire, blood:

Impulsivity. (Klopfer-Developments I)

Fire, blood, injury, internal anatomy content:

Anxiety. (Beck and Molish)

Fire and explosion; chaos; threatening or violent weather; volcano:

Emotional turmoil. (Schafer-Rorschach)

Fire and hell content:

Inadequacy, negativism; masochism; superego conflict. (Schafer-Rorschach)

Fleeing animals, frightening and sinister animals, figures, and places:

Felt weakness with anxiety, inadequacy, negativism. (Schafer-Roschach)

Fleeing or crouching figures, armor, masks, protecting walls, shells of animals, shields:

Paranoid tendency. (Schafer-Rorschach)

Food, mouth content:

Oral-dependent, passive-receptive needs. (Schafer-Rorschach)

Frayed and deteriorated anatomy, objects, and plants:

Concern with aging and death. (Schafer-Rorschach)

Frightening and sinister animals, figures, and places; fleeing animals:

Felt weakness with anxiety; inadequacy, negativism. (Schafer-Rorschach)

Geometrically exact, enclosing, regulating objects:

Emphasis on emotional control. (Schafer-Rorschach)

Guiding beams, beacon, lighthouse, supporting objects:

Felt weakness with need for guidance and support. (Schafer-Rorschach)

Gums and teeth:	Aggressive response to frustrated dependency needs; more common in adolescents and children; resentfulness. (Klopfer-Davidson)
Guns and knives, high places, lake or river bank, ropes (Beck):	Possible suicidal tendency, especially in intelligent persons who display painful affect. (Beck and Molish)
(H), Hd:	Doubt, self-criticality. (Klopfer-Developments I)
Hell and fire associations:	Inadequacy, negativism; masochism; superego conflict. (Schafer-Rorschach)
Helpless, powerless animals or figures:	Felt weakness, impotence, inadequacy; negativism. (Schafer-Rorschach)
Heroic leaders, authority symbols and persons:	Passive-submissive needs which may be denied. (Schafer-Rorschach)
High places, guns and knives, lake or river bank, ropes (Beck):	Possible suicidal tendency; especially in intelligent persons who display painful affect. (Beck and Molish)
House, snake, totem pole:	Sexual symbolism. (Klopfer-Davidson)
Increment of A, and/or At content:	Possible phobic tendency. (Beck III)
Increment anal, oral, sexual associations (anus, breasts, colon, devouring animals, food, mouths, penis, sexual intercourse, testicles, vagina, womb):	Feminine identification, masculine inadequacy in men, masculine identification in women. (Schafer-Rorschach)
Increment oral associations (breasts, devouring animals, food, mouth):	Feminine identification, masculine inadequacy in men, masculine identification in women. (Schafer-Rorschach)
Inert states (sloth, snail):	Inactive tendency; passivity. (Schafer-Rorschach)
Inhuman figures, savage and threatening men:	Sadistic impulses. (Schafer-Rorschach)
Injury, blood, fire, internal anatomy content:	Anxiety. (Beck and Molish)
Instruments of torture or tortured persons, destroyed objects, mutilated parts:	Paranoid tendency. (Schafer-Rorschach)

Internal anatomy, blood, fire, injury content:

Anxiety. (Beck and Molish)

Jaws; concealed, engulfing, and obscured figures and concealing darkness; electrical rays and waves; fangs, pits, poison, teeth, traps, webs:

Possible paranoid tendency. (Schafer-Rorschach)

Kissing and lip associations:

Oral-erotic and passive-receptive tendency. (Schafer-Rorschach)

Knives and guns, high places, lakes or river banks, ropes (Beck):

Possible suicidal tendency, especially in intelligent persons who display painful affect. (Beck and Molish)

Lake or river bank, guns and knives, high places, ropes (Beck):

Possible suicidal tendency, especially in intelligent people who display painful affect. (Beck and Molish)

Lamb, cradle, sleeping infant:

Dependent needs or need for innocence. (Schafer-Rorschach)

Larva, locusts, other plant-devouring insects:

Passive-aggressive ("oral-aggressive") tendency, possible parasitic dependency trend. (Schafer-Rorschach)

Lighthouse, beacon, guiding beams, supporting objects:

Felt weakness with need for guidance and support. (Schafer-Rorschach)

Limp or drooping limbs and organisms:

Felt weakness, impotence, inadequacy. (Schafer-Rorschach)

Lip and kissing associations:

Oral-erotic and passive-receptive tendency. (Schafer-Rorschach)

Lips and lipstick:

Possible homoerotic impulses; sexual preoccupation. (Schafer-Clinical Application)

Lipstick, ambiguous sex differences, sex reversals:

Possible paranoid tendency. (Schafer-Rorschach)

Locusts, larva, other plant-devouring insects:

Passive-aggressive ("oral-aggressive") tendency, possible parasitic dependency trend. (Schafer-Rorschach)

Machines, precision maneuvers, statues:

Lack of spontaneity; possible isolation defense. (Schafer-Rorschach)

Mask; passive, diminutive, or plodding animals:

Caution, delayed response, timidity. (Schafer-Rorschach)

Masks, armor, crouching or fleeing figures, protecting walls, shells of animals, shields:	Paranoid tendency. (Schafer-Rorschach)
Mechanical or athletic associations with masculine connotations:	Feminine identification, masculine inadequacy in men; masculine identification in women. (Schafer-Rorschach)
Mess and dirt associations:	Anality. (Schafer-Rorschach)
Military armament and crushing objects (steamroller, tanks):	Sadistic impulses. (Schafer-Rorschach)
Missing limbs, ragged and worn animal skins, tattered and torn butterflies:	Concern over body integrity, possible castration anxiety. (Schafer-Rorschach)
Missing parts or missing, dead, or mutilated animal, human, and plant limbs:	Concern over body integrity, possible castration anxiety; feminine identification in men, masculine identification in women; inadequacy, negativism. (Schafer-Rorschach)
Monuments; celebrated or powerful persons or religious figures; coat of arms, crowns, emblem, and other kingly paraphernalia:	Paranoid tendency. (Schafer-Rorschach)
Mourning, desolation and decay, weeping:	Depressed or dysphoric mood. (Schafer-Rorschach)
Mouth, food content:	Oral-dependent; passive-receptive needs. (Schafer-Rorschach)
Mutilated, bleeding, crushed anatomy, animals and persons:	Inadequacy, negativism; masochistic. (Schafer-Rorschach)
Mutilated content (Rader):	Aggressive behavior. (Beck and Molish)
Mutilated, dead, or missing animal, human, and plant limbs; missing parts:	Concern over body integrity, possible castration anxiety; feminine identification in men, masculine identification in women; inadequacy, negativism. (Schafer-Rorschach)
Mutilated parts; destroyed objects; instruments of torture or tortured persons:	Paranoid tendency. (Schafer-Rorschach)
Mutilations, explosions, weapons:	Sadistic impulses. (Schafer-Rorschach)

Nature, botany, feminine clothing content:

Pleasantly toned affect, if not countered by negative determinants. (Beck and Molish)

Passive, diminutive, plodding animals; mask:

Caution, delayed response, timidity. (Schafer-Rorschach)

People and animal rear view:

Anality. (Schafer-Rorschach)

Persons or animals arguing, spitting, sticking tongues out, yelling:

Demanding, dependent, passive-aggressive ("oral-aggressive"); possible masochism; rejection of adult role. (Schafer-Rorschach)

Phallic symbols, as arrowhead, cannon, spear; extremely large penis:

Possible paranoid tendency. (Schafer-Rorschach)

Pits; concealed, engulfing, or obscured figures and concealing darkness; electrical rays or waves; poison; teeth, traps, webs:

Possible paranoid tendency. (Schafer-Rorschach)

Plodding, diminutive, or passive animals; mask:

Caution, delayed response, timidity. (Schafer-Rorschach)

Poison; concealed, engulfing, or obscured figures and concealing darkness; electrical rays or waves; pits, teeth, traps, webs:

Possible paranoid tendency. (Schafer-Rorschach)

Poorly prepared or botched adornments, materials, and specimens:

Felt weakness; impotence, inadequacy, negativism. (Schafer-Rorschach)

Powerful animals and figures:

Passive-submissive needs which may be denied. (Schafer-Rorschach)

Powerful celebrated persons or religious figures; coat of arms, crowns, emblem, and other kingly paraphernalia; monuments:

Paranoid tendency. (Schafer-Rorschach)

Powerless, helpless animals or figures:

Felt weakness; impotence, inadequacy, negativism. (Schafer-Rorschach)

Precision maneuvers, machines, statues:

Lack of spontaneity; possible isolation defense. (Schafer-Rorschach)

Protecting clothing, devices, and structures:

Defensive attitude; fearfulness. (Schafer-Rorschach)

Protecting walls; armor; crouching or fleeing figures; masks; shells of animals; shields:

Paranoid tendency. (Schafer-Rorschach)

Ragged and worn animal skins, missing limbs, tattered and torn butterflies:

Concern over body integrity; possible castration anxiety. (Schafer-Rorschach)

Regulating, enclosing, and geometrically exact objects:

Emphasis on emotional control. (Schafer-Rorschach)

Religious figures or celebrated or powerful persons; coat of arms, crowns, emblem, and other kingly paraphernalia; monuments:

Paranoid tendency. (Schafer-Rorschach)

Religious figures and symbols:

Superego conflict. (Schafer-Rorschach)

River or lake bank; guns and knives; high places; ropes (Beck):

Possible suicidal tendency, especially in intelligent persons who display painful affect. (Beck and Molish)

Savage and threatening men and inhuman figures:

Sadistic impulses. (Schafer-Rorschach)

Sex reversals, ambiguous sex differences, lipstick:

Possible paranoid tendency. (Schafer-Rorschach)

Sexually aggressive (H) (satyr); thinly clad female H (show girl):

Sexual preoccupation with socially acceptable expression. (Phillips and Smith)

Shells of animals; armor; crouching or fleeing figures; masks; protecting walls; shields:

Paranoid tendency. (Schafer-Rorschach)

Shields; armor; crouching or fleeing animals; masks; protecting walls; shells of animals:

Paranoid tendency. (Schafer-Rorschach)

Sinister and frightening animals, figures, and places; fleeing animals:

Felt weakness with anxiety; inadequacy, negativism. (Schafer-Rorschach)

Sleeping infant, cradle, lamb:

Dependent needs or need for innocence. (Schafer-Rorschach)

Spider, witches:

Maternal figure conceived of as destructive. (Schafer-Rorschach)

Statues, machines, precision maneuvers:

Lack of spontaneity; possible isolation defense. (Schafer-Rorschach)

Storybook animals and figures (good fairy, lamb) symbolic of innocence:

Superego conflict. (Schafer-Rorschach)

Supernatural, authoritative, or threatening figures:

Authoritarian attitudes; impersonal relationships and sadistic-masochistic orientation. (Schafer-Rorschach)

Supporting objects; beacon; guiding beams; lighthouse:

Felt weakness with need for support and guidance. (Schafer-Rorschach)

Tattered and torn butterflies, missing limbs; ragged and worn animal skins:

Concern over body integrity; possible castration anxiety. (Schafer-Rorschach)

Tattered or emaciated figures (beggar, scarecrow):

Demanding, passive-aggressive ("oral-aggressive"); inadequacy, negativism; masochistic. (Schafer-Rorschach)

Teeth; concealed, engulfing, and obscured figures and concealing darkness; electrical rays or waves; fangs, jaws; pits; prison; traps, webs:

Possible paranoid tendency. (Schafer-Rorschach)

Teeth and gums:

Aggressive response to frustrated dependency needs; more common in children and adolescents; resentfulness. (Klopfer-Davidson)

Threatening and savage men and inhuman figures:

Sadistic impulses. (Schafer-Rorschach)

Threatening, authoritative, or supernatural figures:

Authoritarian attitudes; impersonal relationships and sadistic-masochistic orientation. (Schafer-Rorschach)

Threatening or violent weather; chaos; explosion or fire; volcano:

Emotional turmoil. (Schafer-Rorschach)

Toothless old man; crumbled wall; withered leaf; worn-out rug:

Feeling of decay or deterioration. (Schafer-Rorschach)

Traps; concealed, engulfing, or obscured figures and concealing darkness; electrical rays and waves; fangs; jaws; pits; poison; teeth; webs:

Possible paranoid tendency. (Schafer-Rorschach)

Violent or threatening weather; chaos; explosion and fire; volcano:

Emotional turmoil. (Schafer-Rorschach)

Weakness associations:

Feminine identification, masculine inadequacy in men, masculine identification in women. (Schafer-Rorschach)

Weapons, explosions, mutilations:

Sadistic impulses. (Schafer-Rorschach)

Webs; concealed, engulfing, or obscured figures and concealing darkness; electrical rays or waves; fangs; jaws; pits; poison; teeth; traps:

Possible paranoid tendency. (Schafer-Rorschach)

Weeping, decay; desolation; mourning:

Depressed or dysphoric mood. (Schafer-Rorschach)

Witches, spider:

Maternal figure conceived of as destructive. (Schafer-Rorschach)

Withered leaf; crumbled wall; toothless old man; worn-out rug:

Feeling of decay or deterioration. (Schafer-Rorschach)

Worn and ragged animal skins; missing limbs; tattered and torn butterflies:

Concern over body integrity; possible castration anxiety. (Schafer-Rorschach)

Worn-out rug; crumbled wall; toothless old man; withered leaf:

Feeling of decay or deterioration. (Schafer-Rorschach)

MUSIC
Liberty Bell:

Authoritarian orientation with rebelliousness. (Schafer-Rorschach)

Music:

Feminine attitudes; more than one, superior intelligence. (Phillips and Smith)

MYTHOLOGY
Cornucopia:

Dependent, passive-receptive; rejection of adult role. (Schafer-Rorschach)

Dragons:

Cheerful emotional tone; regressive tendency; rejection of adult role with inadequacy and negativism. (Schafer-Rorschach)

Mythology:

Cultural interests with above-average intelligence; possible homosexual trend; social anxiety. (Phillips and Smith)

NATURE

Cold objects and scenes (ice, snow, etc.): Depressive tendency; feeling of abandonment and isolation. (Beck and Molish)

Concealing darkness: Paranoid tendency. (Schafer-Rorschach)

Dirt associations: Anality; feminine identification and masculine inadequacy in men. (Schafer-Rorschach)

Egg: Concern with reproductive function. (Schafer-Rorschach)

Esthetic forms; (snowflakes, etc.): Adaptive resourcefulness; feminine tendencies. (Phillips and Smith)

High wind: Emotional turmoil; volatility. (Schafer-Rorschach)

Hole: Distrust of others; insecurity in interpersonal relations (Phillips and Smith); possible anal theme. (Schafer-Rorschach)

Ice: Detached emotional tone; unfriendly, unresponsive. (Schafer-Rorschach)

Ice formation in cave: In women concern over childlessness, frigidity, and/or loss of reproductive capacity. (Schafer-Rorschach)

Ice, snow: Rejection by maternal figure. (Phillips and Smith)

Iceberg: Detached emotional tone; unfriendly, unresponsive. (Schafer-Rorschach)

Lightning: Emotional turmoil, volatility. (Schafer-Rorschach)

Mud: Anality; feminine identification and masculine inadequacy in men. (Schafer-Rorschach)

Nature: Normality, superior intelligence (Phillips and Smith); pleasantly toned affect, if not countered by negative determinants. (Beck and Molish)

Pits: Paranoid tendency. (Schafer-Rorschach)

Powerful forces (lightning, etc.): Feelings of tension over impulse-control problem. (Phillips and Smith)

Shell: Constrained emotional tone; defense against sado-masochistic tendency; guarded interpersonal relations. (Schafer-Rorschach)

Shells of animals: Paranoid tendency. (Schafer-Rorschach)

Snow: Detached emotional tone; unfriendly, unresponsive. (Schafer-Rorschach)

Snow, ice: Rejection by maternal figure. (Phillips and Smith)

Spider web: Demanding, dependent, passive-aggressive ("oral-aggressive"); possible masochism; rejection of adult role. (Schafer-Rorschach)

Stagnant water: Concern with aging and death; masochism, possible defeatist tendency. (Schafer-Rorschach)

Sunrise in red: Reaction-formation against hostility. (Schafer-Rorschach)

Threatening or violent weather: Emotional turmoil. (Schafer-Rorschach)

Thunderstorm: Anxiety, depressive tendency, emotional turmoil; volatility. (Schafer-Rorschach)

Violent or threatening weather: Emotional turmoil. (Schafer-Rorschach)

Web: Feminine identification, masculine inadequacy in men; possible paranoid tendency. (Schafer-Rorschach)

OBJECT

Botched or poorly prepared materials: Felt weakness; impotence, inadequacy, negativism. (Schafer-Rorschach)

Damaged, deteriorated, diseased objects:	Concern with aging and death; inadequacy, masochism, negativism. (Schafer-Rorschach)
Damaged, deteriorated, or frayed objects:	Concern with aging and death; inadequacy, masochism, negativism. (Schafer-Rorschach)
Destroyed objects:	Paranoid tendency. (Schafer-Rorschach)

PERSONAL

Botched or poorly prepared adornments:	Felt weakness; impotence, negativism. (Schafer-Rorschach)
Cosmetics:	Feminine identification, masculine inadequacy in men. (Schafer-Rorschach)
Gem:	Narcissistic trend. (Schafer-Rorschach)
Hairdresser's headrest:	Narcissism, sensuality. (Schafer-Rorschach)
Jewelry:	Feminine identification, masculine inadequacy in men; narcissism, sensuality. (Schafer-Rorschach)
Lipstick:	Dependent, passive-receptive; oral-erotic; possible paranoid trend (Schafer-Rorschach); possible homoerotic impulses; sexual preoccupation. (Schafer-Clinical Application)
Perfume bottle:	Feminine identification, masculine inadequacy in men; narcissism, sensuality. (Schafer-Rorschach)
Personal:	Feminine attitudes and interests; normals; women. (Phillips and Smith)
Poorly prepared or botched adornments:	Felt weakness; impotence, inadequacy, negativism. (Schafer-Rorschach)

RECREATION

Baseball bat:	Feminine inadequacy and masculine identification in women. (Schafer-Rorschach)

Bowling pin:	Feminine inadequacy and masculine identification in women. (Schafer-Rorschach)
Carnival:	Cheerful emotional tone; friendly, responsive. (Schafer-Rorschach)
Chess pawn:	Authoritarian attitudes with inadequacy, negative attitudes and submission. (Schafer-Rorschach)
Christmas associations:	Passive-receptive trend. (Schafer-Rorschach)
Christmas stocking:	Dependent, passive-receptive; rejection of adult role. (Schafer-Rorschach)
Circus:	Cheerful emotional tone; regressive tendency; rejection of adult role. (Schafer-Rorschach)
Dance:	Cheerful emotional tone; friendly, responsive. (Schafer-Rorschach)
Frolic:	Cheerful emotional tone; friendly, responsive. (Schafer-Rorschach)
Recreation:	Children, persons with acting-out potential; dependency, irresponsibility, lack of long-range goals. (Phillips and Smith)
Toy:	Cheerful emotional tone; friendly, responsive. (Schafer-Rorschach)
Toy gorilla:	Counter-phobic resistance to passive-submissive needs. (Schafer-Rorschach)

RELIGION

Blatant religious Human or Inhuman-Human content (God, etc.):	Psychotic delusions. (Phillips and Smith)
Decalogue:	Superego conflict with concern over morality. (Schafer-Rorschach)
Halo:	Innocence, denial of guilt as a defense against superego conflict. (Schafer-Rorschach)
Hell associations:	Inadequacy, masochism, negativism;

superego conflict with guilt. (Schafer-Rorschach)

Inquisition:

Superego conflict with concern over morality. (Schafer-Rorschach)

Nonblatant religious Human content (priest, etc.):

Conventionality; guilt over rebellious impulses and sexuality; possible reaction formation. (Phillips and Smith)

Prayer associations:

Passive-receptive trend. (Schafer-Rorschach)

Purgatory:

Superego conflict with guilt. (Schafer-Rorschach)

Religion:

Dependency needs; guilt, especially over severe sexual conflict; religious delusions. (Phillips and Smith)

Religious protective figures, such as angels:

Passive-receptive trend. (Schafer-Rorschach)

Religious symbols:

Superego conflict. (Schafer-Rorschach)

RURAL
Horseshoe:

Passive-receptive trend. (Schafer-Rorschach)

Scarecrow:

Demanding, passive-aggressive ("oral-aggressive"). [Schafer-Rorschach]

SCIENCE
Anemometer:

Constrained emotional tone; guarded interpersonal relations. (Schafer-Rorschach)

Electrical waves or rays:

Paranoid tendency. (Schafer-Rorschach)

Finger or foot print:

Paranoid tendency. (Schafer-Rorschach)

Geometrically exact objects:

Emphasis on emotional control. (Schafer-Rorschach)

Magnified microscopic life form:

Feelings of inadequacy with facade of assurance and confidence. (Schafer-Rorschach)

Poorly prepared or botched specimens:

Felt weakness; impotence, inadequacy, negativism. (Schafer-Rorschach)

Rays or electrical waves:

Paranoid tendency. (Schafer-Rorschach)

Science:

Intellectual inadequacy feelings possibly (Klopfer-Davidson); intellectualization, pedantry; superior intelligence. (Phillips and Smith)

RANGE OF CONTENT

Narrow content range:

Inflexibility (Beck III); mediocre intelligence. (Klopfer-Davidson)

Wide content range:

Above-average intelligence. (Klopfer-Davidson)

SEX (Including Anal Content):

Anal:

Analysands, schizophrenics, self-consciously nonconformist subjects; paranoid or possibly homosexual tendency; sexual maladjustment. (Phillips and Smith)

Breasts:

Orality (Klopfer-Developments I); orality, passive-receptive tendency (Schafer-Rorschach); possible schizophrenic tendency. (Beck III)

Increment sexual associations (penis, sexual intercourse, testicles, vagina, womb):

Feminine identification, masculine inadequacy in men; masculine identification in women. (Schafer-Rorschach)

Increment sex content or references to sex act:

Schizophrenia. (Schafer-Clinical Application)

Many nondeviant sex responses:

Sexually preoccupied analysand, obsessive. (Schafer-Clinical Application)

Negative associations having to do with menstrual or vaginal function:

Masculine identification in women. (Schafer-Rorschach)

Penis (with increment other sexual, oral, and/or anal content):

Feminine or masculine inadequacy; feminine identification in men, masculine identification in women. (Schafer-Rorschach)

Reference to sexual deviation activities or figures:	Feminine identification, masculine inadequacy in men; masculine identification in women. (Schafer-Rorschach)
Semen:	Concern with reproductive function. (Schafer-Rorschach)
Sex:	Analysands, associates of examiner, self-consciously nonconformist subjects, schizophrenics; paranoid or possible homosexual tendency (Phillips and Smith); sexual preoccupation. (Rapaport)
Sex responses to limited number of usual areas:	Possible schizoid tendency; or sexual preoccupation. (Schafer-Clinical Application)
Sexual intercourse with increment other sexual, anal, and oral content:	Feminine or masculine inadequacy; feminine identification in men, masculine identification in women. (Schafer-Rorschach)
Testicles (with increment other sexual, oral and/or anal content):	Masculine or feminine inadequacy; feminine identification in men, masculine identification in women. (Schafer-Rorschach)

STAIN

Blot, spot:	Inhibition of aggression. (Phillips and Smith)
Ink, paint:	Antisocial personalities ("psychopaths"); acting-out tendency. (Phillips and Smith)
Mess associations:	Anality. (Schafer-Rorschach)
Paint, ink:	Antisocial personalities ("psychopaths"); acting-out tendency. (Phillips and Smith)
Smear:	Anality; feminine identification and masculine inadequacy in men. (Schafer-Rorschach)
Splatter:	Anality; feminine identification and masculine inadequacy in men. (Schafer-Rorschach)

"Splattered; splotch":	Direct expression of aggressive impulses. (Schafer-Rorschach)
Spot, blot:	Inhibition of aggression. (Phillips and Smith)
Stain:	Anality; feminine identification, masculine inadequacy in men; superego conflict with both guilt and overt hostility (Schafer-Rorschach); destructiveness, hostility, sadism. (Phillips and Smith)

SYMBOL

Abstract and symbolic letters and figures:	Possible paranoid trend. (Schafer-Rorschach)
Alphabet:	Severe pathology, including schizophrenia. (Phillips and Smith)
Alphabet letters, geometric shapes, or other symbols:	Paranoid schizophrenia. (Schafer-Clinical Application)
Alphabets, letters, and numerals, adult subjects:	Pathology. (Klopfer-Davidson)
Elevated or low social status symbols:	Authoritarian attitudes; impersonal relationships and sadistic-masochistic orientation. (Schafer-Rorschach)
Good luck symbols (horseshoe, wishbone):	Passive-receptive trend. (Schafer-Rorschach)
Heroic authority symbols:	Passive-submissive needs which may be denied. (Schafer-Rorschach)
Symbols of imprisonment:	Authoritarian attitude; inadequacy-negativism; sadistic-masochistic orientation. (Schafer-Rorschach)
Symbols of law and morality:	Superego conflict. (Schafer-Rorschach)
Symbols of rebellion and revolution:	Authoritarian attitude; impersonal relationships, sadistic-masochistic orientation. (Schafer-Rorschach)

TYPE OF CONTENT

Oral content:	Possible addiction or depression. (Beck and Molish)

TRAVEL

Guiding beams (beacon, lighthouse):

Inadequacy, negativism; need for guidance and support. (Schafer-Rorschach)

Lighthouse:

Weakness with need for guidance and support. (Schafer-Rorschach)

Travel:

Adolescents, neurotics, schizophrenics; immaturity. (Phillips and Smith)

VARIABLE CONTENT

Artificial or missing biting and pinching surfaces (false teeth, toothless faces):

(Human Detail or Implement) Denial of oral-aggressive trends; possible emasculation conflicts. (Schafer-Rorschach)

Back-to-back posture of animals and humans:

(Animal or Human) Anal tendency. (Schafer-Rorschach)

Belittled frightening animals (comic-book animals):

(Animal or Art or Inhuman Human) Passive-submissive needs which may be denied. (Schafer-Rorschach)

Bleeding leg:

(Animal or Human Detail) Concern with aging and death; defeatist tendency, masochism. (Schafer-Rorschach)

Blindness:

(Animal or Human) Feminine identification in men, masculine identification in women; inadequacy, negativism. (Schafer-Rorschach)

Cloven hoof:

(Animal or Inhuman Human Detail) Superego conflict with guilt. (Schafer-Rorschach)

Deformed heads:

(Human or Human Detail) Possible sadistic impulses; possible view of others as inferior in intelligence to subject. (Schafer-Rorschach)

Destruction; mutilation responses:

(Anatomy or Landscape) Aggressive, sadistic attitudes. (Phillips and Smith)

Distorted or mutilated animals and humans:

(Animal or Human) Possible feelings of inadequacy. (Schafer-Rorschach)

Drooping or limp limbs:

(Animal or Human) Felt weakness; impotence, inadequacy, negativism. (Schafer-Rorschach)

Drooping or limp organisms:

(Animal or Human) Felt weakness; impotence, inadequacy, negativism. (Schafer-Rorschach)

Ears:

(Animal or Human Detail) Superego conflict with projection as a defense. (Schafer-Rorschach)

Embrace:

(Animal or Human) Cheerful emotional tone; friendly, responsive. (Schafer-Rorschach)

Eyes:

(Animal or Human Detail) Superego conflict with projection as a defense. (Schafer-Rorschach)

Fierce or huge figure:

(Human or Inhuman Human) Authoritarian orientation; concern with authority or power. (Schafer-Rorschach)

Frightening and sinister places:

(Architecture or Landscape) Inadequacy, negativism. (Schafer-Rorschach)

Giant threatening figure on Card IV:

(Human or Inhuman Human) Feeling of anxiety and of vulnerability with paternal figures. (Schafer-Rorschach)

High places:

(Architecture or Landscape) Possible suicidal tendency, especially in intelligent persons who display painful affect. (Beck and Molish)

Horns:

(Animal Detail or Inhuman Human) Destructiveness, hostility, sadism; feminine identification and masculine inadequacy in men. (Schafer-Rorschach)

Huge or fierce figure:

(Human or Inhuman Human) Authoritarian orientation; concern with power and authority. (Schafer-Rorschach)

Increment of water responses:

(Geography or Landscape) Alcoholic tendency. (Beck and Molish)

Inert states:

(Animal or Humans) Inactive tendency; passivity. (Schafer-Rorschach)

Jaws:

(Animal or Human Detail) Demanding, dependent, passive-aggressive ("oral-aggressive"); possible paranoid tendency; rejection of adult role. (Schafer-Rorschach)

Kissing:

(Animal or Human) Cheerful emotional tone; friendly, responsive; passive-receptive trend. (Schafer-Rorschach)

Leaping:

(Animal or Human) Active, lively. (Schafer-Rorschach)

Limp or drooping limbs:

(Animal or Human) Felt weakness; impotence, inadequacy, negativism. (Schafer-Rorschach)

Limp or drooping organisms:

(Animal or Human) Felt weakness; impotence, inadequacy, negativism. (Schafer-Rorschach)

Lip associations:

(Animal or Human Detail) Passive-receptive trend. (Schafer-Rorschach)

Long nose:

(Animal or Human Detail) Possible homoerotic fears or wishes; possible phallic symbol. (Schafer-Rorschach)

Making ferocious animals cartoon figures:

(Animal or Inhuman Human) Denial and inhibition of hostility. (Schafer-Rorschach)

Maternal animals or person:

(Animal or Human) Passive-receptive trend. (Schafer-Rorschach)

Missing or artificial biting and pinching surfaces (false teeth, toothless faces):

(Human Detail or Implement) Denial of oral-aggressive trends; possible emasculation conflicts. (Schafer-Rorschach)

Monuments:

(Architecture or Death) Paranoid tendency. (Schafer-Rorschach)

Mourning:

(Animal or Human) Depressed or dysphoric mood. (Schafer-Rorschach)

Mutilated or distorted animals or humans:

(Animal or Human) Possible feelings of inadequacy. (Schafer-Rorschach)

Mutilated parts:	(Anatomy, Human Detail, or Implement) Paranoid tendency. (Schafer-Rorschach)
Mutilation, destruction responses:	(Anatomy or Landscape) Aggressive, sadistic attitudes. (Phillips and Smith)
Mutilations:	(Animal or Human) Sadistic impulses. (Schafer-Rorschach)
Playing:	(Animal or Human) Active, lively. (Schafer-Rorschach)
Pushing:	(Animal or Human) Active, lively. (Schafer-Rorschach)
Ragged or torn objects:	(Clothing or Household) Authoritarian orientation; felt inferior social status; inadequacy or negative attitudes. (Schafer-Rorschach)
Shrew:	(Animal or Human) Destructiveness, hostility, sadism; feminine identification and masculine inadequacy with fear of women in men. (Schafer-Rorschach)
Sinister and frightening places:	(Architecture or Landscape) Inadequacy, negativism. (Schafer-Rorschach)
Snuggling:	(Animal or Human) Cheerful emotional tone; friendly, responsive. (Schafer-Rorschach)
Springing:	(Animal or Human) Active, lively. (Schafer-Rorschach)
Stomach:	(Anatomy or Human Detail) Dependent, passive-receptive; rejection of adult role. (Schafer-Rorschach)
Storybook figures symbolic of innocence:	(Human or Inhuman Human) Superego conflicts. (Schafer-Rorschach)
Teeth:	(Animal or Human Detail) Demanding, dependent, passive-aggressive ("oral-aggressive"); possible masochism; rejection of adult role. (Schafer-Rorschach)

Throat:

(Anatomy or Human Detail) Dependent, passive-receptive; rejection of adult role. (Schafer-Rorschach)

Torn or ragged objects:

(Clothing or Household) Authoritarian orientation; felt inferior or social status; inadequacy or negative attitudes. (Schafer-Rorschach)

Web:

(Implement or Nature) Feminine identification, masculine inadequacy in men; masculine identification in women. (Schafer-Rorschach)

VOCATION
Dentist's tools:

Demanding, dependent, passive-aggressive ("oral-aggressive"); possible masochism; rejection of adult role. (Schafer-Rorschach)

Vocation:

Masculinity, perhaps compensatory for feelings of inadequacy. (Phillips and Smith)

WAR
War:

Sadistic psychopaths; with Fm obsessive-compulsive, possibly with homosexual fears. (Phillips and Smith)

Determinants

COLOR
Absence color:

Possible withdrawal. (Schafer-Clinical Application)

C, CF:

Lack of secure self-control; impetuosity or marked anxiety. (Schafer-Rorschach)

C, CF-:

Impulsivity, irritability. (Beck and Molish)

CF:

Explosiveness, impulsivity, possible somatization (Rapaport); hypersensitivity, irritability (Beck and Molish); impulsive acting-out tendency; or

	spontaneity (Klopfer-Developments I); impulsivity, inadequate emotional control; or spontaneity. (Klopfer-Davidson)
CF dominance:	Dishonesty; lack of concern over acting-out, lack of integrity and lack of long-range goals. (Phillips and Smith)
CF–:	Impulsivity, poor judgment (Phillips and Smith); irritability; possible impairment of reality contact. (Beck and Molish)
Color:	Extratensive. (Klopfer-Developments I)
Color denial, negative reaction to color:	Overcontrolled affect. (Beck and Molish)
Decrement color:	Asthenic personality or neurasthenic neurosis ("neurasthenia"), depressive neurosis ("depressive"), simple schizophrenia; shyness, inhibition, tension (Rapaport); inhibition (Klopfer-Davidson); withdrawal tendency. (Schafer-Clinical Application)
Emphasis on C and CF:	Manic tendency; possible narcissistic spontaneity. (Beck and Molish)
Exclusive FC:	Formality, overcompliance, social anxiety (Phillips and Smith); lack of spontaneity, passive-compliance, possibly as a defense mechanism. (Schafer-Rorschach)
FC:	Adaptability, conformity, emotional responsivity with self-control; contraindicates assaultiveness (Phillips and Smith); appropriate emotional responsivity; good adjustment (Klopfer-Davidson); appropriate emotional responsivity; good adjustment potential; tact (Klopfer-Developments I); capacity for empathy, rapport (Rapaport); capacity for rapport; positive prognostic sign, social responsivity (Beck and Molish); conformity, submission. (Schafer-Rorschach)

FC−:	Children; in adults impairment of emotional control. (Klopfer-Developments I)
FC only or almost exclusively:	Lack of spontaneity; superficiality in social interaction. (Klopfer-Davidson)
FC only or main color:	Passive; overcompliant. (Schafer-Clinical Application)
Good FC+:	Interest in good rapport with others. (Schafer-Rorschach)
Good form red:	Emotional stability, maturity. (Phillips and Smith)
Inappropriate color (green fire):	Deteriorated schizophrenics; organics, young children. (Phillips and Smith)
Inappropriate color FC ("pink animals"):	Social anxiety, perhaps self-conscious, with need for social approval. (Klopfer-Developments I)
Increment C, CF:	Lability. (Beck and Molish)
Increment CF:	Hysteric (Rapaport); impulsive, irritable, labile. (Beck III)
Increment color:	Contraindicates paranoid condition; hysteria. (Rapaport)
Increment FC:	Inhibition, passive-compliance, possible guardedness (Schafer-Rorschach); obsessive-compulsive (Rapaport); over-control, social dependence. (Klopfer-Developments I)
Increment FC, no other color:	Lack of assertion and spontaneity; overcompliance. (Rapaport)
Increment pure C:	Schizophrenia. (Rapaport)
Low color:	Depression, lack of drive. (Beck and Molish)
Low-form color:	Impulsivity; narcissistic tendency. (Schafer-Rorschach)
Low-form color only (increment CF + C), no FC:	Immaturity, narcissism. (Schafer-Rorschach)
Mutilated C:	Schizophrenia. (Schafer-Clinical Application)

No color:

Anahedonism; lack of capacity for pleasurable experience (Beck and Molish); destructive, querulous; or inhibition. (Phillips and Smith)

One CF only color:

Potential for sporadic impulsive acts. (Schafer-Clinical Application)

Only color C:

Antisocial acting-out (especially with no M or shading). (Phillips and Smith)

Only one type of color-determinant (C, CF, FC):

Lack of flexibility or modulation of emotional tone. (Beck III)

Perseverated, unelaborated CF:

Impulsive acting-out, temper tantrums. (Phillips and Smith)

Preference for cool colors:

Passive-dependency. (Phillips and Smith)

Preference for warm colors:

Activity-independence. (Phillips and Smith)

Pure C (more than one):

Contraindicates depressive trend; demanding, impulsive, wants immediate gratification; schizophrenic (Phillips and Smith); egocentricity, overcompliance (Anderson-Beck); explosiveness, lack of emotional stability (Klopfer-Davidson); explosiveness, organicity (Klopfer-Developments I); impetuosity, acting-out propensity (Beck and Molish); impressionable suggestability; unreflective (Rapaport); inappropriate affect (Schafer-Clinical Application); narcissistic trend. (Schafer-Rorschach)

Pure C perseveration:

Assaultive acting-out. (Phillips and Smith)

Response increment to cool colors:

Repression. (Beck III)

Response to yellow (poor form):

Schizophrenic tendency. (Phillips and Smith)

FORM
Adequate F+ level:

Adequate reality contact. (Beck and Molish)

Decrement F+:

Asthenic personality, neurasthenic

neurosis ("neurasthenics"); hysterical personality ("hysterics"); schizophrenia (except paranoid); impulsivity. (Rapaport)

Diverse range of F+ content: Superior intelligence. (Beck and Molish)

Exclusive form-determined R: Avoidance of conscious awareness of affect; inhibition, intellectualization, isolation. (Schafer-Rorschach)

F-:   Impaired judgment (Beck and Molish); inadequate judgment. (Phillips and Smith)

F+:   Decreases with psychosis, increases with anxiety; unimpaired judgment when optimum (Phillips and Smith); ego strength, intellectual control. (Klopfer-Davidson)

Form accuracy: Ability to concentrate, clarity of associative processes, length of attention span. (Rorschach-*Psychodiagnostics*)

Form-determined F-:   Impulsivity. (Rapaport)

Form-determined F+:   Inhibition; may imply ability to delay impulse gratification. (Rapaport)

Form-determined response first: Inhibition possibly. (Klopfer-Developments I)

High F+:   Anxiety, insecurity (with high P); depression (Phillips and Smith); contra-indicates retardation (Beck and Molish); compulsivity, exactness, literality. (Klopfer-Davidson)

High F+ and extended F+%:   Possible isolation defense. (Schafer-Rorschach)

Increment F%:   Depressive, paranoid, simple schizophrenia; inhibition, lack of spontaneity (Rapaport); lack of spontaneity, possible isolation defense, tendency to intellectual defense. (Schafer-Rorschach)

Increment F+:   Accurate perception; guardedness; lack

of capacity for pleasurable experience and lack of spontaneity (Beck III); constriction, rigidity. (Schafer-Rorschach)

Increment F+, decrement of other determinants:

Constriction. (Klopfer-Developments I)

Increment F+%:

Depression; hysterics, paranoids (Rapaport); perfectionistic, possible compulsive tendency, reaction-formation against hostility. (Schafer-Rorschach)

Low F%:

Subjective reaction to environmental experience. (Beck and Molish)

Low F+:

Inability to concentrate. (Beck and Molish)

Marked increment F% and F+:

Possible overcontrol. (Schafer-Rorschach)

Vague form:

Stereotypy. (Rapaport)

Vague form followed consistently by good form:

Relatively stable defense system or recuperative potential despite vulnerability. (Schafer-Rorschach)

MOVEMENT

Animal Movement
Additional FM, decrement FM:

Tensions blocking constructive self-expression. (Klopfer-Davidson)

FM:

Anxiety, repression, tension; capacity for at least partial insight (Kloper-Developments I); conflict and tension with insight, good adjustment potential, immaturity, with id impulses pressing for immediate expression (Klopfer-Davidson); regressive tendency. (Beck III)

FM much greater than M:

Immaturity, irresponsibility. (Phillips and Smith)

FM (without compensating M):

Immaturity, irresponsibility. (Phillips and Smith)

Increment FM:

Regressive tendency. (Klopfer-Developments I)

No FM:

Repression of id impulses. (Klopfer-Davidson)

Oral-aggressive FM:

Immaturity. (Phillips and Smith)

Human Movement

Additional M, with decrement M:

Inhibition of potential capacity. (Klopfer-Davidson)

Control by external forces, stop-motion:

Contraindicates assaultiveness. (Phillips and Smith)

Dd M:

Caution, chronicity, withdrawal; un-favorable prognosis. (Phillips and Smith)

Decrement M:

Anxiety, depression, hysteria; con-traindicates obsessive-compulsive trend; impulsivity, repression (Rapaport); absense of strong value system, lack of empathy, lack of self-acceptance (Klopfer-Davidson); intolerance of fan-tasy, lack of capacity for insight, un-reflective. (Schafer-Rorschach)

Decrement M (one or less):

Depression. (Schafer-Clinical Applica-tion)

Excessive M:

Obsessive doubting. (Schafer-Clinical Application)

Extensor M:

Good prognostic sign; independence, masculinity, self-assertion (Beck and (Molish); masculine (including in women subjects, where it suggests a homosexual potential); need for inde-pendence. (Beck III)

Flexor M:

Dependence, femininity, submission (Beck and Molish); dependency needs; passive-feminine, submissive tendency (including in male subjects, where it suggests a homosexual potential). [Beck III]

Flexor stance:

Indecision, submissiveness. (Beck III)

Form-plus M:

Potential for empathy, insight and po-

	tential creativity, with constructive fantasy and imagination; ego-strength; emotional stability. (Klopfer-Developments I)
Increment M:	Characteristic of obsessive-compulsive; contraindicates depressive, hysteric, neurasthenic and paranoid trends (Rapaport); obsessive ideas. (Schafer-Clinical Application)
Increment M+:	Possible isolation defenses. (Schafer-Rorschach)
Kinesthetic responses (M):	Creativity; extent of concern with phenomenological as opposed to external events; introspectivity. (Rorschach-*Psychodiagnostics*)
M:	Fantasy activity. (Beck and Molish)
M in A:	Immaturity, regressive attitudes. (Phillips and Smith)
M in A (Klopfer's FM):	Regressive trend. (Beck and Molish)
M in abstraction:	Contraindicates immaturity, psychopathy, psychosis, shyness, tension; superior intelligence. (Phillips and Smith)
M in animal movement, form minus (FM−)	Regressive, possible autistic or reality-alienated fantasy. (Beck and Molish)
M elsewhere than III:	Possible schizophrenic tendency. (Rapaport)
M > average:	Independence of thought, obstinacy; in schizophrenics represents paranoia. (Phillips and Smith)
M > WM:	Social anxiety. (Phillips and Smith)
M in Hd:	Chronicity, immaturity, social anxiety; poor prognosis (Phillips and Smith); immaturity; young children. (Beck and Molish)
M−:	Favorable prognosis (Phillips and Smith); impaired ego strength (Klopfer-

	Davidson); regressive or schizophrenic fantasy. (Beck and Molish)
M+:	Acquisition of self-control with retained freedom of self-expression; capacity for empathy, long-range goals, recognition of individuality in others (Phillips and Smith); capacity to restrain impulses; possible reflective or ruminative tendency (Rapaport); creative potential, ego-strength, good interpersonal relations with self-acceptance. (Klopfer-Davidson)
Movement in full human content:	Interpersonal relations important to subject; sensitivity to others. (Phillips and Smith)
No more than two rare M, one on III:	Obsessive. (Schafer-Clinical Application)
Overemphasis on inactive M:	Passive-submissive. (Phillips and Smith)
Reduction of M:	Anxiety, guardedness, inhibition. (Phillips and Smith)
Small M:	Possible paranoid tendency. (Schafer-Rorschach)
Static M:	Ambivalence with associated anxiety (Beck III); blocked self-expression with inhibiton of hostility; conflict between activity-passivity; obsessive-compulsive or psychophysiologic ("psychosomatic") tendency. (Phillips and Smith)
Underproduction of M:	Conversion neurosis ("conversion reaction"), anxiety neurosis ("anxiety reaction"), psychophysiologic disorders ("psychophysiological states"); depression, immaturity; antisocial personalities ("psychopaths"), organics, retardates. (Phillips and Smith)
WM:	Intelligence, poise, self-assertion. (Phillips and Smith)

Object Movement

Falling animals or humans:	Decompensation fear or tendency. (Schafer-Rorschach)
"Floating" percepts (clouds, etc.):	Lack of long-range goals; passivity. (Schafer-Rorschach)
Fm:	Anxiety (Phillips and Smith); conflict, tension. (Beck and Molish, citing Klein and Schlesinger)
Increment nonabstract F+ Fm:	Contraindicates acting-out, contraindicates psychosis. (Klopfer-Developments II)
Objects collapsing:	Adolescents (anxious), schizophrenics; possible nihilistic fantasy. (Beck III)

MULTIPLE CRITERIA (Determinants)

Animal and human movement:	Intratensive. (Klopfer-Developments I)
Decrement color and M:	Constriction. (Rapaport)
Increment color and M:	Expansive tendency. (Rapaport)
Motion:	Active orientation. (Schafer-Rorschach)
T, V, Y:	Anxiety. (Klopfer-Davidson)
TF, VF, YF:	Anxiety; feelings of inadequacy, lack of worth, rejection with dysphoric affect preoccupation; passivity. (Beck and Molish)

SHADING

Absense of shading:	Blandness, low anxiety tolerance, unreflective. (Schafer-Clinical Application)
Arbitrary and inappropriate FY:	Antisocial personalities ("psychopaths"), deteriorated schizophrenics, retardates; immaturity; lethargic but with impulsive acting-out potential. (Phillips and Smith)
Avoidance of shading:	Lack of capacity for affection or rejection of need for it. (Klopfer-Davidson)

Avoidance of shading or emphasis only on light rather than heavy shading:

Possible denial of anxiety or of sensual needs; possible low anxiety tolerance. (Schafer-Rorschach)

FY:

Contraindicates impulsive acting-out; dysphoric mood, ideational activity; inhibiton of motility (Phillips and Smith); mild-to-moderate anxiety, somatization. (Rapaport)

FY emphasis:

Depression, withdrawal. (Klopfer-Davidson)

FY with form-plus color:

Maturity, possible originality, productivity. (Phillips and Smith)

FY minus color:

Inhibition. (Phillips and Smith)

FY, YF, Y:

Anxiety over frustrated need for affection with intellectualization; FY with more effective intellectualization. (Klopfer-Davidson)

Increment FY:

Tension, worry. (Klopfer-Developments I)

Increment pure Y:

Paralyzing anxiety in certain conflictful situations. (Rapaport)

Pure Y:

Free-floating anxiety. (Rapaport)

Shading:

Intratensive (Klopfer-Developments I); passivity. (Beck III)

Shading increment:

Depression, dysphoric mood. (Beck and Molish)

Y:

Anxiety (Klopfer-Davidson): depression, free-floating anxiety; passivity (Beck and Molish); depressive trend (Schafer-Rorschach); withdrawal tendency. (Beck III)

YF:

Diffuse anxiety. (Schafer-Rorschach)

YF-:

Despair, resignation. (Beck and Molish)

YF + Y:

Free-floating anxiety; possible hysterical tendency. (Schafer-Clinical Application)

TEXTURE

FT: Acceptance and awareness of need for affection; desire for approval and responsivity from others (Klopfer-David son); need for affection, possible sensuality (Beck and Molish); need for social approval; sensitivity. (Klopfer-Developments I)

FT-:   Impairment of adjustment by excessive dependency upon others. (Klopfer-Developments I)

Increment FT: Dependence (Klopfer-Davidson); possible depressive element. (Schafer-Rorschach)

Increment TF: Dependency. (Klopfer-Developments I)

Optimal FT: Awareness, sensitivity, tactfulness. (Klopfer-Davidson)

Overemphasis on texture: Possible homosexual tendency. (Beck and Molish)

Rough texture: Covert hostility; overdeferentiality with indirect expression of hostility for fear of punishment; obsequiousness in conjunction with verbal expression of hostility. (Phillips and Smith)

Smooth texture: Delicacy; femininity; overcontrolled affect with dislike of intense emotion. (Phillips and Smith)

Soft FT: Feminine component (Beck and Molish); oral-dependent tendency. (Klopfer-Developments II)

T: Anxiety; infantile need for nurturance and physical contact (Klopfer-Davidson); negative prognostic sign; possible organicity. (Klopfer-Development I)

T, TF: Emotional instability, social anxiety (Phillips and Smith); lack of secure self-control, marked anxiety or impetuosity. (Schafer-Rorschach)

TF:

Dependence, immaturity, sensuality (Klopfer-Davidson); diffuse anxiety (Schafer-Rorschach); negative prognostic sign. (Klopfer-Developments I)

Texture alone:

Shallow affability. (Phillips and Smith)

Texture (FT):

Conformity, elusiveness (Phillips and Smith): extratensive (Klopfer-Developments I); need for affection. (Beck and Molish)

Texture with other determinants:

Mature adaptability. (Phillips and Smith)

VISTA
Decrement FV:

Possible paranoid trend with other indications. (Rapaport)

FV:

Capacity for insight; potential for good adjustment. (Klopfer-Davidson)

Increment FV:

Asthenic personality, neurasthenic neurosis ("neurasthenic"); schizophrenics (except paranoid). [Rapaport]

V:

Anxiety. (Klopfer-Davidson)

V + VF:

Anxiety over frustrated need for affection. (Klopfer-Davidson)

Vista:

Feelings of inferiority (Beck and Molish, Beck III); inhibition, introspection; perhaps self-derogatory if excessive vista; potential for insight (Phillips and Smith); introtensive. (Klopfer-Developments I)

Vista—architectural structures:

Sense of nonfulfillment of self. (Beck and Molish)

Vista—distances and heights:

Aspirations felt to be unobtainable. (Beck and Molish)

Vista—landscapes, especially islands:

Felt loneliness, isolation. (Beck and Molish)

Vista—reflection (mirrors, water surfaces):

Introspective, self-valuation. (Beck and Molish)

Experience Balance

Ambiequal experience balance (color equal to M):

Ambivalence; compulsive doubting and rituals in neurosis possibly; obsessive neurosis (Beck and Molish); depression, obsessive-compulsivity. (Beck III)

Ambiequal experience balance, with increment of both color and M:

Capacity for change; flexibility; positive prognostic sign for psychotherapy. (Beck and Molish)

Ambiequal experience balance, no more than one color and M:

Constriction; inadaptability; rigidity, with conscious and incessant effort at self-control. (Beck and Molish)

Emphasis on introtensive (M) in experience balance:

Contraindicates manic state. (Beck and Molish)

Experience balance of O:O:

Blocking (Beck and Molish); poor prognostic sign. (Beck III)

Low color and M in experience balance (coarcted EB):

Constriction, rigidity; negative prognostic sign; passivity with anxiety. (Beck III)

Narrow experience balance:

Constriction, inhibition; asthenic personality, neurasthenic neurosis ("neurasthenia"), depression, schizophrenia. (Rapaport)

Fabulization

Fabulization:

Feared or wished-for attitude or prevailing mood with anxiety; contraindicates acting-out and implies above average intelligence; oppressive and morbid self-preoccupation with depressive rumination, irritability and passivity (Phillips and Smith); hysterical tendency. (Schafer-Clinical Application)

Frightening appearance:

Anxiety, hysteria. (Phillips and Smith)

Frightening creatures content:

Apprehension, fearfulness. (Schafer-Clinical Application)

"Strange" appearance:	Apprehension; sexual role conflict. (Phillips and Smith)

Location

Absence or marked decrement of space:	Depression, passivity, suggestibility. (Beck III)
Center D, Dd:	Dependent needs with insight. (Phillips and Smith)
Center detail increment (if M insight is likely to be present into dependent need):	Dependency. (Phillips and Smith)
Cut-off W:	Inhibition of self-expression with lack of determination and drive; social anxiety and restriction with self-doubt and tension. (Phillips and Smith)
Dd:	Evasion, intellectualization, lack of spontaneity (Phillips and Smith); poor prognostic sign to greater degree than vague W. (Rapaport)
Dd (edge details):	Anxiety, avoidance (Klopfer-Davidson); emotional detachment, evasion, intellectualization; meticulousness. (Phillips and Smith)
Dd or edge details:	Avoidance of direct confrontation of problems. (Klopfer-Davidson)
Dd as first response to two or more cards:	Disturbance in judgment and thought; possible psychosis. (Phillips and Smith)
Dd perseveration:	Disruption of formal thought processes; ideational tendencies. (Phillips and Smith)
D and W optimum:	Generalization with appropriate attention to details. (Klopfer-Davidson)
DW responses:	Suggestibility. (Beck and Molish)
Dx and Wx responses:	Perfectionistic tendency; possible reaction-formation against hostility. (Schafer-Rorschach)

Decrement D:	Anxiety; inadequacy; schizophrenia. (Rapaport)
Decrement Dd:	Depression, simple schizophrenia (Rapaport); disinterest in trivia. (Klopfer-Davidson)
Edge details:	Ideational tendency; intellectualizing normal, obsessive-compulsive, paranoid schizophrenic. (Phillips and Smith)
Edge interpretations:	Evasion; inability to tolerate conscious anxiety; lack of insight. (Rapaport)
Emphasis on D:	Limited aspiration. (Phillips and Smith)
Emphasis on D and Dd:	Attention to detail with reluctance to generalize. (Klopfer-Davidson)
Excessive W:	Intellectual pretentiousness. (Schafer-Clinical Application)
F + W:	Possible grandiose ambition and compensatory emphasis on intellectual attainment. (Schafer-Rorschach)
Figure ground reversal space:	In psychiatric patients persistence of delusions; obstinacy, tenacity (Beck III); negativism, stubbornness; possibly desirable self-assertion and ego strength. (Klopfer-Davidson)
Increment arbitrary W:	Possible grandiosity and paranoid attitudes. (Schafer-Rorschach)
Increment D:	Concretism (Beck III); insecure, overemphasis on the obvious (Schafer-Rorschach); possible depression. (Rapaport)
Increment Dd:	Anxiety, avoidance; intellectualization, introspective rumination; addict, character disorder, obsessive-compulsive (Rapaport); compulsivity, denial of affect, pedantry possibly; possible intellectualization, isolation, reaction-formation; possible obsessive-compul-

sive or paranoid tendency (Schafer-Rorschach); criticality, pedantry, obsessive tendency (Klopfer-Developments I); evasion of insight or issues with displacement; obsessive tendency with isolation, reaction-formation, undoing (Beck III); pedantry. (Klopfer-Davidson)

Increment Dd, without obsessive-compulsive features:

Restlessness. (Schafer-Clinical Application)

Increment DW or vague W:

Arbitrary overgeneralization; possible schizophrenia. (Rapaport)

Increment F + D:

Depression; practicality; preoccupation with the obvious. (Rapaport)

Increment F + W:

Abstraction. (Rapaport)

Increment good-form Dd:

Obsessive, pedantic. (Klopfer-Davidson)

Increment poor-form W:

Retardation, schizophrenic tendency. (Klopfer-Davidson)

Increment space:

Assertive or oppositional tendency (Klopfer-Developments I); externalized hostility; may be determination (Beck III); negativism, rebellion (Beck and Molish); possible intellectualization defense; projection, possible paranoid trend, especially if they are figure-ground reversals; unstable defenses (Schafer-Rorschach); possible paranoid condition. (Rapaport)

Increment space in schizophrenic pattern:

May be indicative of paranoia. (Beck and Molish)

Increment space in setting of overconscientious perfectionism:

May represent negativism, obstinacy, or rebelliousness in conjunction with obsessive-compulsive meticulousness. (Schafer-Rorschach)

Increment W:

Possible grandiose aspirations or tendency unless F−; possible intellectualization defense. (Schafer-Rorschach)

Increment Wx:	Critical, possibly perfectionistic. (Klopfer-Developments I)
Interior Dd:	Possible paranoid trend if poor form; social anxiety. (Klopfer-Davidson)
Location response—use of the whole blot (W), of a large usual detail (D), or of a small unusual detail (Dd):	Apperceptive type. (Rorschach-*Psychodiagnostics*)
Mediocre W; underemphasis on W:	Little drive for achievement, limited ambition. (Beck and Molish)
No space responses:	Possible passivity or lack of initiative. (Beck and Molish)
Optimum space in normal personality structure:	Ego strength, positive assertion. (Beck and Molish)
Optimum W:	Generalization from integration of data. (Rapaport)
Overelaboration tiny D:	Paranoid trend. (Schafer-Rorschach)
Overemphasis on D:	Mundane practicality. (Beck and Molish)
Overemphasis on Dd:	Obsessive tendency. (Beck and Molish)
Overemphasis on W:	Tendency to jump to conclusions or to overgeneralize. (Klopfer-Davidson)
Position responses:	Possible suggestibility. (Beck and Molish)
Schizophrenic space:	Negativism, rigidity, resistiveness. (Beck and Molish)
Sequence of location responses:	Logical discipline of thinking. (Rorschach-*Psychodiagnostics*)
Space:	Negativism, rebelliousness (Schafer-Rorschach); oppositional, resistive, stubborn (Anderson-Beck); oppositional tendency (Rapaport); resistiveness. (Beck and Molish)
Space areas viewed as light (luminescence) and/or purity:	Possible hypomanic tendency. (Schafer-Rorschach)
Space in depressive and passive-dependent states:	Absent unless depression is reactive or passive-dependent character is ambivalent. (Beck and Molish)

Space in extratensive setting:	Externalized oppositional behavior; possible antisocial behavior with increment. (Beck and Molish)
Space in intratensive setting:	Self-criticality, self-distrust. (Beck and Molish)
Space in obsessive-compulsives:	Indicative of doubting, excessive inhibition, indecision. (Beck and Molish)
Vague D:	Failure to deal realistically with environment. (Phillips and Smith)
Vague low-form W's:	Looseness of reality testing; narcissistic striving. (Schafer-Rorschach)
Vague W (map, X ray):	Immaturity, inadequacy. (Phillips and Smith)
W at expectancy:	Practicality, realism. (Phillips and Smith)
Wx (cut-off W):	Overcritical. (Klopfer-Davidson)

Multiple Criteria (All Categories)

Adx and Hdx; absence of qualification; combination of space with nonspace areas in crude undifferentiated response; decrement of M; deterioration content; distractability; extreme DW responses; irrelevant conversational remarks; "rocks" and "stones" content (Phillips and Smith); combination of predominant FC with crude CF and C; deterioration content; early appearance of shading; facetiousness with self-distrust; rejection of Card III with H elsewhere; rejection of part of human figure on Card III; war and violence themes (representing fear of loss of control). [Klopfer-Developments II]

Brain damage or organic impairment indicators.

Adx and Hdx; card description; excessive detailing; fabulization; Hd H (social anxiety); haphazard turning; high A percentage; increment D; incre-

Anxiety. (Phillips and Smith)

ment of (H); low M%; M in Hd; pedantically (but not peculiarly) worded anatomy; P beyond expectancy; reduction H, increment of (H); reduction R, increment D; reduction R, increment F+; W below expectancy; "X ray":

Absence of abstraction content; "bee" content; "bird" content; "bug" content; increment "map" content; "monkey" content; multiple rejections (with guardedness); rough texture; sadistic content; stain content; tossing of card back to examiner; underproduction of M; visceral anatomy; weapon content:

Antisocial personalities ("psychopaths"). [Phillips and Smith]

Absence blood content; absence card description; absence clothing content; absence Dd as first response to two or more cards; absence F− to Card I, first reponse; absence M in abstraction; absence pure C; absence religious content; absence stain content; FC; H equal to M approximately; fewer than three Hd; fewer than two art, males; no more than one (H); pleasantly toned shading; positive comments on color; presence H; use of personal pronouns; totem pole content:

Normals. (Phillips and Smith)

Absence or decrement of F+ originals; confabulation; decrement of M; food content; inferior form elaboration; inferior organization; low F+; "smoke" content:

Low mental age and mental retardates ("mental defectives"). [Phillips and Smith]

Absence FC; "bug" content; emphasis on recreation content; possibly shock on Cards I and II, the latter with special conditions:

Assaultiveness. (Phillips and Smith)

Absence of pure C; damage, decay, and death content; decrement color and M; derogatory self-references; dys-

Depression. (Phillips and Smith)

phorically toned abstractions and fab-
ulations; emphasis on FY; F+ ap-
proaching 100%; high A%; Hd > H;
high A%; impotence and perplexity;
low R; rejection Cards IV, V, VI:

Absence of shading; "bug" content;   Acting-out. (Phillips and Smith)
only color C, especially when blood or
fire to Card II or IX and in absence M
and shading (with M or longer record,
perseveration of C):

Abstraction content; anatomy con-   Contraindication to assaultiveness.
tent; blocked or passive M; blood con-   (Phillips and Smith)
tent; emphasis on Hd limbs or projec-
tions; FM responses; part-body M;
presence of FC; shading:

Absurdities; C > CF + FC; confabuli-   Schizophrenia.
zation and contamination; deviant verbalizations; extremely irregular sequence; F+ less than 60%, especially
less than 50%; increment sex content
or references to sex act; marked variability in quality and quantity of response; sex response to Card I, first
response (Schafer-Clinical Application); bizarreness; inappropriate elaborations; contamination; Dd perseveration; decrement H content (except
paranoid); detached "mouth" and Hd;
full-face space and full-face content
(paranoid schizophrenic); generalized
visceral anatomy content; inappropriate elaborations; inappropriate use
of color, as "green fire"; increment
M− (favorable prognosis); increment
religion content; increment sex content; increment travel content possibly; inner details; low F+ and poor-
form responses; low-form color; low
color response to yellow blot areas
possibly; morbid content; mumbling;
mutilated anatomy; mutilated leaf
content; negative responses; over-pro-

duction of M (paranoid); peculiar introductory remarks; possibly "alphabet" content; possibly "bacteria" content; possibly "bee" content; possibly DW tendencies; possibly "food" content; pure C responses possibly. (Phillips and Smith)

Aggressive A or H; color > M; caricatured or inanimate H; increment S:

Externalized hostility. (Beck III)

Anal content; art content; calf content; confusion or perplexity relative to sex of H; "dancing" H; displacing or penetrating Fm content; emphasis on sex content; flower and leaf content; (H) content; mythology content; seeing content usually perceived as one sex as the opposite sex (other than Card III); shock on Cards III and VI; women's clothing content:

Possible homosexual tendencies. (male). [Phillips and Smith]

Anxious, self-derogatory comments; catastrophic reactions; confusion of background and foreground; covering · parts of blot with hand to expose other areas more conspicuously; discrepancy poor performance on Rorschach as compared to Wechsler test; emphasis on projections; good FC (to rule out schizophrenia); good form perseveration combined with emphasis on projections; inability to give alternate responses to the same area; inappropriate combination of good responses to adjacent areas; coherence and reasonable associational sequence (to rule out schizophrenia) with inability to give alternate responses to the same area; passive content Rorschach with aggressive TAT content; perseverated CF content on last three cards; repeated personal references; silly responses accompanied by sensible remarks; use of shading in Cards

Relatively valid signs of brain damage. (Klopfer-Developments II)

I and II; vague W with good form Dd details; variability in response quality:

Automatic phrases; less than 15 R; mostly W responses; not more than one M; perplexity; projection emphasis; response time over one minute:	Classical signs of brain damage. (Klopfer-Developments II)
"Bee" content; cloaking and disguising garments; "eagle" content; "eyes" content; excessive Dd M; excessive Hd faces; face Hd to space area (paranoid schizophrenic); full-face Hd (paranoid schizophrenic); high increment M; looking suspiciously at card back; M > C (also antisocial personalities: "psychopaths"); sex content in schizophrenic men; suspicious remarks about purpose of evaluation or nature of the stimulus; visceral anatomy (vague unsystemized paranoid attitudes):	Paranoid syndromes. (Phillips and Smith)
Blocked or inactive M; diminutive animal content; disgust reaction to cards; flexion M:	Neurasthenic neurosis, neurasthenic personality ("neurasthenia"). [Phillips and Smith]
Blocking, confabulation; contamination; peculiar verbalizations; perseveration:	Possible thought disorder. (Schafer-Rorschach)
Blocking and delayed reaction on color or shaded cards; blood content on II and III; sum of color on Rorschach above M and M is one or zero; CF > FC; CF first on color cards and appears first on II and III; CF limited to blood, botany, clouds, nature content; fabulizations; frightening animals as King Kong, snakes, spiders; low Dd and DW; R below 30; Y and YF content (Schafer-Clinical Application); blood responses to achromatic areas; C and CF responses to red areas, often with expressed conflict over its use; fabulization; underproduction of M (Phillips and Smith):	Hysterical neurosis. ("hysteria")

Bony anatomy content; color 4 X M; color below expectancy; decrement M; F+ color below expectancy; increment F+; low-form color; static M:

Psychophysiologic disorders. (Phillips and Smith)

Botanical parts and reproductive anatomy; childbirth associations; deteriorated or dilapidated pelvic anatomy; emphasis on internal space associations:

Concern with reproductive functions. (Schafer-Rorschach)

Both FC and space responses:

Conflict between conformity-submission and negativistic-rebellious responses. (Schafer-Rorschach)

CF color; + 1C; color-shock; decrement H; decrement pleasantly toned shading; fabulization; Hd H; negative response to color; shock on Card III:

Neurosis. (Phillips and Smith)

Card rejection; delayed reaction time; short total time for card:

Avoidance; repression. (Schafer-Rorschach)

Confusion of sexual characteristics; emphasis on sexual organs or sexual function of animals; possibly pans or satyrs; reversal of usually perceived sex of figure:

Possible homosexual tendency. (Beck III)

Dd perseveration; low F+; M in Dd areas; M- increment; pure C responses possibly; suspicious remarks about content of card or intent of examiner:

Psychosis. (Phillips and Smith)

DW tendency, poor form:

Possible impaired reality testing. (Schafer-Rorschach)

Decrement passive M; decrement shading; possibly impotency reactions:

Narcissism. (Phillips and Smith)

Excessive precision, pedantry, use of esoteric terms; FM content; Hd > H; H at expectancy; increment Dd; increment M; loss of response in inquiry; methodical notation of cards; passive verb forms; precision alternatives; questions about procedure; symmetry comments:

Obsessive-compulsive personality. (Phillips and Smith)

H perceived as double-sexed man and woman; perception of female where male usually seen (other than Card III); uncertainty as to sex (other than Card III):

Homosexuality. (Phillips and Smith)

Increment F+, increment P (Schafer-Rorschach); increment qualification; no turning; precision alternatives; stereotyped phrases; symmetry (Beck III):

Constriction, rigidity.

Increment FC+ S responses:

Conflict between compliance and negativistic hostility. (Schafer-Rorschach)

No FM with evident emotional conflict:

Denial possibly; lack of insight into emotional difficulties. (Klopfer-Davidson)

With anatomical content, conversion; with high F+, compulsive tendencies; with increment M or M other than III, phobic tendencies; with low F+, anxiety and lability; with usual sex content, sexual preoccupation:

Variations of hysterical neurosis ("hysteria"), once basic hysterical syndrome established. (Schafer-Clinical Application)

NORMS
A%:

Optimal 25–40%, but decreases as intelligence and M increases. (Phillips and Smith)

Affective range below 40:

Inertness. (Beck III).

Average R:

20–30 (Normals). [Phillips and Smith]

Color-Naming:

Up to age 5. (Klopfer-Developments II)

Confabulation:

Common in children 4–7 years of age. (Klopfer-Developments II)

D (average R) expectancy:

55–65%. (Phillips and Smith)

D%:

Adults, 67%; Catatonic and hebephrenic, 45%; paranoids 57% (Friendman, H & S). [Phillips and Smith]

Dd%:

Adults, 4%; catatonics and hebephrenics, 3%; paranoids, 15%. (Friedman, H & S). [Phillips and Smith]

Dd (average R) expectancy:	5-15%. (Phillips and Smith)
Decrease of W:	2-4 years of age. (Klopfer-Developments II)
Emergence of fantasy activity:	Age 7-8. (Beck and Molish)
Expected At%:	One (skeletal form). [Phillips and Smith]
F+:	Optimum 70% plus. (Phillips and Smith)
F+ < 60%, especially below 50%:	Schizophrenia. (Schafer-Clinical Application)
F+ 60 to 70%:	Neurotic range of reality contact. (Beck and Molish)
F% Optimum range:	20-50%, objectivity. (Klopfer-Davidson)
F+% of 60:	Minimum for neurotic range. (Beck III)
Form-plus optimum or expected range:	W: 20-30%; D: 45-55%; Dd: 0-15%. (Klopfer-Developments I)
Global perception:	Up to six years of age. (Klopfer-Developments II)
Inappropriate color ("green fire"):	Up to age 5. (Klopfer-Developments II)
Increase D:	5-7 years of age. (Klopfer-Developments II)
Landscape:	Optimal range 1-3. (Phillips and Smith)
M > 5:	Expressivity. (Phillips and Smith)
No perseveration of concepts except color responses to last three cards:	Characteristic of four-to-five-year old child. (Klopfer-Developments II)
Normal range for affective ratio:	40-80. (Beck III)
O + 75%:	Erratic thinking. (Klopfer-Davidson)
Optimal A:	20-35%. (Klopfer-Davidson)
Optimal F:	35%. (Klopfer-Davidson); 20-50%. (Klopfer-Developments I)
Optimal H:	Four (more with superior intelligence);

	lower number H among schizophrenics, except paranoids; also below expectancy in psychotic depression, and with anxiety and neurosis, except obsessive-compulsive. (Phillips and Smith)
Optimal Hd:	<H; <3. (Phillips and Smith)
Optimal M:	At least three. (Klopfer-Davidson)
Optimal O+:	2 × P (with at least 5 P) [superior intelligence]. [Klopfer-Davidson]
Optimal vista:	Two; more is inhibitory and associated with excessive self-criticality. (Phillips and Smith)
P frequency:	Four to six. (Phillips and Smith)
Perseveration of concepts, rejections:	Characteristic of two-to-three-year old child. (Klopfer-Developments II)
S-plus 10%:	Significantly high increment of S. (Beck III)
Sum C less than three:	Decrement of emotional responsivity. (Klopfer-Davidson)
Sum C minimum three:	Normal emotional responsivity. (Klopfer-Davidson)
Ten responses plus:	Normality, although guardedness may be present. (Phillips and Smith)
Use of color:	Begins at three years of age. (Klopfer-Developments II)
Vague W:	Two to four years of age. (Klopfer-Developments II)
W (average R) expectancy:	15–35%. (Phillips and Smith)
W%:	Adults, 25%; catatonics and hebephrenics, 46%; paranoids 16%. (Phillips and Smith)

Originals

O+:	Originality. (Klopfer-Davidson)
Original responses:	Contact with reality; imagination; orig-

inality. (Rorschach-*Psychodiagnostics*)

Perseveration

Perseveration (not produced by organic impairment):

Overcompliance; suggestibility. (Beck III)

Perseveration of organic content:

May suggest brain damage. (Klopfer-Developments II)

Response perseveration:

Organics, schizophrenics. (Klopfer-Developments II)

Populars

Decrement of populars:

Anxiety indicator (Beck III); indifference to conventions, rebelliousness (Anderson-Beck); lack of common sense, possible impaired reality contact. (Rapaport)

High P:

Anxiety, insecurity (with high F). [Phillips and Smith]

Inability to see P on testing limits:

Impairment of reality testing. (Klopfer-Davidson)

Increment P:

Guardedness, stereotypy, depression; hysterical neurosis or hysterical personality ("hysteria"), simple schizophrenia; antisocial personality ("psychopath"); moderately low intelligence (Rapaport); conforming passive-dependency, often with obsequiousness; overconventionality (Beck III); constriction, rigidity (Schafer-Rorschach); overcompliance, overconformity (Anderson-Beck); overconventionality; possible excessive concern with the proprieties (Beck and Molish); overconventionality, possible overconformity. (Klopfer-Developments I)

Increment P (+8):

Conformity, conventionality. (Klopfer-Davidson)

Low P:

Estrangement, impracticality, rebelliousness; schizophrenics, some homosexuals (Beck III) unresponsive to conventional concepts. (Schafer-Clinical Application)

Optimum P:

Appropriate social response. (Beck and Molish); common sense. (Rapaport)

P:

Awareness of the proprieties (Beck and Molish); common sense, conventionality, reality contact (Rapaport); conventionality, sociability. (Phillips and Smith)

Rejection of P after verbalizing it:

Possible impaired reality testing. (Schafer-Rorschach)

Ratios

$(A + H) : (Ad + Hd)$

Optimum 2:1. (Klopfer-Davidson)

$(A + H) < \frac{1}{2} (Ad + Hd)$:

Anxiety, criticality, exacting attitude. (Klopfer-Davidson)

Achromatic to chromatic $> 2 : 1$:

Inhibition. (Klopfer-Developments I)

Achromatic one-half chromatic:

Acting-out tendency. (Klopfer-Developments I)

$C > CF; CF > FC$:

Chronic undifferentiated schizophrenia. (Rapaport)

$C > CF + FC$:

Schizophrenia. (Schafer-Clinical Application)

$C + CF > FC$:

Acting-out tendency, impulsivity (Klopfer-Developments I); demanding, egocentric, irresponsible; lack of perseverance; social isolate (Phillips and Smith); inadequate emotional control (Klopfer-Davidson); possible narcissism. (Schafer-Clinical Application)

$C + CF > FC : 2$ texture:

Acting-out tendency without excessive dependency. (Klopfer-Davidson)

$C + CF$ twice shading:

Acting-out impulsivity relatively unrestrained by social disapproval. (Klopfer-Developments I)

CF > FC:	Emotional instability, impulsivity. (Klopfer-Developments I)
Color > M:	Externalized hostility (Beck III); hysterical neurosis, hysterical personality ("hysteria"), schizophrenia; impulsivity, inappropriate affect (Rapaport); impulsive, obstinate. (Phillips and Smith)
Color < M:	Psychopathology. (Rapaport)
Color > 2 texture:	Optimum social interaction. (Klopfer-Davidson)
Color responses < non-color responses:	Inhibition, withdrawal tendency. (Klopfer-Developments I)
Extended F+ below 80% (including F):	Impaired reality testing; maladaptive; unstable defense system. (Schafer-Rorschach)
Extended F+ 80–90%:	Stable defense system, unimpaired reality testing. (Schafer-Rorschach)
Extended F+ > 90%:	Constriction, rigidity. (Schafer-Rorschach)
F% about 50, F + FT + FV 75% or below:	Constrained but reasonably comfortable social interaction. (Klopfer-Davidson)
F% > 50%:	Compulsive tendency, constriction. (Klopfer-Developments I)
F + FT + FV > 75%:	Lack of emotional spontaneity, neurotic contriction. (Klopfer-Davidson)
FC = C + CF:	Social anxiety with need for social interaction. (Klopfer-Developments I)
FC > C + CF:	Appropriate response in social interaction. (Klopfer-Developments I)
FC > C + CF; FC equal to M (approximately):	Normality; stability. (Phillips and Smith)
FC > CF:	Excessive control of spontaneity; lack of uninhibited responsiveness; superficiality in social relations. (Klopfer-Davidson)

FC increment, minimum or no C + CF:

Lack of spontaneity; superficiality. (Klopfer-Developments I)

FC only, equal number of M and FC, above-average intelligence:

Intellectual resources which may be dissimulated or utilized for neurotic defense purposes primarily. (Schafer-Rorschach)

FM equal to M:

Awareness of impulses and acceptance of them; FM > 2M, immaturity, lack of long-range goals if CF > FC (if FC dominant, behavior may be immature but still socially acceptable); M > 2, exceeds FM which is greater than zero, maturity and capacity to work for long-range goals (Klopfer-Davidson); optimal FM : M 2 : 1. (Phillip and Smith)

FM (+) equal to M > Fm, few Fm:

Self-control, stability. (Klopfer-Developments I)

FM equal to 2M:

Impulsivity, lack of long-range goals, need for immediate gratification. (Klopfer-Developments I)

FM + Fm > 1½M:

Potential reducing anxiety. (Klopfer-Davidson)

FT + FV < ¼F:

Denial or repression of dependency. (Klopfer-Davidson)

FT + FV > ¾ F:

Overwhelming dependency. (Klopfer-Davidson)

FT, FV, FY < T, TF, V, VF, Y:

Dependency of such degree as to impair adjustment. (Klopfer-Davidson)

H equal to Hd:

Anxiety neurosis ("anxiety reaction"); depressive neurosis ("reactive depression"); obsessive compulsive neurosis, obsessive-compulsive personality ("obsessive-compulsive"). [Phillips and Smith]

H < Hd:

Constriction, retardation (Beck and Molish); obsessive compulsive neurosis, obsessive-compulsive personality ("obsessive-compulsives"); phobic neurosis ("phobics"); depressive neurosis ("reactive depression"). [Phillips and Smith]

M approximately equal to FM, CF present:

Spontaneity. (Klopfer-Developments I)

M approximately equal to FM, no color:

Egocentricity, psychophysiologic states. (Klopfer-Developments I)

M balancing sum C:

Sporadic breakdown and reinstitution of controls, as with ambulatory schizophrenic, manic. (Schafer-Clinical Application)

M > H:

Manifest and social anxiety; overideational. (Phillips and Smith)

At least 2-3 M Present, minimal or no sum C:

Assaultiveness, emotional instability. (Phillips and Smith)

M > 2 sum C, F% > 50:

Repression, withdrawal. (Klopfer-Developments I)

M equal to or > FM + Fm:

Stability (if < 3 Fm). [Klopfer-Developments I]

M > FM, FM at least half of M:

Ego strength, motivation for long-range goals, self-acceptance. (Klopfer-Developments I)

M > FM, FM < ½M:

Lack of spontaneity, overcontrol, tension. (Klopfer-Developments I)

M- :M ratio 1:3:

Psychosis. (Phillips and Smith)

M > color:

Delusional, obsessive, phobic; ruminative (Rapaport); persistence of defenses. (Beck III)

M equal to sum C:

Not striving, passive-submissive. (Klopfer-Davidson)

M equals 3 X sum C:

Antisocial personality ("psychopaths"); paranoid schizophrenics (may be assaultive); poor prognosis. (Phillips and Smith)

M equals 2 X sum C, increment F:

Inhibition, withdrawal. (Klopfer-Developments I)

Marked increment M to minimum color, as 10 M to zero sum color:

Unstable defenses. (Schafer-Rorschach)

M > sum C (when M > 2 and C is at least 1:

Introspective. (Klopfer-Davidson)

Sum C > M:

Extrotensive. (Klopfer-Davidson)

Optimal color:

FC:CF + C is 2:1; spontaneity with mature impulse control. (Phillips and Smith)

Optimal H:M:

Equal. (Phillips and Smith)

Optimal M to other determinants (M at expectancy):

Dd M + M in A + M Hd + M− equal to less than 1; sum C:M about equal; FC:M about equal, with FC:CF + C: ratio 2:1; W+ to M 1:1; W:M ratio 2:1. (Phillips and Smith)

Shading twice number of color responses:

Fear of rejection; inhibition. (Klopfer-Developments I)

Sum C above M and M is one or zero:

Hysterical tendency. (Schafer-Clinical Application)

Sum C > 2M, F% < 30:

Impulsivity. (Klopfer-Developments I)

Sum C 3–4 × M:

Psychophysiological disorders ("psychophysiologic"). [Phillips and Smith]

T + Y, TF + YF > FY + FT:

Dependency so great as to disrupt adjustment. (Klopfer-Developments I)

Texture > 2 × color:

Social anxiety; withdrawal for fear of rejection. (Klopfer-Davidson)

W:D ratio 1:2:

Anxiety, inhibition. (Rapaport)

W > 2 × M:

Unrealistic ambition or level of aspiration. (Klopfer-Davidson; Klopfer-Developments I; Rapaport)

W < 2 × M:

Antisocial personality ("psychopathy"), concreteness (Rapaport); aspiration below potential capacity (Klopfer-Developments I); creative potential not adequately expressed. (Klopfer-Davidson)

W:M:

Average 2:1. (May drop as W+ or M increases.) [Phillips and Smith]

W:M ratio 2:1:

Ambition for accomplishment with potential for it (Klopfer-Davidson);

	realistic aspiration with minimum 3 M, 6 W. (Klopfer-Developments I)
W : M ratio 3 : 1 :	Grandiosity, unrealistic ambition. (Phillips and Smith)
Zero color and M :	Psychotic depression. (Phillips and Smith)

Rejections

Excessive rejections :	Guardedness, impairment of judgment. (Phillips and Smith)
Increment rejection :	Asthenic personality or neurasthenic neurosis ("neurasthenia") paranoid conditions ("paranoia"), simple schizophrenia; depression, inhibition. (Rapaport)
Rejections :	Anxiety indicator, avoidance or withdrawal tendency (Beck III); guardedness, repression; may be evoked by association a particular card suggests. (Schafer-Rorschach)
Rejection IV, V, VI :	Depressive tendency. (Phillips and Smith)
Rejection VIII, IX, X :	Schizophrenic tendency. (Phillips and Smith)
Rejection of all ten cards, or all but one or two cards :	Guarded antisocial personalities ("psychopaths"). [Phillips and Smith]
Rejection of cards; rejection of response after verbalized :	Possible hypercriticality and negativism. (Schafer-Rorschach)
Rejection of poor form percept :	Adequate reality testing to that degree. (Schafer-Rorschach)
Rejection without evidence of guardedness :	Avoidance or withdrawal in presense of stimuli like that suggested by the card rejected. (Schafer-Rorschach)

Response Time

Delayed reaction time for first response :	Anxiety indicator. (Beck III)

Lack of variability in time for first response:

Possible neuroticism or schizophrenia; rigidity. (Beck III)

Long reaction time:

Anxiety, blocking, doubting. (Rapaport)

Response time 10″ or less:

Impulsivity; lack of planning ability; passive-suggestibility. (Phillips and Smith)

Optimum reaction time:

30″. (Klopfer-Davidson)

Response time 5″:

Impulsivity, lack of long-term goals. (Phillips and Smith)

Response time 40″ or more:

Avoidance reaction; cautious, rigid; may be indicative of shock. (Phillips and Smith)

Response time more than one minute:

Depression, slow mental process. (Klopfer-Davidson)

Slow response time:

Conflict area, possible blocking. (Beck and Molish)

Very rapid response time for first response, color cards:

Impulsivity; tendency to act before reflecting. (Beck III)

Very slow response:

Blocking. (Beck III)

Very slow time for first response:

Blocking possibly; possible regression of speech function. (Beck III)

Response Total

Decrement R:

Depression, paranoid schizophrenia, simple schizophrenia. (Rapaport)

Excessive R total for VIII, IX, X as compared to other cards:

Autism, daydreaming, excessive immersion in fantasy. (Beck and Molish)

High R (with other positive indices):

Potential for productive activity. (Beck and Molish)

Increment R:

Contraindicates hysteria as primary process; possible reaction formation (Beck III); obsessive-compulsive (Rapaport; 40+ R, possible intellectualization defense; possible reaction-formation against hostility. (Schafer-Rorschach)

Large number of R:

Reduction in productivity:

Reduction R:

Drive. (Beck and Molish)

Anxiety indicator. (Beck III)

Anxiety, guardedness. (Phillips and Smith)

Sequence

CF response followed by form-determined response:

Even response Card IX, increment R Card X:

Extremely irregular sequence:

Fm in conjunction with or following FT:

Fm following or in blends with CF:

Following response with anxious or hostile implications by one with more innocuous content (As "blood" followed by "jam"):

Precision alternatives:

Recovery on subsequent card after shock on previous card:

Sequence orderly:

W followed by Dd:

Impulsivity followed by attempt at repressive control. (Klopfer-Developments I)

Normality. (Phillips and Smith)

Schizophrenia. (Schafer-Clinical Appplication)

Anxiety relative to dependency needs. (Klopfer-Developments I)

Anxiety over impulsivity, at conscious level. (Klopfer-Developments I)

Defense of undoing. (Schafer-Rorschach)

Average or above-average intelligence; indecision, obsessive-compulsive tendencies, self-evaluation. (Phillips and Smith)

Good adjustment potential. (Beck III)

Potential for orderly procedure. (Beck III)

Schizophrenics, young children. (Klopfer-Developments I)

Shock

Cards most likely to elicit color shock, in decreasing order of shock frequency:

Cards most likely to elicit shading shock:

II and IX about equally; VIII, X. (Beck and Molish)

IV, VI, VII, about equally, followed by V and I. (Beck and Molish)

Color-shock:

Anxiety, neurosis; favorable prognostic sign (Beck and Molish); good prognostic sign in schizophrenics; neurosis (Beck III); neurosis, repression. (Phillips and Smith, citing Rorschach)

Color-shock in schizophrenics:

Favorable prognostic sign. (Beck and Molish)

Indices of shock:

Adx, Hd, and Hdx as first response; absence of P when P is frequently given; absence of W in five responses to card when W is at expectancy elsewhere; card rejection and turning when not extensive elsewhere; Dd initial response to card; DW when not prevalent elsewhere; deviant content not found elsewhere (anal, sex, etc.); fabulized or hesitant verbalizations; inadequate form level of more than one response to card when form level is adequate elsewhere; increased time for first response; initial cut-off W when not frequent elsewhere; initial edging exclusive to card where shock is presumed present; initial F− when not given extensively elsewhere; low number of responses compared to that elsewhere; M in A when M is in H elsewhere; M not perceived on III; responding to card only in turned position when responses to other cards are to blot in presentation position; reversed sequence when not extensive elsewhere. (Phillips and Smith)

Severe shock, Card V:

Possible homosexual tendency, with latter a source of anxiety. (Beck and Molish)

Shading shock:

Anxiety, dysphoric and painful affect, guilt (Beck III); apprehension (Phillips and Smith); hysteroid trend with obsessive defenses, as obsessive phobic anxiety; obsessive rumination; reaction-

	formation tendency, possibly with undoing. (Beck and Molish)
Shading shock, Cards IV and VII:	Possible oedipal conflict. (Beck and Molish)
Shock on Cards I and IV:	Anxiety relative to attitude toward same-sex parent. (Beck and Molish)
Shock on Cards II and VII, female subject:	Possible anxiety over sexual curiosity and impulses. (Beck and Molish)
Shock on Cards II and VII, male subject:	Heterosexual anxiety with possible feminine identification. (Beck and Molish)
Shock on Card VI:	Heterosexual conflict; or homosexual anxiety. (Beck and Molish)
Shock on Card VI, male subjects:	Castration anxiety, possible fear of injury. (Beck and Molish)
Shock indicative of anxiety:	Most prevalent on Cards IV, VI, VII. (Beck III)
Unlikely to elicit shock:	Card III. (Beck and Molish)
White space shock:	Cards II, VII, IX; heterosexual anxiety. (Beck and Molish)

Symmetry

Comments on asymmetry of cards:	Possible conflict over ambivalence; possible obsessive-compulsive tendency. (Schafer-Rorschach)
Increment of symmetry:	Constriction, rigidity. (Beck III)
Reflection responses:	Possible obsessive rumination. (Beck and Molish)
Symmetry comments and responses:	Ambivalence (Beck and Molish); average or above-average intelligence; obsessive-compulsive traits; tension over repression of intense impulses pressing for expression (Phillips and Smith); possible obsessive-compulsive trend (Schafer-Rorschach); undoing. (Beck III)

Task Orientation

Abruptness:

Impulsivity. (Phillips and Smith)

Absence of any asperity or assertion; overcompliance with test procedure:

Possible reaction-formation against hostility. (Schafer-Rorschach)

Absence of elaboration, avoidance of additional responses to cards, terse style:

Attitude of detachment, lack of responsivity to social pressures. (Phillips and Smith)

Absence of excessive verbiage and of anxiety and prolonged doubting in an obsessive-compulsivity setting, if evidence of psychosis is not present:

Effective defense system. (Schafer-Rorschach)

"Any time limit?"

Dependency. (Phillips and Smith)

Apologetic attitude, redundancy:

Lack of self-confidence. (Beck III)

Appearance of response only during inquiry; long pause before response:

Possible repression or repressive tendency. (Schafer-Rorschach)

Apprehension, impaired attention and concentration:

Anxiety neurosis ("anxiety state"). [Schafer-Clinical Application]

Asking for confirmation of adequacy of the response and for reassurance:

Dependency; need for help and support. (Schafer-Rorschach)

Asking for further explanation of Rorschach before performing:

Obsessive; paranoid. (Rapaport)

Attention fluctuation, blocking, forgetting, inaccurate recall:

Emotional tension. (Beck III)

Attitude that tests are "crazy"; egocentric, naive responses:

Repression. (Schafer-Rorschach)

Attributing to test or examiner's attitude or assumed expectation responses unacceptable to patient although produced by him:

Paranoid trend. (Schafer-Rorschach)

Automatic phrases (Piotrowski):

May be indicative of low intelligence. (Beck and Molish)

Automatic phrases, no organic impairment:

Inflexibility, rigidity. (Beck III)

Bland detachment relative to both neutral and "taboo" or emotionally provocative responses:

Isolation. (Schafer-Rorschach)

Card turning without inquiry as to whether it's permissible, after developing previous R:

Freedom of self-expression. (Phillips and Smith)

Comment on inquiry that blot no longer appears like original percept:

Schizophrenia; unstable interpersonal relationships. (Phillips and Smith)

Comment on similarity between cards:

Possible paranoid trend. (Schafer-Rorschach)

Complaint that all cards look alike:

Possible rigidity of defense system. (Schafer-Rorschach)

Completely unmodified, unqualified, terse responses:

Children; organics; people in trouble with the law; persons resistant to social pressure. (Phillips and Smith)

Complimentary remarks about card following by disparaging comments:

Ambivalence; ingratiation followed by provocation; inhibition of action for fear of punishment alternating with acting-out of hostility. (Phillips and Smith)

Complimentary remarks about cards:

Desire for dependency, fear of punitive reactions from others, ingratiation. (Phillips and Smith)

Conservative responses:

Contraindicates character-disorder. (Schafer-Clinical Application)

Consistent self-depreciation:

Depression. (Rapaport)

Constant speech:

Anxiety; manic tendency. (Beck and Molish)

Covering part of blot with hand to exclude non-percept area:

Immaturity; passive-suggestibility. (Phillips and Smith)

Criticism of blot:

Possible rejection of feeling of inadequacy. (Schafer-Rorschach)

Criticism of card, with overpoliteness to examiner:

Possible depressive trend. (Rapaport)

Criticism of cards:

Externalization of hostility and of responsibility; possible self-righteous attitude. (Schafer-Rorschach)

Criticism of self for unproductiveness:

Depressive introjection of hostility. (Schafer-Rorschach)

Crude euphemisms, swearing, "yeah": Low socioeconomic level. (Phillips and Smith)

Decline of R as test continues; complaining about demands of test or time it takes: Anxiety over repressed impulses; demanding querulousness; passivity. (Schafer-Rorschach)

Delayed reaction time and/or expression of uncertainty and inadequacy feelings: Anxiety, often evoked by associations a particular card suggests. (Schafer-Rorschach)

Derogatory remarks about the cards: Hostile; negative attitudes. (Phillips and Smith)

Derogatory self-references: Depression; low self-esteem; request for assurance. (Phillips and Smith)

Detached but introspective test approach: Lack of spontaneity; possible isolation defense. (Schafer-Rorschach)

Detailing: Social anxiety. (Phillips and Smith)

Disparagment of Rorschach and test figures (Toubin): Aggressive attitudes. (Beck and Molish)

Doubt expressed about adequacy of a percept: Indecision, self-doubt with self-consciousness, social anxiety; organicity. (Phillips and Smith)

Doubting rumination, excessive emotional constraint, pedantry: Obsessive-compulsive neurosis, with defenses of intellectualization, isolation, and rationalization. (Schafer-Clinical Application)

Dropping or throwing a card to table with expression of fright or repulsion: Morbid anxiety. (Phillips and Smith)

Edging: Eccentric element in personality; or obsessive-compulsive tendency. (Beck III)

Egocentric, facetious, weak empathic and introspective capacity: Antisocial personality ("narcissistic character disorder" type). [Schafer-Clinical Application]

"Either-or" alternatives: Obsessive-compulsive tendencies. (Phillips and Smith)

Elaboration of basic percept: Average or above-average intelligence. (Phillips and Smith)

Emotional reaction to response as reason why it was given:	Egocentricity, naiveté; hysterical trend; possible phobic tendency. (Schafer-Rorschach)
Enumeration of parts:	Apprehension, inhibition, manifest anxiety; conventionality. (Phillips and Smith)
Esoteric phrases and terms; pedantry:	Ideational, obsessive-compulsive. (Phillips and Smith)
Evasion, vagueness:	Limited capacity for reflection and self-confrontation; low anxiety tolerance. (Schafer-Rorschach)
Evidence of emotional disturbance without color-shock:	Anxiety at least partially bound by characterologic defenses. (Beck and Molish)
Excessive card turning:	Tension. (Beck III)
Excessive prefatory remarks and qualifications:	Apprehension, caution, social anxiety, with self-distrust; phobic tendency. (Phillips and Smith)
Excessive qualification:	Apprehension, self-devaluation, submissive tendency (Beck III); phobic tendency. (Phillips and Smith)
Excessive or too rapid verbalization followed by apologies or repeated questions as to whether verbalization is excessive or too rapid:	Possible defense of undoing. (Schafer-Rorschach)
Excessive unsystematic turning uninterrupted by interpretations:	Manifest anxiety; may be greater for cards relating to conflict areas. (Phillips and Smith)
Exhibitionistic display of sexual areas by dress and posture; flirtatiousness:	Seductiveness and possible promiscuity as way of relating to others. (Schafer-Rorschach)
Facetious closing remarks to terminate card responses:	Effort to make a game of Rorschach testing; it's not to be taken seriously. (Schafer-Rorschach)
Facetiousness, negativistic resistance to testing:	Defense against passive-submissive needs. (Schafer-Rorschach)

Failure to turn card after asking permission:

Ambivalence; dependency needs countered by negativism. (Phillips and Smith)

Failure to turn cards:

Fearfulness, inhibitory tendency. (Beck III)

Further inquiries about turning after permission is given:

Conforming, passive-dependent; resistive tendencies within limits. (Phillips and Smith)

Great show of industry with banal responses and evasion:

Antisocial personality ("psychopathic") trend. (Schafer-Rorschach)

High intelligence with resignation:

Increases chances of suicide. (Beck and Molish)

Holding card after terminal remarks until examiner removes it:

Passive-submissive. (Phillips and Smith)

"I":

Self-assertion, self-respect. (Phillips and Smith)

Ideas of reference relative to intent of blot configuration:

Paranoid schizophrenia. (Schafer-Clinical Application)

Immediate consistent turning, usually with R given to upright position:

General negativistic attitudes; immaturity. (Phillips and Smith)

Impulsive, unreflective:

Possible repressive trend. (Schafer-Rorschach)

Inability to perceive responses to some blot areas, no difficulty with perception on other areas:

Hysterical neurosis, hysterical personality ("hysterics"). (Klopfer-Developments II)

Inability to recall a percept:

Rejection of the wish contained in the percept. (Beck III)

Inappropriate or strange vocalizations:

Psychopathology. (Phillips and Smith)

Incongruent, irrelevant conversational remarks:

Organicity. (Phillips and Smith)

Incorrect grammar:

Low socioeconomic status; possible lack of middle class aspirations and mores. (Phillips and Smith)

Increment euphorically toned associations:

Possible denial. (Schafer-Rorschach)

Increment perplexed qualification:

Possible obsessive-compulsive trend. (Schafer-Rorschach)

Increment qualification:

Constriction, rigidity. (Beck III)

Increment qualifications, including question form of response:

Feeling of insufficiency; guilt. (Beck III)

Ingratiation followed by petulance as testing continues:

Passive-receptive tendency. (Schafer-Rorschach)

Ingratiation; minimizing of negative or painful reaction to life experiences and test stimuli; pollyanna attitudes:

Denial. (Schafer-Rorschach)

Inquiry as to what to do with card after responding to it:

Passive-compliance with obsessive-compulsive features. (Phillips and Smith)

Inquiry as to whether it is permissible to turn cards:

Dependent, submissive. (Phillips and Smith)

Inquiry by subject in regard to how he is expected to perform:

Attempt to structure the situation by establishing rules; obsessive-compulsive traits. (Phillips and Smith)

Lack of qualification:

Lack of inhibition or of self-control. (Beck and Molish)

Lackadaisical comments on mild disparity between R and blot outlines:

Apathy, immaturity, indifference (except when indifference is due to resistiveness). [Phillips and Smith]

Laying card down after response:

Cooperativeness; freedom from pathology. (Phillips and Smith)

Legalistic attitude; traits of overcaution, suspicion:

Paranoid personality ("paranoid character"). [Schafer-Clinical Application]

Looking at back of cards:

Curiosity, ideational tendency, suspicion; paranoids. (Phillips and Smith)

Marked evasiveness:

Possible paranoid tendency. (Schafer-Rorschach)

More than one response to cards, quick response, response to disturbing card areas:

Ability to recuperate from stress; fairly effective counter-phobic defenses. (Schafer-Rorschach)

Mumbling:

Lack of interest in social exchange; schizophrenics. (Phillips and Smith)

Negation or withdrawal of a response, negative attitude toward test elements or toward examiner:

Unstable defenses. (Schafer-Rorschach)

Negative emotional tone (lack of appropriate humor, and cooperation, presence of moderate-to-severe anxiety, unresponsiveness):

Unstable defenses. (Schafer-Rorschach)

No turning:

Authoritarian tendency with conformity, rigidity, tension (Phillips and Smith); constriction, rigidity (Beck III); rigidity possibly. (Klopfer-Developments I)

Nonconsistent immediate turning of card:

Shock; card represents conflict area and turning is avoidance reaction. (Phillips and Smith)

Nonderogatory remarks about the grotesque or strange appearance of the cards:

Ambiguous sexual role; apprehension; self-doubt. (Phillips and Smith)

Nonderogatory self-references:

Egocentricity. (Phillips and Smith)

Overpoliteness:

Hostility. (Rapaport)

Overqualification:

Lack of self-confidence. (Beck III)

Perplexity:

Avoidance (Beck and Molish); depression; self-criticality, uncertainty in regard to sexual and social role. (Phillips and Smith)

Personal pronouns:

Assertion, self-respect, stable value system. (Phillips and Smith)

Pleasantly toned color comments:

Appropriate emotional responsivity; favorable prognostic sign in schizophrenia. (Phillips and Smith)

Positive emotional tone (humor, responsivity, relative freedom from manifest anxiety):

Stable defenses. (Schafer-Rorschach)

Preliminary remarks connoting hesitation:

Average or above-average intelligence; passive-submissive tendencies; reluctant conformity to social pressures. (Phillips and Smith)

Qualification of bizarre responses:

Suggests reality contact is still at least partially retained, although it may be deteriorating or impaired. (Schafer-Rorschach)

Qualifying response to make it more innocuous in significance, as "a devil; a friendly sort of devil":

Defense of undoing. (Schafer-Rorschach)

Questioning:

Passive-dependence. (Phillips and Smith)

Questioning of own response:

Anxiety; unstable or weak defenses. (Schafer-Rorschach)

Recognition of Rorschach percept as untenable, followed by its reaffirmation:

Schizophrenic tendency or loose contact with reality; possible latent schizophrenia"). [Schafer-Clinical Application]

Redundancy, superfluous elaboration:

Conflict area. (Phillips and Smith)

Refusal to hold cards:

Anxiety over aggressive impulses. (Phillips and Smith)

Reluctance to produce a response; demurring remarks but not refusal or stated inability:

Resistance to self-revelation; withholding of perceived material. (Phillips and Smith)

Remarks implying response source is intrinsic to blot or objects it resembles:

Detachment, inhibition, intellectualization; obsessive-compulsive, passive-receptive. (Phillips and Smith)

Remarks suggesting feeling of resignation over inability to produce response or further responses:

Discouragement; low self-esteem; passive-submissive tendency. (Phillips and Smith)

Remarks suggesting R is contingent and possible rather than certain:

Average to above-average intelligence; capacity for good adjustment; good prognosis. (Phillips and Smith)

"Reminds me":

Intellectualization tendency. (Phillips and Smith)

Resignation formulas, as "that's all I can think of ":

Depressed tendency. (Beck III)

Selection of common areas for percept:

More likely to occur with brain damaged than schizophrenic patients. (Klopfer-Developments I)

Self-disparagement with rejection of reassurance, together with implicit provocation of rejection by examiner:

Masochistic. (Schafer-Rorschach)

Self-references:

Autism or self-absorption (Schafer-Rorschach)

Self-references to justify response:

Egocentric trend. (Schafer-Rorschach)

Sincerely accepting or positive attitude toward Rorschach determinants; expression of pleasure relative to color or the nature of the task:

Stable (or rigid) defenses. (Schafer-Rorschach)

Smiling at examiner:

Denial of hostility; dependency; guardedness with self-confidence. (Phillips and Smith)

Smiling at Rorschach cards but not examiner:

Detachment; possible delusional tendency; secretive. (Phillips and Smith)

Stated inability to produce a response:

Contraindicates malingering; inadequacy with passivity and resignation; narcissistic or voyeuristic tendency. (Phillips and Smith)

Statement that blots do not suggest a response:

Avoidance of self-analysis and insight; lack of empathy for others; malingering or resistiveness. (Phillips and Smith)

Stroking or touching cards:

Passive-receptive tendency; skin eroticism. (Phillips and Smith)

"Suggests to me":

Passive-receptive attitude. (Phillips and Smith)

Suspicious remarks about the cards or the examiner's motives:

Paranoid tendency. (Phillips and Smith)

Systematic examination and rotation:

Obsessive-compulsive. (Phillips and Smith)

Tender descriptions:

Sensitivity. (Schafer-Clinical Application)

"To me":

Egocentric, passive-receptive. (Phillips and Smith)

Tossing back card:

A provocative act; hostile antisocial

Traits of histrionic behavior, lability, naiveté:

personality ("psychopath"). [Phillips and Smith]

Hysterical neurosis ("hysteria"). [Schafer-Clinical Application]

Turning beyond normal expectancy:

Manifest anxiety. (Phillips and Smith)

Turning cards without asking permission:

Some freedom of self-expression. (Phillips and Smith)

Turning, few or no responses with card turned:

Anxiety, doubting tendency. (Klopfer-Developments I)

Turning head rather than card to alter view of blot:

Passive-submissive defense system with authoritative persons. (Schafer-Rorschach)

Use of editorial "we":

Pomposity, perhaps to compensate for feelings of inadequacy. (Schafer-Rorschach)

Use of term "weird":

Possibe phobic tendency. (Schafer-Rorschach)

Volubility:

Narcissistic, negativistic, provocative. (Schafer-Rorschach)

Whimsical content:

Creative potential, good adaptive capacity, intellectual superiority. (Beck and Molish)

"You" forms:

Evasion, insecurity, lack of self-reliance. (Phillips and Smith)

BIBLIOGRAPHY

1. Beck, Samule J.: *Rorschach's Test;* vol. I, New York, Grune, 1962; vol. II, *A Variety of Personality Pictures*, 2nd ed., with Molish, H. B. [Beck and Molish]; and vol. III, *Advances in Interpretation*, 1952 [Beck III].

2. Beck, Samuel J.: The Rorschach test: A multi-dimensional test of personality. In Anderson, Harold H., and Anderson, G. L.: *An Introduction to Projective Techniques.* New York, Prentice-Hall, 1951 [Anderson-Beck].

3. Bender, Lauretta: *A Visual Motor Gestalt Test and its Clinical Use.* New York, American Orthopsychiatric Association, 1938 [Bender].

4. Gilbert, Joseph: *Clinical Psychological Tests in Psychiatric and Medical Practice.* Springfield, Thomas, 1969.

5. Halpern, Florence: The Bender visual motor gestalt test. In Anderson, Harold H., and Anderson, G. L.: *An Introduction to Projective Techniques.* New York, Prentice-Hall, 1951 [Anderson-Halpern].

6. Hammer, Emanuel F. (Ed.): *Clinical Application of Projective Drawings.* Springfield, Thomas, 1963 [Hammer].

7. Hutt, Max L.: *The Hutt Adaptation of the Bender-Gestalt Test*, 2nd ed., New York, Grune, 1969 [Hutt, 1969].

8. Klopfer, Bruno, Ainsworth, Mary, Klopfer, Walter G., and Holt, Robert R.: *Developments in the Rorschach Technique.* New York, Harcourt, 1956, vols. I and II [Klopfer-Developments I and Klopfer-Developments II].

9. Klopfer, Bruno, and Davidson, Helen H.: *Rorschach Technique: An Introductory Manual.* New York, Harcourt, 1962 [Klopfer-Davidson].

10. Machover, Karen: Drawing of the human figure: A method of personality investigation. In Anderson, Harold H., and Anderson, G. L.: *An Introduction to Projective Techniques.* New York, Prentice-Hall, 1951 [Anderson-Machover].

11. Machover, Karen: *Personality Projection in the Drawing of the Human Figure: A Method of Personality Investigation.* Springfield, Thomas, 1965 [Machover].

12. Mayman, Martin, Schafer, Roy, and Rapaport, David: Interpretation of the Wechsler-Bellevue Intelligence Scale in personality appraisal. In Anderson, Harold H., and Anderson, G. L.: *An Introduction to Projective Techniques.* New York, Prentice-Hall, 1951 [Anderson-Mayman-Schafer-Rapaport].

13. Phillips, Leslie, and Smith, Joseph G.: *Rorschach Interpretation: Advanced Technique.* New York, Grune, 1953 [Phillips and Smith].

14. Rapaport, David; Gilland, Merton M., and Schafer, Roy.: *Diagnostic Psychological Testing.* New York, Int. Univ., 1968, revised edition edited by Robert R. Holt. [Rapaport].

15. Rorschach, Hermann: *Psychodiagnostics*, 5th ed. New York, Grune, 1951. [Rorschach-Psychodiagnostics].

16. Schafer, Roy. *Clinical Application of Psychological Tests.* New York, Int. Univ., 1948 [Schafer-Clinical Application].

17. Schafer, Roy. *Psychoanalytic Interpretation in Rorschach Testing.* New York, Grune, 1954 [Schafer-Rorschach].

18. Tolor, Alexander, and Schulberg, Herbert C.: *Evaluation of the Bender-Gestalt Test.* Springfield, Thomas, 1963 [Tolor-Schulberg].

APPENDIX
Rorschach Symbols and Symbol Equivalents

Component	Beck	Klopfer	Phillips and Smith
Whole Response	W	W, Ŵ	W
Common Details	D	D, d	D
Uncommon Details	Dd	dr, dd, de, di	Dd
Space	Ws, Ds, Dds	S	Ws, Ds, Dds
Form	F+, F, F−	F+, F, F−	F+, F−
Human Movement	M	M	M
Animal Movement	[Animals in Humanlike actions scored M]	FM	FM
Object Movement	Excluded	Fm	Fm
Form Dominant Color	FC	FC	FC
Form Secondary Color	CF	CF	CF
Pure Color	C	C	C
Form Dominant Shading	FY	FC′, Fk	FC′, Fk
Form Secondary Shading	YF	KF, kF, C′F	KF, kF, C′F
Pure Shading	Y	K, C′	K, C′
Form Dominant Texture	FT	Fc	Fc
Form Secondary Texture	TF	cF	cF
Pure Texture	T	c	c
Form Dominant Vista	FV	FK	FV
Form Secondary Vista	VF	Excluded	VF
Pure Vista	V	Excluded	V

Note: 1) For the sake of clarity, double content categories under the Beck system are separated in the text with a period (i.e., Human.Religion) rather than with the comma employed by Beck for this purpose.

2) Beck's *Alphabet* category is excluded from the content listing and the author's *Symbol* is used as a more inclusive category. Phillips and Smith's *Stain* and *War* are employed as additional categories to Beck's. Klopfer categories utilized, not included in Beck but utilized in Phillips and Smith, are *Animal Movement* (FM), *Object Movement* (Fm), *Emblem* (Em) and *Inhuman Human* (H). The category *Anal* is also utilized by the author as perhaps more representative of a number of responses which do not seem entirely appropriate under the categories of *Anatomy*, *Human Detail*, or *Sex*.

Index

Index

W (Whole Response), Rorschach, 83, 85,
87, 88, 89, 90, 91, 92, 93, 94, 95, 96,
202, 203, 204, 205, 206, 207, 210,
213, 214, 220, 221, 223, 224
War Content, Rorschach, 188
Withdrawal, 4, 5, 7, 9, 14, 26, 27, 28, 34,
35, 36, 37, 40, 43, 44, 48, 69, 79, 82,
85, 96, 188, 189, 194, 198, 217, 219,
220, 221
WM (Human Movement Whole Response),
Rorschach, 195, 196
Women, 136, 178
belittling of, 68
competitive women in involutional
period, 101
conflict with, 4, 5, 17
derogatory attitude towards, 80, 106
fear of, 101, 124
hostile designations for (Rorschach), 73

hostility towards, 32, 150
impaired relationship with, 136
regarded as sexually rejecting, 28
rejection of as sexual objects, 81
sadism towards, 111
Wx (Cut-off Whole Response), Rorschach,
202, 205, 206

Y (Pure Shading), Rorschach, 96, 197, 198,
210, 218, 220
YF (Form Secondary Shading), Rorschach,
85, 94, 197, 198, 210, 220
YF– (Form Minus and Secondary Shading),
Rorschach, 198
YF+Y (Form Secondary and Pure Shading),
Rorschach, 198

Z (Integration Tendency for Location
Areas), Rorschach, 84, 90